BAY COUNTRY

TOM HORTON

BAY COUNTRY

Reflections on the Chesapeake

Ticknor & Fields
New York

for Cheri

For information about permission to reproduce selections
from this book, write to The Johns Hopkins University Press,
701 West 40th Street, Baltimore, Maryland 21211.

Library of Congress Cataloging-in-Publication Data

Horton, Tom, date.
 Bay country : reflections on the Chesapeake / Tom Horton.
 p. cm.
 Reprint. Originally published: Baltimore : Johns Hopkins
University Press, c1987.
 ISBN 0-89919-837-6
 1. Chesapeake Bay Region (Md. and Va.)—Description and
travel. 2. Natural resources—Chesapeake Bay Region (Md.
and Va.) 3. Environmental protection—Chesapeake Bay
Region (Md. and Va.)
 I. Title.
F187.C5H67 1989
975.5'18—dc19   88-37388
                                                              CIP

Printed in the United States of America

s 10 9 8 7 6 5 4 3 2 1

Ticknor & Fields paperback 1989
Published by arrangement with
The Johns Hopkins University Press

Contents

Preface

This is a collection of personal essays, the distillation of what has seemed truest and best through a decade of reporting on the Maryland environment. The choice of subjects inclines toward the Chesapeake Bay, as does most of the state's land and water. Only in the western third of Garrett County, where the eastern continental divide shrugs the Casselman and the Youghiogheny rivers off one shoulder toward the Gulf of Mexico, does the state pay appreciable tribute to a watershed other than the bay.

From their titles, the sections of this book may seem mostly about fish and the seasons, trees and rivers, and islands, birds, and assorted other natural objects; but these are only starting points.

Take fish, for example. Like quotes, they must always be placed in context if the reporter is worthy of his craft. A context I have always favored for fish is Windmill Point in lower Dorchester County, Maryland. It long ago lost its windmill and reverted to being largely undifferentiated from the rest of several thousand miles of salt-marsh coast on Maryland's Eastern Shore—which is to say that when the sunset of a calm summer evening suffuses sky and water equally with a seamless, pastel coloration, and a flood tide sets the green marsh afloat between heaven and earth, it can be a place of infinite charm and contentment.

That is how it was at Windmill Point the time I caught surely the biggest silver- and black-striped rockfish that a boy of twelve ever saw. It scarcely matters that I can't recall exactly how big. What I can tell you unequivocally is how good I felt when I boated it, how good I felt watching my father admire it, and how good it was fried in cornmeal back at the lodge that night, dwarfing the lesser specimens of the rest of our party of grown men. Feeling good about that rockfish is a rare touchstone, one of the few things I can count on to stay constant the rest of my life.

Now this is far from a selfish reason for assigning importance to a

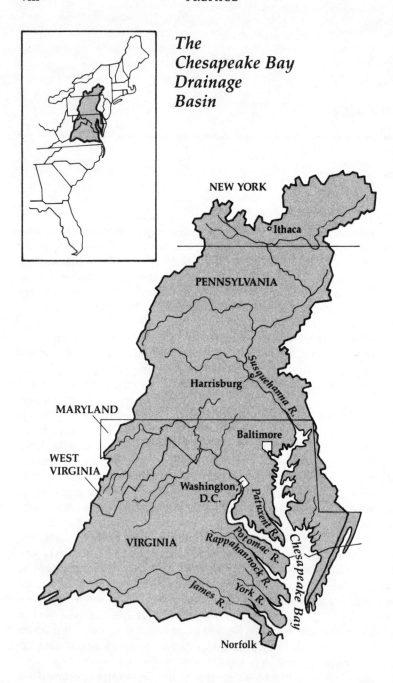

*The
Chesapeake Bay
Drainage
Basin*

cold-brained, scaly vertebrate. Remember that the Chesapeake Bay has at least a thousand places like Windmill Point, and close to a thousand times a thousand fathers and sons and mothers and daughters who fish its waters each year. And every one of them, until pollution and overfishing of the last decade depressed the old rock's numbers to where it is now illegal to catch them, had a fair chance of hooking into something silver and striped, whose value far transcended the ability to measure it of any economics we have yet developed.

A man who lived and wrote decades ago on a scrub farm in the Sand Hills of Wisconsin and, as far as I know, never caught a rockfish, came closest to explaining their allure. Aldo Leopold, the conservationist, understood there are values to living creatures that, although unquantifiable, are as universal as any of the laws of science; "the physics of beauty," he called it—one department of natural science still in the Dark Ages: "Everybody knows for example, that the autumn landscape in the north woods is the land, plus a red maple, plus a ruffed grouse. In terms of conventional physics the grouse represents only a millionth of either the mass or the energy of an acre. Yet subtract the grouse and the whole thing is dead."

So it is that I have not dropped anchor at Windmill Point for several years now—have not even thought about the place until recently, as my own son nears fishing age. It would still be pretty enough, but something vital would be lacking. The pastel sunsets and the flood tide in the marsh would no longer be invested with the marvelous energy that comes from the lurking presence there of a rockfish—whether a real presence or only one that could be reasonably anticipated did not matter. But let us insist on the full context in this matter. Any honest lament for the rock must confront the hard-eyed scientific truth that a decline of any one species in nature often represents not so much a diminution of life as it does a shift from one form to another.

Nature abhors a vacuum. Although conditions in the Chesapeake Bay no longer seem to favor the rockfish, this does not mean there are fewer fish in the bay. In fact, most measurements of total fish landings for the Chesapeake indicate that in recent years the total biomass is up. The more polluted conditions of the late twentieth-century bay appear to favor the oily little menhaden, and the bluefish that feed on them. No sportier fish ever existed than the sharp-toothed, strong-swimming bluefish. It is no trick, when blues are in one of their frequent feeding frenzies, to catch them by the freezerful. Pound for pound, their fight makes the rock seem sluggish; and while they are still not considered the culinary equivalent of the rock, new recipes for bluefish are being published every day, and a lot of them are very tasty.

Perhaps, it is suggested, our extraordinary attachment to rockfish is a perception that will not outlast the aging generations of us who grew up used to having them at our disposal. Our sons and daughters may someday wax as eloquent on the charms of catching bluefish. But no. There is more to the quality of fish than that. Bluefish spawn and pass the bulk of their lives far at sea, out of our sight and minds, moving about almost exclusively in great, impersonal shoals and sticking to the deep channels much of their time in the bay. We encounter the rock, above most fish species, in habitats ensorcelling to us—wherever land and water mingle seductively in the marshy skirts of the Atlantic coastal plain; in the moonlit tide rips off Martha's Vineyard; in the wildest crashing surf along the beaches and jetties of a coastline stretching from the Outer Banks to Maine.

The rock may live several decades and attain nearly the length and weight of a man; and during all that time, they choose to hug our coastal edges, feed in the shallows, and return each spring from the length of the East Coast to procreate in Chesapeake rivers almost to the doorsteps of our towns and cities—accessible to, and vulnerable to, us as are few other wild species of their stature. Sharing many of the same waters where it is most convenient for human beings to build their power plants, dump their sewage, and fill for waterfront development, rockfish keep us honest. How we treat them says a good deal about our progress in learning to coexist with nature.

That we need fish to teach us peaceful coexistence is evidenced by the recent case of the Westway, a mammoth highway and commercial development long-planned for the Hudson shoreline in Manhattan. Backed by a steamroller coalition of the Rockefellers and organized labor, Westway was avidly supported by four successive U.S. presidents, three governors of New York, and three mayors of New York City. Opposed to Westway for more than a decade were thousands of New Yorkers who said it would pollute their air, destroy their neighborhoods, and cost an unconscionable $1 million for every ten feet of its twelve-lane roadbed, at a time when the city's subway system was falling apart for lack of transportation funding. None of these arguments made even a ding in Westway's progress; but the rock—or striped bass as they call them outside the Chesapeake—stopped it cold. A federal judge found that a landfill, needed for the project to achieve its lucrative commercial potential, would illegally devastate acres of rockfish habitat along the Hudson's edge. New York, stymied, scaled back the project and shifted the rest of the funds into mass transit.

On the Chesapeake, if we lose the rock for good, we lose more than a potent reminder that the waterfront must remain habitat for more than human beings. We also lose the rivermen of a dozen bay tributaries who each spring greeted the rock's return to spawn with small boats and hopeful nets, perpetuating the ageless rituals of the season observed on other bays and rivers for thousands of years. Count the occupations left on this continent where people still depend on knowing nature's ways for their daily living and you see that when a fish goes, so does a unique subset of ourselves. Wipe out a river's spawning run and you have diminished the very springtime.

It was in the winter of 1984, a few weeks before Maryland's indefinite moratorium on catching rockfish took effect, that I sat drinking coffee with an old schoolmate, Bill Price, a fifth—and now, possibly last—generation gill netter on the Choptank River. Bill, whose school career was less distinguished by academics than by his ability to work a duck call during basketball games, seemed eloquent now. He could not help but be impressed at how smart people were in this world, able to build spaceships and land people on the moon. But for all that, he said, "we have never figured out what to do with our water, and that's gonna put an end to the world, not just to my living."

If not an end to the world, at least to its quality. Catching bluefish in the old rock's stead is like chugging Coke is to sipping wine—the former may stimulate and refresh, but the wine contains infinite subtleties and associations. So does the rock, which is, in a word, *connected* to us as the bluefish never can be; and you can no more weigh the worth of rockfish disentangled from those extraordinary webs of place and emotion and responsibility than you could rate a vintage wine by the number of grapes per bottle, or describe a sunset by its B.T.U. content.

And all that is just what is attached to one fish. We bay dwellers move in a far richer and more extensive matrix of subtle relations and ancient connections with nature than we can yet explain or admit. Often we sense it—the exhilaration brought by a crackling blue autumn sky over the limitless sweep of golden marsh; in the inexplicable yearning created by Canada geese migrating over our cities; in the vague, pleasurable homecoming we feel amid particular unchanged landscapes; and in the quick, secret dismay we feel, watching the legal rights of private property development overwhelm the rights of the forest and its wildlife. To preserve the full diversity of such connections into the next century will require a broader view of environmental protection than is likely to evolve through our legal and political systems alone. Carl Jung, the great psychoanalyst, once said he had never been able to cure a patient who did not have a firm belief that he or she was part of something larger. Thus we need our religions, our cosmologies, and equally, I think, a greatly expanded appreciation of all the ways in which we and nature fit together. To the extent we can comprehend it, rediscover the familiar in what has become unfamiliar—to that extent we may experience what Kenneth Grahame, in *The Wind in the Willows*, called "the most priceless possession of the human race . . . the wonder of the world."

Wonder lies in the bay and its watershed in full measure. It is nothing alien or mystical, or reserved for the expert. It is a different way of looking at things, a scarcely plumbed literature awaiting only skillful enough translation and properly attuned ears, to which these essays may contribute a bit.

Acknowledgments

In a very real way, my father and mother collaborated on this book. She, the first female reporter on the *Salisbury Times* until marriage and family intervened, contributed a love of language. He, an Eastern Shore poultryman, showed me the outdoors whenever he could; and when he couldn't, farmed me out to two Hooper Island watermen, Ackley Tyler and Levin Tolley, who knew a thing or two about rockfish and black ducks.

Much of the material in the book was developed during a decade of writing on the Chesapeake Bay for the *Baltimore Sun.* I am indebted to a long line of editors there for affording me an extraordinarily long leash in pursuit of whatever seemed intriguing—also for never making me wear a necktie.

Many, many persons were involved in educating me about the Chesapeake Bay and its environs, but a few seem in retrospect especially important:

Gene Cronin, the dean of the bay's scientific community, who has been encouraging and supportive almost from the first story I ever wrote on his beloved Chesapeake; Tom Wisner, whose songs and words and presence have anchored and buoyed me; a trio of Baltimore ladies, Ajax Eastman, Judy Johnson, and Beth Hartline, who taught a young reporter what the environmental movement was all about.

Also Joe Mihursky, Walter Boynton, and Mike Kemp, ecologists with the University of Maryland's bay laboratories, and their colleague Court Stevenson, at whose dinner table I have spent a number of stimulating evenings; Nick Carter, environmental regulator and bullfrogger *par excellence;* Don Baugh of the Chesapeake Bay Foundation, a marsh mucker after my own heart; and Bill and Barbara Smith, proprietors of the most hospitable way station a reporter traveling on the Eastern Shore ever could want.

Thanks also to Nancy Essig and Jane Warth, of the Johns Hopkins

Press, who have edited this book, and tolerated the author's eccentricities better than he could have hoped.

Finally, special thanks to Helen Winternitz, whose guidance, comments on the manuscript, and frequent availability for lunch and for bull sessions on writing were simply invaluable.

What Is Natural, What Is Right

It is winter in Harford County, and, crouched in a blind, I am watching, almost forgetting to breathe as dozens of bald eagles glide silently down the long shafts of setting sun to roost in the tall, dead trees. It is one of the largest concentrations of this magnificent and endangered species outside wild Alaska. Ah, wilderness! Well, hardly. The roost is downrange on the U.S. Army's Aberdeen Proving Ground, and there is scarcely a minute when the calm is not punctuated by the pounding of 120-millimeter howitzers. The eagles seem not to mind. Their numbers increase here with each winter.

It is summer at the Chincoteague National Wildlife Refuge, and I am marveling to a ranger at the eye-stretching sweep of pristine marsh, dune, and ponds. All about, a diverse population of migratory wildfowl is strewn like confetti. It is inspiring—also "100 percent managed," the ranger proudly replies. The dunes have been bulldozed up and stabilized with plantings of beach grass. The ponds were dug to catch fresh water, and equipped with floodgates to divert the annual coastal run of young eels into the impoundments as a food supply to hold the birds there. At night, floodlights attracted crab larvae to a nearby ocean cove, where a powerful pump sucked them through a pipe laid across a road and into one of the ponds, where crabbers would exclaim at nature's bounty in months to come.

It is fall at Horsehead Farm, a waterfowl preserve in Queen Anne's County, and a photographer friend is remarking at the frosted, natural beauty of dawn light illuminating the feathery plumes of tall reeds that surround us. I tell him the reeds are phragmites, an introduced species despised as a weed by all card-carrying environmentalists, because it outcompetes the indigenous bay grasses and offers little food value to wildlife.

1

What is it we mean anymore by the "natural environment"? The closer
we look, the harder it seems to know. The forestry ecologists sneer at
reporters who throw around terms like *virgin forest*. There probably
aren't ten acres of a really unaltered climax forest ecosystem in the
state anymore, they say. Meanwhile a peregrine falcon, symbol of all
that is fierce and untamed and free, hatches eastern North America's
first chicks (called *eyases*) in the wild in thirty years—hatches them in
downtown Baltimore, on a granite ledge of the United States Fidelity
and Guaranty Building's thirty-third floor. Cities, it turns out, concentrate pigeons and rats, candy to peregrines, better than nature ever
could.

It is often said by managers in environmental agencies that the
hardest step in saving the Chesapeake Bay, or any ecosystem for that
matter, is deciding what kind of environment we want to preserve. As
natural an environment as possible, you say—but how to define that?
We lament the vanishing of fish and animal habitat before civilization's
march, but any wildlife expert will tell you there are far more deer in
Maryland, and in most of the nation now, than ever existed in the days
of the Indians. And consider wild geese, whose numbers around the
bay have grown from a few thousand in the 1930s ("you could get your
picture in the paper for shootin' one then," a Cambridge resident told
me), to nearly one million nowadays. Likewise, although we have become so alarmed about the decline of the state fish, the rockfish, as to
place a moratorium on catching them, the bay's crab population is
booming, and total production of fish in the estuary quite possibly has
never been higher. If pollution is killing the bay, it seems awfully
selective.

What else can we say about the "natural" state of things?

We learned, during five days in June 1972, that events occurring in
nature can be so catastrophic as to overwhelm our best efforts at pollution control. Tropical Storm Agnes so accelerated the natural sedimen-
tation processes that are gradually filling in the bay, it was said to have
"aged" the estuary many decades in less than a week. Another century
of enforcing the state's sediment pollution laws on every developer and
farmer scarcely will offset Agnes.

The natural state of things can also be overstated, and come to represent an impossible goal. Legislators, watermen, and even scientists
who should know better often cite the fifteen million–bushel oyster
harvests of a century ago as an example of the bay's prepollution productivity. But that Everestian peak of harvest (current ones are about
one million bushels annually) was mostly indicative of uncontrolled
rape, as huge steam vessels scraped the bottom bald with their gaping
dredges, taking shell and undersized oysters along with the adults. It

was a harvest rate insupportable for more than a few years by the most pristine bay that ever existed.

Another example: some knowledgeable fisheries experts have speculated that the capacity of the bay to produce large numbers of rockfish may well have been greater in the mid-twentieth century than in the days of Captain John Smith. True, the explorer's party described rock so thick one could nearly walk on their broad backs, and that was probably not too far-fetched, because there was very little harvest pressure, and the fish can live for several decades. But as for the *rate* of reproduction, the betting is that up to a point (perhaps now exceeded) our injection of more nutrients into the system, via sewage and farm fertilizers, probably grew far greater supplies of microscopic aquatic life whose supply is critical to how many baby rockfish survive each year.

What, then, are we to make of our conventional image of human beings as spoilers—numbers of people up, pollution up, and environmental quality down? How do we interpret environmentalist urgings not to manipulate or intervene with nature when *natural* seems such an elusive quality, and sometimes not what we'd like it to be? I would be suspicious of anyone who claimed to have all the answers, but a few guidelines suggest themselves. You must be wary of using any single species as an indication of natural quality. There are at least a couple reasons why deer are more abundant now than in Indian days. We have killed off all the big predators, cougar and wolf and the like; and our massive forest-clearing activities, while polluting streams and destroying habitat for many deep-woods species, have nonetheless created lots of what game biologists call *edge habitat*, or areas where forest debouches on field or pasture. It just happens that such junctions favor deer, especially when one side includes a cornfield.

It is the massive proliferation of corn-growing since World War II that has led to the abundance of wild geese. Ironically, our expanded grain agriculture resulted in a huge increase in fertilizer, washed by rains into the bay in such unremitting quantities that it has killed the submerged grass beds. And these grasses were the prime food of ducks like the canvasback, which will not feed in cornfields. So we have more geese, but few canvasbacks. The trade-off is more than geese for ducks. It is a loss of balance and diversity, which are pretty good indications of health and resilience and stability in natural systems. The submerged grasses also were critical in absorbing pollutants from sewage, and in harboring dozens of aquatic species during one stage or another in their life cycle.

As for the paradoxical health of crabs even as their fellow bay dwellers, the rockfish, have declined, it is misleading to treat them equally as indicators of pollution just because we find them in the same waters as adults. Rather, look to where each species spends its most vulnerable, larval stages. The crab spawns in the clean, oceanic environment of the bay's mouth, whereas the rock, and virtually every other species that is reproducing poorly—shad, herring, yellow and white perch—spawn in the streams and rivers close to the polluting influences of civilization. Again, we have a natural system that, in terms of gross seafood landings, seems booming right along, but is seriously out of kilter. You must look at all the parts, and their relations to all the other parts. Only then can you begin to judge what is natural.

Of the eagles at Aberdeen, it was in retrospect a happy accident, the army's sealing off eighty thousand acres of open field, forest, marsh, and water on Harford County's bay shore during World War I. Given the ferocity of development that has consumed so much of the surrounding natural waterfront, it seems likely nothing less than the fire power of an army division could have kept Aberdeen Proving Ground sacrosanct. It is profoundly humbling that constant cannon fire has been far less destructive to the environment than the condos and suburbs and marinas; and that our national symbol, the eagle, would rather endure the sounds of war than the sight of human settlement.

The havoc wrought by natural catastrophes like Tropical Storm Agnes often is used by the unthinking or the unscrupulous as an excuse not to bother with environmental protection. Don't worry about more control of a certain air pollutant, they say; one eruption of a volcano can dwarf our manufactured quantities of it. I prefer the Boy Scout philosophy—leave the campsite as you found it, if not better, for you are just passing through. The only responsible course is to do whatever we can to put the least possible burden on the environment, because we cannot predict the frequency of a volcano or an Agnes, which some feel was at least a once-in-500-years storm. It is intriguing to reverse the natural-catastrophe argument and ask: Has anyone ever stopped developing the Ocean City beach front because at some point a hurricane is likely to offset our efforts?

What is natural? What is right? Here are some absolutes. Curves are natural. We grow up hearing so often that a straight line is the shortest distance between two points that we end up thinking it is also the *best* way to get there. A river knows better—it has to do with how it dissipates the energy of its flow most efficiently; and how, in its bends, the sediment deposited soon turns into marshes and swampy islands, harboring all manner of interesting life, imparting charm and character to the whole waterway. I would defy you to find a river on this planet that prefers to run straight, unless it has been taught so by the U.S. Army Corps of Engineers. People do exist who seem to prefer the straight line to the meander, the ditch to the creek, but it is mostly a failure of education that they are so unaware of the natural beauty and values of the curve.

Changelessness, or at least the diligent pursuit of it, is a good. Many environmentalists and ecologists feel that precisely because it is so hard to know what is natural, we should, in any decision affecting the environment, consider first how *not* to change the existing order. Aldo Leopold once wrote: "If the biota in the course of eons has built something we like but don't understand, then who but a fool would discard seemingly useless parts. To keep every cog and wheel is the first premise of intelligent tinkering." Of course, the "no-build" alternative is a required consideration of all federal Environmental Impact Statements nowadays, but we seldom accord it the seriousness it deserves. When we do, the results can be gratifying. A California law requires a power company proposing say, a $1 billion power plant, to first calculate whether that same billion, spent on conservation, solar power, storm windows, and so forth, could not save more energy than the new plant would generate. The law has avoided several new plants. I wish every schoolchild in Maryland could be allowed to hike, hunt, fish, swim, and breathe the clean air at some of the sites in rural Maryland reserved by the state and by utility companies for future power plants. It would do much to make them lifelong advocates of energy conservation.

At the extreme in promoting changelessness are some Indian tribes who hold certain lands so numinous they have made them holy places. I make no such pretensions, but it is true that one of my favorite fishing spots, on the remote Honga River in Dorchester County, has not yielded a fish for me in years. I go there for the view of pine and salt marsh and bay; it is one of the few places to have remained just the same as in my boyhood memories. I suspect mine is not an isolated or silly sentiment. It may be one reason that close to one million fishermen a year keep coming back to the bay even though, according to state creel surveys, more than a third of all their trips produce no fish at all. They must be hooking into something else, something natural and deeply satisfying, and it may have to do with changelessness.

Finally, I would propose the quality of *wildness* as a valuable aspect of what is natural. Yes, it can be partly a created thing, like the lovely, constructed scene at the Chincoteague Refuge; but there we have only provided a setting, a way station. Crab, osprey, canvasback duck, great blue heron, and migrating eel—all bear witness that larger natural systems, far beyond our ability to concoct, still survive. There is considerable energy being expended these days around the Chesapeake Bay to build hatcheries to produce more rockfish, resurrect the American

shad, and repopulate the bay with waterfowl. It would only be to augment depleted natural populations until we can turn the environment
around to let them come back naturally, the hatchery proponents say.
But the concept has such power, you can see the undercurrent of their
thinking—if worst comes to worst, don't worry, we can just hatch our
fish and birds for our sport; and if the migratory flights of the herons
and ospreys should ever flag, well, a small hatchery tucked away in the
pines at Chincoteague, one supposes, could supply the ponds indefinitely. If it worked, why knock it? A heron is a heron is a heron.

But that is to confuse nature with zoos. A wild trout implies a
whole watershed still forested enough, still enough removed from human pollution, to maintain a clean, cold, constant flow in its streams. A
canvasback duck, as it plops down on the bay's surface one fall morning, brings with it the certitude that some of the vast, lovely prairie
pothole marshes of Saskatchewan, its nesting and summering
grounds, remain inviolate. A hatchery trout or a hatchery duck would
be just as beautiful, but something natural would be missing, something would not seem right. The author and Maryland native John
Barth, in a discussion on the bay's future, once speculated that perhaps, just perhaps, our technologies could succeed in keeping the waters clean and productive even as we ringed the estuary with "wall-to-
wall Glen Burnies." We would still have oysters, crabs, and rockfish,
but we would not have the bay, he said. "The spirit," he said, "would
have gone out of it."

Killing Geese

Deep Neck, Talbot County, Winter

It is thrilling to watch the flock of wild geese winging confidently
on the crest of dawn, closing rapidly the last few hundred yards that
separate us. It is rare, when you think about it, for human beings today
to see free living creatures that are not running away, shying, freezing
in their tracks, programmed long ago to avoid the most deadly species.
It's been a trade-off, our becoming lords of the earth. In so doing, we
have been exiled from the paradise of peaceful coexistence with our
fellow creatures, says Konrad Lorenz, the pioneer animal behaviorist
who won the Nobel Prize for living with geese in the wild to learn their
ways. In those rare moments when wildlings approach us, he says, it is
almost as if the exile had been lifted.

Perhaps some notion of this does flicker across our deeper consciousness as the geese sideslip to lose altitude, tumbling like leaves, recovering effortlessly. They swirl down all around us, honking low, soft moans of contentment, feet down, great wings set, cupping the wind, mastering its every caprice and buffet so surely that they seem to descend through some more viscid, stable medium than air. But what we seek so avidly this bright, cold December day is not exactly the paradise of Konrad Lorenz.

"Let's take 'em," murmurs Elmer Crawford, letting fall the goose call he has been blowing so seductively; and the four of us, guns roaring, leap almost in unison from our concealment near the decoys bobbing on the water of the cove.

Even as we rise, the geese have sensed the fatality of their commitment to landing. They struggle to gain altitude, appearing to lumber because they are such big birds; but actually they are gaining about four feet with every wing beat, and I try to lead my targets accordingly. The flock fades quickly from sight, leaving two of its number shattered on the water. Later the dogs will sniff out a third, a cripple, that had glided unnoticed into the marsh during the excitement. By sunset, with another goose and two mallard ducks also in the bag, the hunt will have qualified as a memorable one. Three times we will flirt with the peaceful coexistence paradise of Lorenz and three times we will respond by pulling the trigger.

It seems worth examining whether it must be that way; because when you kill a goose, you have ended something special. Geese, the late Edgar Merkle used to say to me, are smarter than you and I; they mate only once, they protect their children, and they feed their young first. At his Patuxent River farm, Merkle's breeding and conservation efforts through several decades established a flock of more than twenty thousand wild geese on the bay's western shore, where historically there had been none. Why geese? I asked him. He said, "Because I knew the pleasure geese would give to people . . . just to watch 'em, to hear 'em talk just before they take off; just to know they were around. Also they are mostly all Geminis [hatching in May and early June on their Arctic breeding grounds], and Gemini is a good sign."

In his convictions, Merkle, who would avidly shoot ducks, but never a goose, was pretty much in agreement with the learned ethologists like Lorenz who have documented the wild goose's extraordinarily close-knit family structure, and a potential for living nearly as long as we (though in the wild it is undoubtedly less). They pair for life, and the loss of a mate can provoke an uncannily human response. "They possess a veritably human capacity for grief," writes Lorenz, who also noted that animals in general, "in terms of emotions. . ., are much more akin to us than is generally assumed."

I have observed geese that appear to be calling for a lost mate, or a lost flock, and I have no trouble believing they are grieving. In the most ancient parts of the brain, where the deep emotions and instincts are seated, we do not have such different apparatus than a goose. Of course, it is those outsized frontal lobes, sprung forth in just the last few hundred thousand years, that set us apart from the animals. They give us the capacity for rational thought, for choosing between hunting geese and going bird-watching with the Audubon Society, a group, it must be noted, that officially does not oppose hunting. Our big forebrain lets us love geese, even as we love to kill them. That hunting is part of our heritage is as certain as the pointed canines we have in our head, the better to rend meat with. "Man cannot re-enter Nature except by temporarily rehabilitating that part of himself which is still an animal," wrote José Ortega y Gasset, a Spanish philosopher who saw hunting as a necessary, brief escape from the twentieth century. But we are long past those old needs to kill other animals for survival, even to eat meat at all; and so, there we hang, as the geese swirl down to the decoys—civilized hunters, balancing between our canines and our molars, between paradise and exile, faced with a succinct little question posed by the naturalist Joseph Wood Krutch: "Why should anyone kill anything for pleasure?"

Ironically, "the kill" is probably the aspect of hunting that Rooney Crawford, the gunner to my immediate right in the blind, has considered least as a reason for pursuing his sport, which makes him fairly typical of most hunters in the numerous surveys that have been done on what makes them tick. Rooney, forty-one, an affable data-processing engineer from Greenville, South Carolina, has been coming up here every goose season for more than a decade with his older brother, Elmer, fifty-one, a real-estate salesman from Bessemer City, North Carolina. Elmer says he sent away to Maryland for a list of professional goose-hunting guides and picked Sam Leonard's Friendship Farm, here in Talbot County, by closing his eyes and sticking a dart into the page. The brothers, Rooney says, grew up on a farm in little Clover, South Carolina, hunting squirrel and rabbit as their natural birthright, an easy contact with the land and its wild crops that he feels society is less and less privy to nowadays.

Rooney says he hunts to be in the outdoors, for the suspense, for the challenge; and the Crawfords love to eat wild ducks and geese. Mostly, though, Rooney hunts for the pleasure of bringing along the fourth member in our blind, his sixteen-year-old son, Mitch. "Mitch began coming here when we had to stand him on a concrete block to shoot over the edge of the blind," Rooney says. There is an easy, joshing camaraderie between the two out here, which reminds me that some of the best times I ever had with my father—some of the best times I ever had—were in hunting situations. I don't know that it couldn't have been just as good in other circumstances, but for us it happened on hunts; on kills, if you will.

"The killing," Rooney says with a little uneasiness, but no uncertainty, "it is almost an after-part to the rest . . . unfortunate, but . . . " But it has to be there? Yes, it does, he agrees. There is the uncomfortable paradox. Take just about any of the justifications people give for going killing/hunting—being outdoors, obtaining meat, camaraderie—and they all seem things you could experience just as well separately from the hunt. Or maybe not. Up to the time we first shot, the morning had been typical for a hunt at Friendship Farm, which is to say filled with staggering beauty and a senses-swelling awareness of our surroundings. The first fierce blush of dawn kindled cold fires on the smooth surface of Elberts Cove, which edges Sam's farm. The sky was a parfait of creams, pastel blues, palest oranges, and raspberry ices. Increasing daylight developed the landscape like a photographic print as cedars, marshes, and cornfields tugged apart from the featureless grays of night and assumed their own forms, textures, and colors. Crows sallied eastward, cawing. A great blue heron swept silently along the near shore, pursuing solitary routes more ancient, even, than the migrating geese. A swan, big as a ship, sailed fearlessly into our goose decoys, pecking one on the back. We have not hunted its race for centuries, and the swan seemed to know it.

I thought about what Sam Leonard said in the toasty farmhouse kitchen before we walked out to the blind; how he often called his paying customers to give them a chance to back out when he thought the hunting would be poor the next day. They almost never do, Sam said. They just like to be out there . . . getting a goose is just a bonus. But of all the hunters he has seen, Sam can only recall one who did not go out there at least in anticipation of the kill. He just sat there for three days, never fired his gun, happy as a lark just watching, Sam said. But he was very, very unusual.

Sam doesn't say so, but there is also bonus enough for most of his hunters in spending a day in the blind listening to Sam, or his son, Bobby, who helps out with guiding. Both are as close to natural predators as modern human beings get. They oyster and crab and fish from the waters that edge their farm. They hunt and eat goose, duck, coon, deer, rabbit, quail, dove, and squirrel from the woods and hedgerows that checker their grain fields. I doubt seriously whether they spend a hundred dollars a year on meat from a store. They crop Friendship Farm and its environs in the fullest sense of the word. They know the price of waterfront land—Sam was offered close to a $1 million for the farm recently; and they also know its value—he turned it down with little thought. Virtually every night of his life between October and March, Bobby, thirty, has gone to sleep to the sound of goose music from the cove by the farmhouse. One Sunday in midwinter, he told me, he had decided to get away, take a drive somewhere. He drove straight to Blackwater National Wildlife Refuge, forty miles away. "I just got the urge to see some geese," he explained.

In the blind, it is nearing noon and nothing much is flying. I have taken advantage of the lull to wander among the decoys and pick up a half-dozen oysters from the clear, elbow-deep water. The water is so icy I have to quit. We open them on the wooden seat of the blind and down them in their cold, salty liquor, with a liberal sprinkling of winter sunlight and clean-smelling air. Good chow, and plucked from nature like that, it somehow satisfies more than just the belly. This is the time of the hunting day to stretch, walk out behind the blind to piss, explore the shoreline, and tramp across a couple fields in hopes of scaring up a rabbit, or quail. Today the noontime entertainment comes from a hawk, whose dazzling power dive undoubtedly translated into death for some hapless creature scurrying frantically through the winter-weary stubble of Sam's cornfield.

"The hawk, the swoop and the hare—all are one," wrote the poet Gary Snyder, in as terse and true an ecological statement as I ever read. The awesome thrill of the swoop, the panic of the cowering prey, beauty and cruel death—each is integral to the very existence of the raptor, and there is not much gain in discussing any part out of context. Suddenly, we are startled by a flash of birds that have moved silently up behind us in the air just off the corner of our sight. I almost spill my mug of coffee. They are only blackbirds, not geese, but it is not unusual for this to happen several times in a day's hunting. Sometimes it is a lone seagull wandering into the periphery of your field of vision; even a sparrow can trigger it.

The reason, I think, is that far from being relaxing, hunting generates a constant and fairly high level of tension, a keen, sense-stretching state in which every subtlety of the tides, winds, weather, lunar cycles, every speck flying on the horizon, becomes worthy of intense scrutiny and endless and pleasurable debate. I have gone birding with expert ornithologists, trekked the Western Maryland mountains with the region's foremost botanists, and pondered the flora and fauna of beaches with noted coastal scientists; but nothing expands my senses to such limits as scanning the horizon, armed, from a goose blind. When seeking to kill, it all *matters* in a way it doesn't seem to when you are not.

Konrad Lorenz and some others no doubt can extract at least as rich an awareness of nature as any hunter, and on a more intellectual, nonviolent basis; but for the bulk of the 20.6 million Americans who hunt, there may be no fully satisfactory substitute for their sport. As I write, I can hear those who will say that even use of the word *sport* is loading the dice. So yes, "killing for kicks" is also what it is, reduced to its essentials; but surely it is "kicks" that have some pretty complex and not wholly unsavory aspects to commend them. It may be that there are no satisfactory resolutions to the question of killing. Its roots run so deeply, are so interlaced with tradition, and evoke so many poignant yesterdays; roots that are too deep to be pulled up and examined, in the opinion of John Madson, a conservation writer.

A national survey by Stephen Kellert of Yale's Forestry School indicated that only about 17 percent of hunters feel compelled to rationalize the deeper urges behind their trigger fingers. I don't wonder. Those are urges for which you can summon some powerful, bloody, and unflattering interpretations: "Men are not friendly, gentle creatures wishing for love," wrote Sigmund Freud, who felt we are motivated by an undeniable, instinctual urge for aggression. He is seconded by the anthropologist Raymond Dart, who believes we have an inbred proclivity for killing, an inherited blood lust, a concept that has been popularized by writers like Robert Ardrey in *The Territorial Imperative* and Desmond Morris in *The Naked Ape*. Certainly I have hunted with people who in their passion for killing come on, as one writer put it, "Like a U-boat commander upping his periscope at Noah's Ark." And I can recall a time, in my teens, when I competed fiercely with a companion in a numbers game to down the most ducks, legal limits and other game laws be damned. I suspect this blood lust, given the nature of teenage boys, is more hormonal than genetic, because it seems a pattern that the need to kill declines in most hunters as they age, though the love of going hunting may never waver. As Chan Rippons, an old Hooper Islander who has quit after slaying more than his share of waterfowl, says, "the older you get, the more you respect life."

At any rate, I prefer the hypothesis of the anthropologist Richard Leakey, who believed that aggression and the hunting instinct are not so interwoven as we had thought. Our capacity to slaughter our own kind in warfare, Leakey thought, is not the product of a hunting society, not the result of something dark and uncontrollable inherited from prehistoric human predators. It is rather a by-product of agriculture. The human economy had to include planted fields and stable settlements as spoils before war became worth the tremendous expenditure of resources it entails. Ultimately, probably all one can certify about our shedding of goose blood today at Friendship Farm is that its motivation lies on a plane above lustful killing and yet surely below

Emerson's transcendental communion with the spiritual through nature. To the geese hung behind the blind, it can't make much difference.

Now the sun is almost down. Only the long, red wavelengths of its light linger, stretching across the land, burnishing everything with a warm, coppery glow that belies the fast-falling temperature. Flying so fast they rend the air audibly, six big ducks, creamy undersides luminously rosy in the sunset, wheel across our decoys with a military precision the Blue Angels would envy. Trigger fingers tighten briefly and ease. These are canvasbacks, a protected species since severe habitat loss and hunting pressure devastated their numbers several years ago. "Beautiful, though, aren't they?" says Elmer.

Marsh grass is golden
Under a late sun,
And wild ducks' wings
Whistle with the wind.
We are one,
Wild duck and setting sun.

The young hunter who wrote that half a century ago lives just across the Choptank River from Sam's place. Gilbert Byron is old now, and a renowned poet of the Chesapeake Bay. The poem that contains those lines is still his favorite. He long ago lost the urge to hunt, but the beauty endures, he says. A cuticle of new moon is rising as we pack up geese, guns, and shared memories and head back to Sam's farmhouse, boots breaking thin ice forming in the low spots. Far out on the darkening, slatey water a chorus of goose music is piping up that will last all night.

Nettlesome Facts of Life

July, somewhere on the bay, but definitely not in it. The language of the federal Clean Water Act promised to make this place not only "fishable," but also "swimmable"; obviously Congress didn't know about jellyfish.

Spissitudinous, viscid demons" is what a *Baltimore Sun* editorial of July 1934, called them; and it is doubtful that *Chrysaora quinquecirrha*, the summer sea nettle that scourges Chesapeake Bay as no other place, has risen in the public estimation since. This is the time of year when everyone suddenly craves the opinion of David Cargo, the ranking jellyfish expert at the Chesapeake Biological Laboratory of the University of Maryland, down on the Patuxent River at Solomons. Some years he seems a bit weary of his status as a man for one season, a sort of Chesapeake version of Punxatawney Phil, the Pennsylvania groundhog whose annual emergence is covered by the national media; but he bears his burden amiably. With jellyfish, one must learn, above all, accommodation. The only things that seem to damp populations of jellyfish in the bay, he says, are wet years, warm winters, and cold springs. This year has been dry as a bone. The winter was frigid, and the spring blissfully warm. He thinks, come August, we are going to see a blossoming of *Chrysaora* to equal the vintage of 1969, which was what you call a 100 percent year. A 100 percent year simply means that if you swim in the bay you get stung—anywhere, anytime.

We have not always been so accepting of our fate as that. In the 1930s, Maryland officials were experimenting with a variety of control measures. They found a poison that worked, copper sulfate, but concluded that to eradicate the jellyfish, it would take all the sulfate mined . . . and kill everything else in the bay. Always pushed by Maryland's delegation, Congress flirted with declaring war on the stinging nettles for the next few decades. In 1970 President Richard Nixon signed the Jellyfish Control Act. It authorized research into the creature's life cycle, in hope of finding a weak link that could be exploited to control it (by then there was no more talk of eradication).

If the subsequent research achieved anything, it was to give us new appreciation of just how marvelously fit *Chrysaora* is for life in our estuary. Above all other places it ranges, from New England to the tropics, the bay is elixer to the species. Oyster shells form a perfect substrate to which the jellyfish can attach the ice cream cone–shaped polyps that are its overwintering stage. There, *Chrysaora* can encyst itself for years, and perhaps decades, effortlessly enduring times unfavorable for reproduction, such as during high flows of fresh water. Then, the polyps will resume their asexual budding-forth of young jellyfish in the spring. These in turn will mature sexually in late summer—we call it the medusa stage—and produce larvae that sink to the bottom, attach to oyster shells, and form more polyps.

It also appears that not much of anything else in the bay preys on jellyfish, and that they have a virtually unlimited supply of their favorite food, the gelatinous, transparent creatures called comb jellies, or *Ctenophores*. The latter are destructive to crab and oyster larvae; but before we give a gold star to jellyfish for protecting crabs and oysters, be aware that some scientists think they eat even more crab and oyster larvae than the comb jellies do. In sum, one is tempted to paraphrase Captain John Smith, the early explorer and publicist of the bay, and conclude that "heaven and earth never agreed better to frame a place for *jellyfishes* inhabitation."

You have to look hard for a silver lining to jellyfish. The ecologist may thrill to such elegant adaptation of a creature to its environment; and personally, I have always given the jellyfish high marks, along with the mosquito and the greenhead fly, for making large sections of the bay seasonally inhospitable enough to discourage dense human settlement there. But most of us are left to console ourselves with Adolph's Meat Tenderizer, a favored amendment for jellyfish stings, and to ask the eternal questions: "Why did the Lord make jellyfish? What good are they to the bay? Why must the bay have jellyfish?"

In search of a better perspective on that universal plaint, to get me through this "100 percent" summer, I passed an afternoon watching two *Chrysaora* bobbing in the mouth of the Choptank River. Their opalescent bellshapes undulated as one with the bay swells, and their tentacles rippled sensuously in the current. The effect was hypnotic. I could swear I overheard them in this conversation. . . .

Nettle 1: Damn nuisances. Does anyone even know where they come from?

Nettle 2: No one knows for sure, but every summer, just about the time the weather's getting great for swimming, here they come, out of nowhere, great grotesque, thrashing hunks of raw meat, jumping off boats, piers, and riverbanks. It gets so by August its almost impossible for a nettle to avoid touching one of them.

Nettle 1: Aren't they even good to eat?

Nettle 2: Nah. Too big to paralyze—a waste of your poison.

Nettle 1: But surely anything that numerous must have some role, some niche in the ecosystem, if not useful to us nettles, at least important to the bay?

Nettle 2: You would think so. They are obviously estuarine-dependent organisms. Worldwide, seven of their ten biggest cities are located on estuaries.

But the connection isn't obvious. All they seem to do is take crabs, take oysters, take rockfish, take, take, take. All they put back is sewage and chemicals. All the evidence is that the bay could exist just fine without them.

Nettle 1: What's known about their life cycle? Where do they go in the fall? How do they survive cold weather?

Nettle 2: Most of them seem to retreat in September up two major tributaries, the Potomac and the Patapsco, which we surmise may have some unique habitat essential to their spawning and overwintering.

We know that they're a tough, resilient species. They can stand even wet years like Tropical Storm Agnes in June 1972—remember how all that fresh-water inflow knocked the nettle population for such a loop for years afterward? Well, by August of that very year the humans were back in the bay like nothing had happened.

Nettle 1: I've heard talk they've increased their population dramatically in the bay in the last century. Some say if it keeps up, there may soon be no room left for nettles.

Nettle 2: I don't think so. It's nothing you can prove, but if the bay hadn't been made for us jellyfish, would we have prospered so here? I can't believe we're not a part of some grander design of nature that may or may not include humans.

Look at it this way. We *Coelenterates* have been around for close to a quarter-billion years with very little change. That's what you call a success story, if I may speak evolutionarily. Now, the entire human existence has spanned only about 1 percent of that time—certainly not enough to judge their staying power.

What you see in the last century or so may amount to a fluke, a temporary outbreak, like a virus or an epidemic of flu—rough while it lasts, but over as quick as it came, poof!

Trees

I have traveled widely because of trees, usually to document their mass destruction and the disenfranchisement of their wildlife: to the Amazon, where the pace of ill-conceived development could wipe from the planet by the middle of next century much of the billion-acre rain forest that harbors 40 percent of all the earth's plant and animal species; to the threatened New Jersey Pine Barrens, where for the moment you can still mount a fire tower that is an hour's drive from New York City's outskirts and drink in a great, green hush of untrammeled forest and clean rivers flowing to every horizon; and to South Carolina's brooding, cypress-sentineled I'On Swamp, where biologists prowled the blackwater recesses listening vainly for the notes of perhaps the last Bachman's warbler on earth, and loggers readied to pounce on the species' last likely deep woods refuge should it be declared extinct.

Intellectually, I lament all of these; but it is humbler change in more familiar places which hits one like a slap in the face with the fate of forests. In Caroline County, where I grew up, I can now see, riding out the old Hurlock Road by where George Evans's bar was, all the way north to American Corners. Cutting across a half-dozen little back roads and flat-land farms and creeks that used to seem like separate parts of the county, it is more of a view than I ever wanted to have. The impact of the shorn forest, carried away on a limitless tide of soybeans, has somehow been to diminish the landscape, unravel it, demystify and impersonalize it. My mood is not improved on seeing, a few miles more down the road, that a local farmer has hung a fancy, prosperity-proclaiming sign at the entrance to his lane announcing: "Clearcut Acres."

In just twelve years, between 1964 and 1976, Caroline County cut off eleven thousand acres, or around two square miles, or 13 percent of its forests. The forest cannot compete in any short-term economic sense with booming grain markets or against the demands of ever-larger farm equipment and irrigation systems for unbroken blocks of cleared land on which to operate effectively. "Clean farming" is the name of the game now, and every year the quail and rabbit hunters find that another few miles of favored hedgerow has vanished to it. A lot of farmers say: We live in a hungry world. Would you rather have trees or food? I think many of them believe this. Certainly the thought of feeding the world produces a warm glow in a job that offers a pitiful monetary return compared to the investment of cash and time. But most of their grain is used to feed cattle and chickens and hogs; and it takes fifty-five acres of soybeans, fed to steers, to produce the protein that one acre could produce if fed directly to people. Our forest losses are fueling history's most luxurious diet, not staving off starvation.

Perhaps that begs the issue of whether forests are competitive at all in our modern schemes of existence. Although Eastern Shore agriculture in the twelve-year period for which statistics are available accounted for 87,000 acres of forest clearing, development for houses and shopping malls in the five-county Baltimore metropolitan region claimed another 130,000 acres. All told, the changes produced the most drastic rate of deforestation in the northeastern United States, and reduced the forest which covered virtually 100 percent of Maryland when the colonists arrived, to about 40 percent. The economic forces arrayed against forests seem unlikely to lessen. We have no strategy for checking the losses, no bottom line beyond which we mean not to let forest acreage decrease.

Acreage figures also tend to understate the seriousness of loss, for there are also quality considerations to forests. The woodland warblers and vireos whose sweet, liquid songs are an increasingly rare delight need as much as a thousand acres of forest in unbroken blocks to survive. The red-cockaded woodpecker, who took nourishment only in old-growth pines, has virtually vanished from its last refuges in Dorchester County. I read about a forester there recently who expressed great relief at convincing an old farmer to fell some of the biggest, oldest loblolly pines in the state. The farmer had been "just letting his trees go," the forester said. Letting it go to red-cockaded woodpeckers perhaps.

The "overmaturity" feared by the professional forester, the stage at which trees have ceased to add new wood at a rapid rate, can occur centuries before a forest would approach its natural life span. This was until recently the sin of a unique stand of oaks and tulip poplars known as the Beltwoods, which had grown, nearly untouched, for more than 250 years on ninety acres near the Capital Beltway and Central Avenue in Prince Georges County. There were few forests left in the eastern half of the country to rival the Beltwoods. Trees soared a hundred feet before branching. Surveys of breeding birds there in 1947 and again, in 1975, showed some of the greatest population densities ever recorded. The ancient trees were surprisingly disease-free, and for a while seemed as if they might last, an island out of time, well into the twenty-first century or beyond. The late Seton Belt, a semireclusive banker and gentleman farmer whose family had owned the forest for generations, stipulated in his will that the giant old trees never be logged off.

But the bank entrusted with administering Seton Belt's estate, and the church to which he left his goods, found that the forest earned the highest accolades not just from naturalists and woodland songbirds. "Veneer quality," eager buyers from the world's leading timber concerns adjudged the massive, knot-free, straight trunks of the oaks. Debarked, steamed until soft, then sliced and peeled on huge machines into sheets just $1/42$-inch thick, just a few of the Beltwoods giants would decorate acres of executive conference-room walls in warm wood tones.

The church said it needed money over and above the $10 million that old Belt had left it to build an urban home for the elderly. With the bank, it broke the will in court, and half the mighty Beltwoods fell to the chainsaw (the rest ultimately was bought by the state and preserved). The forester hired by the bank explained to me his satisfaction when the veneer deal went through. From the standpoint of annual, new cellulose production, he said, the old oaks were well into the area of diminishing returns, even though they might live another century or two. "The only thing left for that particular stand of trees to do was to die and fall over," he said.

Given our track record with even forests as magnificent as the Beltwoods, it is legitimate to ask whether we care much at all about them. Because we love individual trees, celebrate our biggest and oldest ones, glory in their shade and beauty in our yards and along our urban streets, and marvel at their fall color—because of all this, we may assume we love forests; but the evidence is to the contrary. Even our wildlife managers tend to be most enamored not of the true forest but of its fringes. It is on the forest edge, and in its clearings, that deer and quail, rabbits and most of the species we hunt abound.

More basic than this, however, is the compelling, if forever speculative, evidence that the primary edge species on the globe is us. Most biologists agree that the place where *Homo erectus* first crawled down from the trees to stalk the abundant game so temptingly nearby was where the jungle opened out onto the East African savanna—one of the richest edges on earth. There was enough open space to make hunting good, and trees close by to scramble back into should predators threaten. We still, I suspect, innately feel most comfy around such edges. A classic study in Michigan with deer mice found that even after being bred for twenty generations in a laboratory cage, the latest descendants showed an uncanny preference for the natural habitat of their ancestors. They learned to adapt and survive in a lab cage, but they knew in their genes where they fit best. Certainly our modern parks and estates and golf courses emulate that primal savanna edge habitat to a surprising degree.

As an increasingly urban population, we tell our children, "Don't go in the woods . . . walk where there are streetlights." Read the papers any day; the wooded areas seem always to be where rapes occur and bodies are dumped. The Washington, D.C., police recently had to clear-cut a nice block of forest on the edge of the city after trying fruitlessly for years to halt the drug trafficking that had overtaken the place. To city dwellers, whose votes more and more shape public policies, the deep woods may be as fearful a place as it ever was for their early ancestors (yes, and as full of wild animals).

Perhaps, as innate lovers of the forest's edge, we should be in our glory in modern Maryland, which increasingly has little but edges and fringes of forest left: but we are discovering, belatedly, that with the loss of the great forest, there was a loss of more than trees and even the wildlife that needs deep-woods habitat, like the warblers. You can find in old fisheries records evidence of sizeable oyster populations in Maryland's upper Chesapeake Bay as far north as the Gunpowder River, which has mystified scientists. Conditions there, even before the water got polluted by sewage and industry, would seem to have been inimical to the oyster. That part of the bay is so far removed from the ocean as to be almost totally influenced by the flow of rivers. They flood in the spring and run almost not at all in some summers, causing major fluctuations in environmental conditions. Additionally, they carry such loads of sediment from farms and development sites that choking silt and dredging to clear boat channels are constantly degrading the environment. In short, the upper bay environment seems too unstable ever to have hosted the shellfish populations that it clearly did at one time.

Recently a possible explanation has emerged as some scientists have begun rethinking what the watersheds of the upper bay were like when the virgin forest canopied them. The force of rainstorms was diffused through multiple stories of leaves and branches: and what fell to the ground, fell upon a centuries-old accumulation of leaf duff that came to a man's waist, according to accounts of early settlers. The land back then was like a giant sponge, trickling water slowly into the bay, filtering it, metering it evenly throughout the year. Spring floods were smaller, and summer droughts were less severe: the water was clearer. Sediments corresponding to that period indicate the upper bay was saltier, evidence that the rivers and the ocean struck a more consistent balance back then. Controlled by the forest, the environment of the upper bay was more stable and lovely than anything that now exists, or probably can exist again.

No one dreams of bringing back the forest primeval, but slowly the forest is gaining recognition as a key to water quality. The silt from farm and developed land runs into the bay at a rate fifty times that from woodland. Phosphorus, another prime pollutant, comes eighty times as much from cropland as from forest, and forty times as much from residential areas. For nitrogen and toxic chemicals the story is similar. Recently the Maryland legislature, in a historic session tabbed the Year of the Bay, passed a law recognizing forest, for the first time, as a "least polluting landuse." It is only the narrowest extension of protective consideration, applying just to the trees nearest major waterways; but from ever-expanding numbers of a race that loves its edges and its grain-fed beef, it is about as good as the forest can hope for right now.

Elms

I never met a tree I didn't like. I pity anyone who has never lolled away a summer day in the deep-shaded boughs of a maple, or snuggled in the crotch of a willow while the wind and sun fooled with its green-golden tresses; who has not delighted in hiding beneath the ground-sweeping skirts of a hemlock; or who has never been lulled by the woodwinds of a tall pine forest.

We all marvel at certain individual trees of extraordinary stature, age, or historical import, but whole species may also have powerful personalities. The oaks are a robust, confident lot, thrusting brawny limbs at angles from their trunks that dare gravity, the wind, and time itself to do their damnedest. The sycamores are big, raw-boned country boys, graceless and blotchy complexioned, more at home next to the stream in a cow pasture; but their blocky catcher's mitts of leaves are so spaced as to dapple city sidewalks with the perfect mix of sun and shadow.

Gingkos, a Japanese import, I like for the way they combine sumo-wrestler size with pretty little leaves resembling nothing so much as a geisha's delicate fan. One girthy old gingko on Northern Parkway in Baltimore is a personal favorite—a survivor of the city's overwhelming allegiance to concrete. Just approaching 150 years of age—early adult-hood for this species that evolved with the dinosaurs—it was to have been destroyed by widening the highway; but for three years city for-esters laboriously dug successively deeper ditches around the old Brobdingnag's root system to "shock" its system, toughening it to the point it could accept a concrete retaining wall that separates it by only inches from the busy expressway.

In my travels to some of the globe's remotest corners, I have taken time to inspect champion trees of every stripe: the great neem trees that line the Blue Nile at Khartoum, the bizarre, elephant-skinned baobabs of Tanzania's arid interior: giant acacias of the Red Sea deserts; the magnificent Brazil nut tree of the Amazon rain forest, soaring tall as a redwood. Nothing I have ever seen is the equal of the American elm. Cities and towns nationwide have planted some twenty-five mil-lion for their graceful, boulevard-arching shade in summer; but it is winter that reveals them as true artists. Any landscape painter can tell you that rendering a tree faithfully has to do not only with branches and leaves but also with how space and light are scattered among them. Along with their overall contours, it is this interior architecture of trees that visually differentiates an elm from an oak, a beech from a birch.

Notice an elm silhouetted against a sunny winter sky, how ele-gantly and cleanly its sinews compartment regions of bright, blue space. No other tree is as adept. In winter it frames great, uncluttered swatches of light in fantastic borders of wrought iron, strength and del-icacy in a combination that would shame the best creations of an Alex-andre Eiffel. Leaved-out for the summer, the elm is a vase, holding the atmosphere of the day in sensuous, curved grandeur. In spring, the long, strong arching of its major limbs, seen through a negligee-thick-ness of newly minted green, is simply seductive—there is no other word for it.

Almost as if their extreme beauty had angered the gods, the elms all are dying. More than half of the twenty-five million in America's yards and streets have already gone, and each year another 400,000 succumb, victims of Dutch elm disease, a beetle-spread fungus. Bal-timore loses several hundred elms annually, and is down to its last couple of thousand. The city is replacing them on major streets like Thirty-third and Gwynns Falls with Japanese zelkovas, which are highly resistant to disease and pollution and in time will provide ex-cellent shade—but not excellent architecture. The zelkova is rather twiggy and tends to mushroom rapidly toward its top. We are replac-ing elegant vases with umbrellas.

If some exotic, imported termite were set loose which had a pre-

dilection for chewing up all our finest old buildings, doubtless the nation would spare no expense in controlling the pest or inventing a way
to termite-proof the architectural treasures. As near as I can tell, after a
check with the private Elm Research Institute of Harrisville, New
Hampshire, the grand total of all corporate, government, foundation,
and academic budgets for research to stop the demise of America's
most beautiful tree is about $200,000 a year—this in a nation that can
spend that much and more for each few yards of modern interstate
highways.

Why have we not done more for the elm, arguably our finest natural architecture and the only city public-works project that accrues in
value for a century or more after it is put in place? Perhaps it has to do
with our difficulty in putting beauty down on municipal account
books. The value of the elm cannot be quoted on any stock exchange,
or even expressed in board feet (it is lousy lumber and firewood, tough
and resinous, almost impervious to splitting).

With the demise of the elm, we are courting the distinction of having lost in half a century both our primest urban tree and also the best,
most valuable tree that ever grew in American forests. The spreading
chestnut tree has gone the way of village smithies, with even less of a
nod from society than the elm has received. You can still see old
chestnut stumps scattered throughout the state's Piedmont and Appalachian forests, valiantly sprouting new shoots each summer. But
the airborne fungus imported from Asia in the early 1900's, which virtually extirpated our dominant woodland species by 1920, still lurks,
waiting to strike with deadly results. It is rare that a chestnut offshoot
survives more than a few years before it develops the deadly cankers of
the fungus.

As with the elm, research efforts to restore the chestnut, viable
groves of which survive in pockets of Wisconsin and Washington State,
are piddling. Probably it says something about our society's move away
from dependency on, and proximity to, the forest. Only a few generations ago we had a discerning knowledge for wood that would astound
most moderns. We understood the different working qualities of
dozens of woods, which types complemented one another; which best
served every function, from ladles to barn beams. We have lost that
refined sense of quality, both in our wood and in our forests, and we
and they are the poorer for it.

A tree is a tree is a tree, to paraphrase Gertrude Stein. Not to me. I
write this next to a favorite picture that hangs on my office wall. Its
rendering of wild geese is pleasing enough, but that is secondary to the
frame, which is of virgin chestnut. If you have ever marveled at the
grain and color of oak in furniture, then you have never been spoiled

by chestnut. Its tawny blonde luster and flowing grain are striking; and its extraordinary workability and resistance to rot made it our finest all-around building material during the bulk of the nation's history. It still stands in the beams of old barns and in split-rail fences around Maryland's more rural areas. Many are still as sound as the day they were erected. Perhaps someday an industrious botanist will employ the burgeoning science of genetic engineering to create a disease-resistant elm and, in the process, a chestnut too. The botanist will obviously win the Nobel Prize for science, but I would award it also for art.

Roots

From what we see of corn, it is no wonder we celebrate it. Its tender green sprouting signals spring as much as robins and pussy willows. All summer, growing higher than a man's head across fully a tenth of the state's surface, it defines the Maryland landscape as few other species; in autumn, it is the ripe, golden coin of the realm, the mounded, shining symbol of the harvest. The soil is fertile, the land bountiful, corn constantly reassures us. Even in winter, the drear stubble of cornfields blossoms with legions of wild geese that glean there nearly until planting time rolls around.

The roots of corn we seldom notice, but ought to heed; for they speak as eloquently as the golden ears and luxuriant foliage topside, but a different message indeed. Pull up a stalk sometime and the first thing that will strike you is how easy it was to do, and how scanty are the underpinnings of so statuesque a plant. Pushing up its glossy green regiments across a thousand square miles of Maryland, this giant, wild grass, bred into the aristocrat of cultivated cereals, epitomizes the pride and problems of our agriculture—and of more than agriculture—I venture there is more profound social commentary in a cornfield than in some libraries, if one is willing to dig for it.

Corn is the superstar of a food system whose mammoth productivity has enabled 98 percent of us to only consume, while just over 2 percent need produce; and that handful produces enough extra to export some $40 billion of grain annually, the greatest single offset to our nation's balance of payments deficit from importing oil. From yields of fifty bushels an acre only a few decades ago to bumper harvests now that may triple, even quadruple, that figure, corn has led all major field crops in productivity gains. Genetic engineers now envision transferring from other plants into corn abilities such as capturing its own fertilizer from the air, and there sometimes seem no limits on the bounty of our farm system.

But the roots of corn say different. There are severe and unyielding limits to growth that have always applied to corn and every other plant on this good, green earth. They are limits that tend to be overlooked in our Western, reductionist approach to science, where researchers learn amazing details about toenails without peering up to see the elephant to which they are attached—or the jungle in which the elephant must survive. The limits are most real to the ecologists, who study how all the parts mesh and communicate to sustain whole systems in nature. To them, the staggering increases in corn yields appear less a straightforward improvement on nature than they are an elegant shell game, where for every gain, one must ask, "Where has the trade-off been made?"

The ecologist sees that for all their thoroughbred lineage and scientific cultivation, the very best, most potent, highest yielding, fastest growing hybrid corn varieties are still terribly close to the scraggliest weeds in one critical aspect. In their basic life process of photosynthesis, the conversion of sunlight into food and structure, all plants can utilize no more than about 4 percent of the solar energy that falls on them to fuel their growth and maintenance. How can that be? Four percent efficiency. In three billion years of selection, cross-pollination, trial and error, how has nature's highly touted evolutionary process not been able to do better? And for all the high-yielding, superplant varieties developed in our Green Revolution successes of the 1960s and 1970s, we have not been able to improve on that overall efficiency one jot.

The reason is that, while there is plenty of "excess" sunlight for photosynthesis, that is no more what limits plant growth than the size of your car's gas tank limits its ability to crack the sound barrier. There are chemical and physical factors involved in photosynthesis which impose far more severe constraints on corn plants that would become oak trees, bearing ears like Doric columns. These primarily involve the scarcity in the atmosphere of carbon dioxide, which plants need to breathe, and the inevitable waste of some available energy at each of the multiple steps in the plant's work of converting sun, water, and carbon dioxide into usable food for itself.

The only known ways around this, the only ways to make the finest corn that science can breed any more *efficient* at using solar energy, would entail increasing the amount of carbon dioxide in our atmosphere; or repealing the second law of thermodynamics, which dictates that any time work is performed, as in converting sunlight to plant food, some of the energy expended is lost as useless heat. The repeal of the second law's limits would require trading for another universe, where the physical laws of matter and energy did not apply, and this does not seem likely.

As for carbon dioxide, it now seems we are, however inadvertently, increasing its mix in the global atmosphere through industrial society's wholesale combustion of fossil fuels, which releases CO_2. Whether this will actually increase corn production is highly debatable, as enough added CO_2 will also cause the celebrated greenhouse effect, raising global temperatures, which in turn will shift the earth's best grain-growing climates substantially northward, where soils are not as good as in our American breadbaskets. This seemingly poor job nature has done through the eons in maximizing the growth of plants is only so if we misconceive what the evolutionary process is about. Evolution strives to maximize only one thing, whether in a corn plant or any other living thing, and that is long-term survival of the species. In that context, look again at the pitiful bundle of roots dangling from the cornstalk we have pulled up. Here is the shell game—albeit an ingenious one—that we have played with corn and other food crops. Operating within corn's severely limited abilities to use energy, we have cleverly selected for varieties that shifted more and more energy into the parts of the plant from which we and our livestock take our nourishment, the fat, golden ears of grain.

That has meant drawing energy away from the plant's resistance to pests, and diseases; from corn's ability to reproduce unaided by human beings who now cross-pollinate it by hand on commercial seed farms. It has meant drawing energy away from the extensive root system that wild plants put down to see them through droughts and to glean every bit of nourishment from the soil. The genius of the once-great American prairie lay in its extensive below-ground root structures, conquerable by agriculture only after tempered steel plows became available. The roots of the prairie could sustain it indefinitely, even through frequent fires (in fact, the fires, killing all but the prairie plants, were what kept the Great Plains from undergoing natural succession to a forest). Sustained also by the prairie roots system were the buffaloes that grazed it and the Indians with their buffalo-centered economy and culture.

There is a story from the Midwest of an old Indian buffalo hunter, standing on what was then the edge of the American frontier, watching a settler's new steel plow churn a rich black wake, raising a sound almost like singing as the blade snapped the roots of the virgin sod, grown tough and tight as piano wire. After a time the Indian shook his head and said, "Wrong side up." What he saw turning over was not just soil, but a whole culture. All the staying power of the original prairie has long since been shifted topside with modern corn farming, and the upshot is marvelous and scary. If you measure the carbon dioxide in the air over a big Maryland cornfield, you will often find it less than a fourth of what it normally is in the atmosphere. Those plants sitting there so quietly, rustling like taffeta in the slow summer breeze, are in reality running near the limits, sucking air like world-class athletes sprinting at a record-setting pace.

Just as we coddle our modern Olympians, insulating them from life's normal travail to focus on propelling themselves a distance in the shortest possible time, so do we bolster our corn with lavish injections of the finest imported energy. We liberally apply petroleum-based herbicides and insecticides to help it outcompete pests. For drought resistance, we fuel mighty irrigation pumps around the clock. For nutrition, we strip nitrogen fertilizer from natural gas in factories the size and complexity of oil refineries, and strip mine phosphates from large sections of Florida and Morocco for shipment around the globe. We refine these and other essential plant nutrients to highly absorbable forms and slather them onto the depauperate root systems for easy uptake.

In the process the corn plant and we, its benefactors, have come almost to ignore the soil. The plants seem to just perch there, as if it were a convenient substrate onto which water and food and pest protection can be pumped as needed. For us, the notion of *soil* is an increasingly abstract term, pleasantly nostalgic perhaps, but less and less connected with the concept of a living organism that holds literally tons of microbial life per acre. Take a spade into a field anywhere in Maryland which has been plowed and doctored to grow corn for a few successive years and see if you can find enough earthworms anymore to catch a mess of perch. Put the soil under a microscope and compare its biological activity to the soil from a woodland or fallow field. It has become a relative desert—a productive one, to be sure, but fertile? Only in the sense that a brain-dead patient lives while hooked to the heart-lung machine and i.v. tubes of a shock-trauma ward.

This is the pitfall of modern agriculture, its Achilles root, if you will. It is not a sustainable system. The prices of nonrenewable energy resources on which the corn plant's lack of roots and other natural defenses make it so highly dependent are rising, as reserves of oil and gas are depleted. And the efforts of the plant breeder to offset this by shifting more and more of the plant's resources into grain yield are meeting rapidly diminishing returns. Even if the genetic engineers succeed in their long-held dream, devising a corn that will capture its own nitrogen fertilizer from the air, there is reason to question whether yields will increase, or even hold stable, because the plant still will be drawing against that same 4 percent photosynthetic efficiency.

The dilemma, to the 98 percent of us who no longer work the soil for a livelihood, might seem at first to be agriculture's alone. As a grain-exporting nation, and one that feeds fully three-quarters of domestic production to such inefficient converters of grain into protein as beef cattle, the United States is scarcely in danger of not being able to meet its own nutritional requirements. But if the roots of corn do not individually run wide and deep, collectively they are connected to the quality of all our lives. Just look at what else turns up as we trace the ramifications of growing corn in the 64,000-square-mile watershed of the Chesapeake Bay.

Before World War II, cornfields in the region were small and far between, interspersed with fruit orchards, tomato patches, watermelons, canteloupes, strawberries, pasture, and hay. With changing markets and the advent of mechanical grain harvesters, the situation began by the 1950s to change radically. Corn was well on the way to its present status as the dominant plant species in the watershed. The harvesting machines, or combines, not only made large fields of grain an efficient proposition but also left a good deal more corn on the ground than in the old days when it was harvested with more hand labor. The farmers' waste became the golden opportunity of migrating Canada geese, whose presence in the bay region paralleled the rise of corn, going from several thousand geese to more than a million in the space of a few decades. A huge domestic poultry industry arose hand in hand with the easy availability of feed grain. It became possible for Maryland farmers to make money growing corn, raise poultry on the side, and then to extract a bonus crop from their fields by renting them to goose hunters for a few winter months at prices that sometimes range into the tens of thousands of dollars.

At the same time, hunters, bird-watchers, and biologists began to fret at the mysterious decline of another bird, the magnificent canvasback diving duck. Flocks, which once clotted the bay in great winter rafts, now numbered only several thousand baywide. Redheads, another diving duck popular for shooting and eating, also were in precipitous decline. Some of the problem, it was known, was the loss of the ducks' nesting habitat in Canada, where farmers were draining prairie potholes. But that alone did not seem to explain the direness of the ducks' circumstances. In the late 1970s two scientists confirmed that canvasbacks wintering on the bay had changed their diet from feeding 90 percent on the estuaries' succulent underwater grass beds, to foraging almost exclusively on hard-shelled little clams. Surveys began to detail how the grass beds, the ducks' preferred diet, had nearly vanished across thousands of square miles of bay bottom. Had a similar loss of wildlife habitat occurred on land, it is likely the state would have been declared a disaster area, eligible for millions in federal aid.

It was to be several more years before a firm link would emerge between the rise on land of the giant grass, corn, and the fall of the lush underwater meadows. The lavish use of manufactured fertilizers, combined with the highly erosive agricultural practices used to bully the maximum grain production from the land, had so polluted the water that the submerged grasses could no longer compete. (In fairness, the increase in human sewage from urban areas was also fingered as a major contributor). Worse, it turned out that the fertilizers, washing bayward by the thousands of tons every time it rained on the region's cornfields, were, along with sewage, also major culprits in causing a growing depletion of oxygen from the bay's bottom waters. Oysters and clams were beginning to die when the spread of oxygen-poor water peaked in the hot summers; and even crabs, creatures so hardy that watermen call them "bay buzzards," were sometimes driven by low oxygen to crawl onto the shores for relief.

Across the bay's watershed, in Harrisburg and Annapolis and Richmond, legislatures voted millions to assist farmers in controlling their polluted runoff. Agriculture, traditionally exempt from most state and federal water-quality regulations, fought successfully to make sure the task would remain voluntary. Buttons were made up showing a corn plant against a background of blue water, reading, "Farmers, Partners with the Bay."

A lot of citizens wondered why such major impacts on the natural system as that wreaked by agriculture hadn't been recognized a lot sooner. In retrospect, it was the failure, even by knowledgeable scientists, to recognize its combined effects along with known threats from sewage, that caused overoptimistic assumptions about the Chesapeake Bay's health. But in a sense our ignorance was not so surprising. A society uncoupled from the land, an agriculture divorced from the soil —how likely was it that either would be sufficiently sensitive to the subtle web of relationships that ties topsoil to bay bottom, corn to canvasbacks, and good goose hunting to scarce oysters? Only close scrutiny of the roots of corn might have warned us earlier, and those roots hardly exist anymore.

Interstate Wilderness

Western Maryland, summertime, in the time of Ronald Reagan and James Watt

Somewhere between the exit ramps for Big Pool and Clear Spring we crossed a tall-grass meadow and entered the deep woods, with the thrill of knowing we walked paths sequestered from others for decades. The solitude of the leafy dell was broken only by the gentle sussurus of highballing eighteen-wheelers. The fragrance of the forest floor mingled with the piquance of carbon monoxide. In the median strip of a six-lane interstate we had found a wilderness preserve. With a president whose stated belief is that trees cause air pollution, and a secretary of the interior who favors drilling and mining in the nation's most pristine public lands, perhaps our most secure natural areas are these linear reservations protected by concrete and the Federal Highway Trust Fund. If we are not too picky about what we call natural, there is precedent for this hope. Conservationists noted more than forty years ago that one of the last places the rich flora of the original prairie had not been turned to growing corn was within railroad rights of ways, established before serious sodbusting got started.

Interstate hiking may someday be the last cheap thrill available to the eco-conscious among the rapidly conurbating corridors of the East Coast. There are, if one searches diligently, miles and miles of places in between modern society's fast lanes where, strictly for economic reasons, it was found more prudent to engineer around nature rather than over or through it. Thus the archenemy, the highway engineer, has left swaths of field and forest ample enough to make hikers virtually forget that they are sandwiched between thick slabs of concrete. What remains in the median is a biopsy of what once existed there, a tissue section left in an outdoor laboratory. I am convinced that such is our allegiance to the automobile and all its support systems that there is no land use in America likely to remain more stable through the centuries than our interstate system. Its medians are firmly off-limits to farming, development, or timber management, fit only to be left alone. Welcome to Interstate 70 National Park—Don't pick the hubcaps!

We had chosen two segments of I-70 for our maiden expedition into the wild delights of the median strip. Both lie between Hagerstown and Hancock, within a couple hours of Baltimore, and both range in width from about eighty to two hundred yards, with mildly undulant stretches of thick forest cover. Good cover is important, because

Section 21-509 of the Transportation Article of the Maryland Code is not yet attuned to those who would gambol on the state's median strips. A trespasser could be busted for up to $500 and two months in jail for getting caught between ribbons of a limited-access interstate. "But you know, I bet they *would* be neat to hike on," mused the attorney general who researched the issue for us.

From the moment we plunged into the wilds of I-70, we were impressed by the diversity of trees and other plant life there. This used to be orchard country, and literally overhanging the eastbound lanes was a tree begging to be divested of its perfect, ripe apples. A little farther along, another stop yielded a horde of small, sweet pears. Further exploration yielded representatives of cedar, oak, beech, willow, black walnut, hawthorn, horse chestnut, sycamore, ash, dogwood, and other species beyond divining with our *Golden Guide to Trees*. Every space between the trees was decorated with gauzy spider webs as big as bushel baskets, attesting to the lack of human transit. A half mile or so "deep" into the woods, we found a bona fide babbling brook, looking trouty as one could wish, and furnished with commodious, sun-dappled flat rocks for lunching. After vainly searching for a trout, we broke out eats, supplementing our store-boughts with crisp, interstate pears.

It was while lying there, munching crunchy granola and listening in stereo to the muted whishing-by of traffic from the equidistant lanes of I-70 East and I-70 West that an unexpected delight of the median strip became apparent. It was the delicious feeling of *hiding out*, a feeling perhaps not experienced since you crouched as a child behind the big chair in your living room, undiscovered, while the grownups came and went; or when you made a hideout of the big cardboard box that the new washing machine came in. That is how you feel eating wild pears by a brook, hidden behind a thin screen of trees and brush from a hundred thousand unsuspecting passers-by on the interstate. Even more than the woods, the flora of the old, reverting fields, the clearings and the ditch banks and stream bottoms in the median were a botanist's cornucopia. Our *Golden Guide to Weeds* was quite overwhelmed. In the space of ten minutes we tramped through mustard, two different species of thistles, prickly pear cactus, wild carrot (Queen Anne's lace), wild lettuce, the delicate blue flowers of chicory, goldenrod, and the purplish plumes of tall redtop.

The second stretch of median was farther west, shorter, and more precipitous. In the span of less than half a mile, the terrain changed from old-growth hardwood forest to skunk cabbage growing in the cool mud of an oozing, deeply shaded stream; then into a fresh-water cattail marsh. Clambering back up a sandy hill, we discovered a miniature pine barren. There we spotted our first rare and endangered species: a chrome, baby-moon hubcap gleaming at us from a copse of staghorn sumac. There had been no reports of such a creature in the wild since the early 1960s. We searched for signs of its mate, but fear no breeding pairs may remain outside of antique auto shows. Idly following a strand of rotting barbed wire grown into the trunks of some hardwoods, we came on a real find, a row of chestnut fence posts. This was prime range for the American chestnut in the early years of the century, before the blight nearly extinguished this premier wood and shade tree from the continent. The wood in the fence was still rot-free and sturdy, and perhaps will yet outlast the concrete that has, for the moment, superseded it in these parts.

Wildlife was not much in evidence between the interstate corridors, but ever-inventive wildlife managers are at work on the situation. Researchers at the federal Patuxent Wildlife Refuge in Laurel have a major contract to study the potential habitat on four different interstates; and a recent national highway conference devoted several sessions to the subject of highways as an environment for wildlife. It is known that migrating Monarch butterflies frequent the abundant stands of milkweed on highway medians to fuel up for a journey that takes them across the United States to wintering grounds in Mexico; and at least one species of mole is thought to flourish principally within median strips.

I am not at all sure I want to see the professional natural-resources crowd gain an interest in the median strip, because they might feel compelled to manage and improve it. Already a local forester in Western Maryland has won recognition for using a piece of median to demonstrate the effectiveness of pine plantations in this part of the state. It is claimed the median was chosen only for its visibility and would never be considered for serious tree farming. I pray it is so, because that would create as much of a monoculture, in its own way, as does concrete. Some quixotic souls no doubt will sneer at my modest proposal for interstate wilderness, preferring to keep fighting the powers in Washington to preserve whole ranges of the Rockies, and half of Alaska. But right now, the future of wilderness looks brightest here in the median. The more we drive—and we drive more every year—then the more sacred do its borders, the highways, become. Ultimately the median, grown hoary with climax oak forests, old-growth beeches, and soaring tulip poplars, will acquire all the privilege and holiness that ever the ancient Greeks and Romans accorded the sacred groves of their gods.

Coming and Going

O*ne of the* truest statements I ever heard about the Chesapeake Bay came from Douglas Ritchie, Jr., a University of Maryland marine researcher at Solomons. He had been painstakingly explaining the myriad factors in the decline of a certain species of fish when I asked him, with all the brash naïveté of a new reporter on the beat, to please get to the bottom line; forget that fish and tell me, Was the health of the bay good or bad? Was it coming back or going to hell? "Is the bay coming or going?" Ritchie looked bemused, but only for a moment. "I guess it's always either coming or going. It's sure never standing still."

Every year, my appreciation grows for how fundamentally "coming and going" characterizes the nineteen or so trillion gallons of water we know as the bay. Not even that volume is truly a constant. It began coming about fifteen thousand years ago, after the retreat of the last ice age. As the ice melted, the seas rose and innundated the narrow defile through which the Susquehanna River flowed to the ocean, forming the bay as we know it. Perhaps at the height of that process some three thousand years ago the bay was, for the merest geological moment, in perfect equilibrium; but for all practical purposes it has been "going," filling in with the sediment from its rivers ever since, and by every expectation it will become a marsh some ten thousand years hence.

Those scientists who began around half a century ago to monitor the bay's vital signs paid little attention, year to year, to that heaving and sighing of eons. They measured salinity, which sets the boundaries of where life and reproduction can occur for species ranging from marsh grass to white perch. They found that salinity is determined by yet another fundamental coming and going within the bay. The salt ocean at its mouth is always flowing, irrespective of the tides, up the bay, while fresh water from its forty-odd rivers is always heading seaward. The constant mixing of salt coming and fresh going sets the standard for salinity, but the only standard seems to be change. Between extremes of flood and drought, the flows of dominant rivers such as the Susquehanna and Potomac can vary by factors of five hundred and more. They can send all vestiges of the salt ocean reeling back to near the Virginia line or, at low flows, allow the salt to penetrate far enough upbay to contaminate the water supplies at Havre de Grace on the Susquehanna Flats. Anything in between these situations can, and constantly does, occur. Similarly, wet years and dry can alter by as much as a *hundred million pounds* the quantities of primary pollutants like farm fertilizers that come washing down the rivers for the bay to absorb.

Continual and dramatic redefinition of the basic parameters of existence is the rule in the bay, and it follows that everything adapted to living there also is prone to coming and going with a caprice and magnitude that so far have mocked most of our attempts to manage the system. We understand a considerable amount about the individual players, the crabs and oysters, the fish and the wildfowl; but the script they follow, which is constantly getting rewritten, still may confound us.

"Crabs are scarce, oyster reproduction is down, continuing an ominous trend, and rockfish are scarcer than most people can remember," I wrote in the draft of a news article in November 1976. I was about to conclude, authoritatively, that the death of the bay was clearly in sight when I checked the fisheries records from two decades earlier. In a nutshell, I could have written the same article back then without changing a word. I have not felt so authoritative since. However, I haven't felt alone. The bay's comings and goings have fooled the experts, degreed and otherwise, just as badly.

"It's over. Natural set [reproduction] of oysters in the bay is over," I was told solemnly by Dr. George Krantz, the University of Maryland's chief oyster scientist, in June 1977. Shocking as it was, his pronouncement, coming after oysters had failed for eleven consecutive years to have a hugely successful spawn, seemed a safe enough prediction. I had occasion to recall it twice during the early 1980s, as the bay's oysters erupted with two of the greatest years of "natural set" that Krantz or anyone else had ever seen.

"Crabs is like flies. You don't know where they come from, or where they go to, but they always come around," said Chandus Rippons of Hoopersville, one of the bay's savviest old seafood packers. He was explaining to me, in the early summer of 1976, that he was already seeing the end to what had appeared the scarcest year for crabs in history. Even as crab-house owners read his reassuring words in the *Baltimore Sun* and began phoning in orders, the crabs took a monumental dive again. Chan still takes a fierce ribbing about those "flies."

Ironically, our growing sophistication in recognizing the boombust potential of the bay and its creatures has been partly responsible for ignoring, until very recently, that the goings of a lot of species have been getting all too common, while the comings occur more infrequently. By the late 1970s many astute scientists were convinced this signified an ominous new chapter of the estuary's environmental history—too many species were down at the same time. But the state's top natural-resources bureaucrats could still make a case for natural cycles; and it would have been a bold scientist indeed who publicly disagreed, betting his or her reputation against a great comeback in a system where the only sure thing was enormous flux. Now we are all pretty much agreed that the scientists were right. The oyster, the rockfish, the canvasback duck, the great underwater grass beds that were vital food and habitat to so many species—all these are going. Just going. They are in no natural cycle, and will continue to ebb until we repair the massive and fundamental damage done to them by pollution and overfishing.

But even with such declines, the bay as a whole cannot really be said to be going. Shifting is more like it. As the grass beds have declined, the nutrients in the water column on which they fed are available to grow more free-floating algae; and even as some fish species sink toward historic lows of abundance, others that are adapted to feeding on algae have come on like gangbusters. Amid all the coming and going, it is doubtful whether the total of the bay's biomass, the pounds of life growing there in one form or another, has changed much. All you can say with certainty is that the bay sure hasn't been standing still.

Woven intricately through all the preceding are comings and goings of another sort, the richest and most complex of all, forming the very fabric of what many of us love most about the bay. These are the annual migrations. They range from the spectacular, the arrival of the geese in October, to the mysterious, the great exodus of eels on the dark of the moon in November for the Sargasso depths. They include journeys long and exuberant—the lusty thrashing of sea-run herring and rockfish and shad up every river and stream in April and May; and journeys short and subtle—the vertical migrations of larval oysters and crabs, covering the space of only a few feet, from the seaward-flowing fresh water at the bay's surface to the upward-creeping salt wedge on its bottom. The wedge will take them where they need to go against currents and tides they could never battle alone.

It never seems to end, this coming and going. Even when the bay becomes a marsh, fills in with the sediment of its rivers in a hundred centuries or so, it will not be the end. Geologists assure us there have been many Chesapeake Bays throughout time as the ice ages have come and gone, and earth's seas have risen and fallen. Our bay is only the latest in a long string. All the species that use and depend on the bay dance to the tune of coming and going—all except one. Our own history on the estuary is too short as yet to say for sure, but there seems no reason to think people will continue to do anything but increase. Coming without ever going—it seems a good trick if you can get away with it; but judging from what all else has been going without coming back in recent times, I wonder who we think we are fooling.

Eau de Rock Creek

Rock Creek, Washington, D.C., Spring

No finer parade, or one more unappreciated, ever swung through this capital than the quicksilver legions of *Alosa pseudoharengus,* the common river herring, that engorged Rock Creek on the annual spawning return from the sea this week. A herring run is one of earth's great enthusiasms, but for all that the homecoming was not well-publicized here. I only heard of it at the last minute through Jimmy Hancock, downriver in Charles County, who heard about it from some ospreys on the Potomac below Mount Vernon. Their frenzied diving at this time of year could only mean a big run was on, Jimmy said. I hurried to rendezvous with the *Alosa,* donning hip boots and taking a position below the Potomac Parkway just past the Watergate.

I considered toasting the vanguard with something appropriate . . . perhaps a white wine, dry and crisp; but on second thought that seemed better suited to opening day on a trout stream, altogether too refined for this exuberant reunion of alewives—and Rock Creek is no trout stream, either. I packed a Diet Coke in my slicker's pocket. I caught the run more perfectly than I had in several years. Reaching upriver to the Georgetown Channel, the schools of 8-to-10-inch fish executed smart right faces at Rock Creek's mouth, first by the dozen, then by the hundreds and thousands, pulled by incredibly powerful chemical and evolutionary machinery.

Penetrating a scum of oil and debris under the Whitehurst Freeway, they moved upstream. Past the M Street bridge into Georgetown they coursed. They rounded the P Street beach, their progress exclaimed by bursts of forsythia along the triumphal avenue. Budding creek maples flushed deep maroon with the excitement as the run gathered strength and shot past the Q Street gauging station and under Massachusetts Avenue. Violets massed on the banks craned their stalks at the occasion and murmured with purplish wonder as crashing shoals of herring pulled abreast the National Zoo and kept on going. Only Pierce Mill Dam, a 1930s Civilian Conservation Corps project that plugs Rock Creek six-feet high with concrete about five miles above the Potomac, stopped the charge. Before it was there, the fish ran nearly to Laytonsville, twenty-five miles upstream in Montgomery County, and a place where, if you ask, all but the oldest natives will say they are landlocked.

But no matter. The nation's political power center on this morning once again has been renewed with power of a sort that transcends politics. It is still plugged in, no matter how tenuously, to the oceans, to wildness, to one of the planet's primal cycles, so long as a single little *Alosa* still mounts the gravelly, sun-washed creases of the Rock Creek watershed. The journey of the silver *Alosa* is set in motion by nothing less than cosmic events. It is concluded by forces so specific and precise as to mark Rock Creek unique and irreplaceable among every other waterway in the world. It begins when the hemisphere seems most tired, the land in Maryland most winter-weary. Something massive sighs, shrugs, the planet's tilt alters, oceanic currents shift, and, far out in the cold, gray Atlantic, millions of herring sense that it is time to go home. Scarcely a waterway the length of the East Coast will not vibrate with their response by the time it climaxes weeks later.

"The skirts of the sun's robe, passing over the ocean, stir the deep, and its mysterious peoples move north on the fringes of the light," wrote the naturalist Henry Beston, many decades ago. And recent scientific research bears him out, if less poetically. At sea, the lengthening of days after the winter solstice triggers hormonal changes that give the first nudge coastward to the sexually mature members of the school. The youngest of these adults, those returning for the first time, have been at sea nearly four years since they left the stream where they were spawned. Others will be returning for the second, third, and, for a few, the fourth time. This repeat spawning capability gives the herring considerable resilience as a species. Even after a disaster such as Tropical Storm Agnes, whose rains swelled creeks and blasted the 1972 spring hatch to oblivion throughout the bay's watershed, there were adults left at sea to run again the next year.

As the great oceanic schools begin purposefully to move inshore, Pamlico Sound herring branch off toward North Carolina. Chesapeake Bay herring seek the Virginia capes. New England herring take their separate path, and so on. In the next few weeks they will unerringly navigate from the ocean to the vicinity of the river system whence they sprang. How they navigate to this point is less understood than the remainder of the journey they will make. Scientists know that fish can ascertain latitude and longitude from the sun. They know they can detect polarized light. They know they can receive signals from the earth's magnetic field. They know they are exquisitely sensitive to gradients of temperature, salinity, and current movement. Of these, take your pick as to which the herring use to get from ocean to river mouth, the scientists say; or better, perhaps, choose them all.

Now, eggs and milt (sperm) are rapidly maturing as water temperatures approach the minimum 54°F needed to inspire spawning, and the *Alosa* surge up the rivers, seeking the fast-flowing, fresh-water, gravel and sand stream bottoms their eggs require to survive. Partly, they seem to be kept on course upriver in this phase by a phenomenon called *rheotaxis*, orientation against the current. But increasingly there is something else operating now, an influence of almost mystical properties. It prods them on even when there is no current, or a reversal of current, even when, in experiments, they are blinded. In the Potomac it pulls the *Alosa* spawned in Rock Creek past stream after choice spawning stream lower down the river, as surely as if drawn by a line hooked in their jaw. Dr. Arthur D. Hasler of the University of Wisconsin has attempted to define this in *Underwater Guideposts*, a text on the much more studied homing instincts of Pacific salmon: "We think each home stream acquires from the soils and plant communities of its drainage basin, and in its bed a unique organic quality which young salmon learn in the first few weeks of life." The same is thought to hold true for herring, shad, and other members of the family *Alosa*.

Call it an organic bouquet, "eau de Rocque Creek," or what you will, it seems to beckon to the *Alosa* so seductively that no other than the natal stream will do for its spawning. They can follow the heady essence to its source through daunting overlays of competing odors, on the way braving pollution zones that would turn most aquatic life around in its wake. What more eloquent testimony to this ability exists than the fact that remnant herring runs still mount the vile Anacostia River as far as Hyattsville and seek the junky Patapsco even to Baltimore's Inner Harbor? Through it all, apparently, the bouquet, the fragrance of home, prevails: "The smell and taste of things remain poised a long time, like souls, ready to remind us, waiting and hoping for their moment . . . and bear unfaltering, in the tiny and almost impalpable drop of their essence, the vast structure of recollection."

That might have come from *Underwater Guideposts*, but it came from Proust's *Remembrance of Things Past*, in the overture to *Swann's Way*. Evocative as taste and smell may be to us, we are insensitive as stones compared to the fishes. Research with the humble bullhead indicates a highly complex chemical language through which fish interact with their environment. At the very least, the bullhead can use organs of taste and smell to ascertain another fish's species, mood, sex, age, size, reproductive state, individual characteristics, and, probably, family background. The notion of parallel universes is a popular one in science fiction, usually predicated on something exotic, like a time warp, or black hole in the galaxies. More and more, I think they exist, complete and resplendent, no farther than the nearest creek, in the sensory powers of common fish.

No one, of course, knows just what the cold brain of a Rock Creek herring feels or senses when it begins to pick up the organic trace of its ancestral stream far down the Potomac. Work with salmon makes scientists think that if fish traveled in a constant "cloud of odor" their olfactory senses quickly would become overwhelmed. Rather, they think, the herring follow the trail on a "presence-absence basis," crossing back and forth across the odor like a dog on a scent, picking up a whiff here, a whiff there. Several years ago two scientists captured salmon as they entered their home stream and hooked them to an electroencephalograph. Their brains were almost shut down, except the portions that controlled the sense of smell. When water from the home stream was passed through the captive salmons' tank, their olfactory bulbs began firing madly, sending spikes leaping across the recording paper of the brain-wave machine. The natal water was diluted by half with distilled water, and again the same response. It did not disappear until the diluted water had been again diluted, and so on, for the tenth time.

Dr. William Richkus, a scientist with the Martin Marietta Corporation in Baltimore, did his Ph.D. work on *Alosa pseudoharengus* and is an acknowledged authority on their migration habits. He says he has seen tagged herring return from the ocean with amazing (although not total) accuracy to streams in Rhode Island no more than five feet wide. Once he watched a fish ladder installed over a dam that had prevented herring from spawning in a stream. Adult females, laden with eggs, were placed in the stream to spawn. Within three or four years the stream had a herring run. That would seem to have profound implications. We can create a whole new tribe of *Alosa*, responsive, for all time, to one stream.

And destroy, too. If a stream loses its *Alosa*, it is not just a few tons of fish that are gone, but a separate and distinct tribe, unique in all the world. The stream may continue to broadcast its organic come-hither message, but there will be none of its own to renew the romance. Another stream's song will ring hollow; some important notes will be gone from spring's symphony. This can happen—in fact is happening with alarming pervasiveness around the Chesapeake Bay. Jay O'Dell, head of the Anadromous Fish Survey team of the Department of Natural Resources, has spent more than fifteen years slogging the thousand or so streams of Maryland's sixteen tidewater counties which have spawning potential. He has about another decade to go to finish. His report from the bay's capillaries is that they seem diseased. Severn Run in Anne Arundel County has lost most of its run. Development has wiped out Sawmill Creek in Glen Burnie, a tributary to Furnace branch, which runs by Wilkins Buick. Cattail Creek off the Magothy River is another excellent run that has gone under to the siltation caused by shopping centers, O'Dell says. The broad cause of these declines is clear—too many people; but lately something more subtle, but quite ominous, seems to have come into play. The very rain that falls across the whole bay region now is highly acidic, a result of air pollutants from fossil-fuel combustion in power plants as far away as the Ohio River Valley. O'Dell speculates—and research is still struggling to confirm—that the acid rain leaches the abundant aluminum in the watershed's soils into the spawning streams, where the metal can be highly toxic to larval herring and other species in concentrations of as little as a few parts per million. Combined with a generally heightened acidity in the spawning areas, it may be negating most of the efforts of the *Alosids'* long run from the ocean to perpetuate themselves.

The survey has also documented more than five hundred dams and obstructions to spawning, put there over the decades by road builders; by industries and farmers, wanting to pool water for cooling and irrigation; and by waterfowlers, wanting to dam up a pond for shooting; and even by beavers. So many interests are not in free-flowing water. The largest of these is the hydropower company that owns Conowingo Dam on the Susquehanna. The dam looms more than one hundred feet high across what once was the mightiest spawning river of the bay—perhaps equaled only by the Columbia for migratory fish runs. Once shad and herring used to travel all the way from the bay's mouth to creeks above Binghamton, New York, to deposit their eggs. These mightiest of all *Alosa* nations have all but ceased to exist in the Susquehanna in the last decade. Maryland's plan to build an $11 million fish ladder over Conowingo Dam has been languishing in the Federal Energy Regulatory Commission's proceedings on the utility company's responsibility to fish. The FERC must weigh the costs and benefits of the fish ladder, and one wonders how they will value the cost to the Chesapeake springtime of doing nothing.

The FERC should be aware that streams that hold *Alosa* are vital to more than fish. I speak as one who used to belong to a tribe on the Eastern Shore which each spring was drawn to a cluster of Nanticoke River streams just as surely as the herring. You could hear spring coming. We hunkered at night on the damp, sandy bank, our capacious wire dip nets wedged in narrow channels where the herring must pass, and waited tensely for the waves of spawners leaping and crashing upstream toward their destiny. We always wondered why they leaped so, even where there was no obstacle to surmount. No fisheries scientist has been able to explain it. Perhaps they were glad to be home.

Often, with youth's disdain of foreplay, we rushed to consummate the affair, leaping three abreast into the cold stream and beating to a froth the water ahead of us, routing frogs and snakes and chasing all that swam, pell-mell, into the dip net. I can recall catches that snapped the handle, a pole the diameter of one's wrist. The net was hoisted, spilling its load of herring like bright coins to quickly beat out their lives against the bank. We fell on them like savages, squeezing each one near the vent to see if it contained the prized light-amber roe. It was finer grained than even shad roe, and considered a treat for breakfast, scrambled with eggs of chickens. When the weather promised a hot weekend, we sometimes saved a few dozen herring for mailbox stuffing. A metal mailbox so filled on a Friday night and shut to bake until Monday never failed to impress its owner.

In later years I have joined the ranks of civilized herring dippers, who operate by day, preferably seated on a peach basket in the shade of a tree. The fish are not so active as they are at night, but they will come if you are patient; and waiting, I have found, has its own pleasures. When a few herring tentatively enter the deep wire cone of the net about halfway, one deftly tips it upward and then lifts it clear of the stream. You catch only the number needed for roe and for salting and pickling. I like to think there is hope for mankind if a former stream-beater and mailbox-stuffer can mellow so.

On Rock Creek, sad to say, the human symbionts of that stream's *Alosa* have deteriorated to a level that would scarcely be tolerated on the Nanticoke. I questioned three of them this spring. One was trying to snag a herring with a bare hook. Another was fishing with a hook baited with corn (herring don't eat on spawning runs). The third was trying to dip-net with a white plastic shopping bag. Did they know what manner of fish they pursued so ineptly? "Halibut," the snagger announced brightly. His companion, the bagger, thought that was right. And when had they first noticed the run beginning this year? "Oh, they're here all year. They just show themselves certain times."

A federal park policeman of some years service along the creek was no more able to identify the fish as herring. A steady flow through the park of joggers and cyclists never noticed their existence, even when crossing a bridge over a stream where several dozen herring were sunning themselves. People do not seem to look into the water much in Rock Creek Park, perhaps because they do not expect to see anything. Maybe it is foolish to worry about the *Alosa* of a stream losing its human tribe, but I wonder: Can a stream expect the fierce protection and care it needs from a human constituency that has lost its sophistication about natural objects? When people are no longer aware of all the parts of the machine, will they be alert to its deterioration? The very concept of water quality, without such awareness, seems empty, an abstraction at best. And a stream that has lost both its tribes is truly dead, though it continues to waft its organic bouquet for all time to come, like some radio signal beamed randomly to far galaxies. Because nowhere will the essence of such a stream be tended any longer in the souls of people or fish, to be rekindled in the great sigh of nature that comes when winter hangs heaviest on the land.

Shad

> *Poor Shad, where is thy redress?*
> —*Henry Thoreau*

*T*he creek, named the Marshyhope by early settlers, provided drainage for flat Caroline County farmland and a haven for catfish and sluggish gar. In the summers, bright red tomato peels from the John N. Wright Cannery floated bank to bank on its lazy current, mixing sometimes with shoals of yellow feet and shiny guts fresh from the Caroline Poultry Company. Nothing warned it was a high-voltage natural area until an idle cast, made there on the way to fish the town lake, hooked the shad. The sea-run spawner's fight was sparked with all the desperate, procreative amperage of springtime. The afternoon yielded a half-dozen more charged encounters, great slabs of silver hauled, precious as ingots, from the tea-colored water, opening an everlasting emotional circuit among angler, creek, springtime, and the oceans.

The grander implications didn't crystallize until years later. My immediate reaction was to work the handlebars of my bicycle through the mouths and gills of the four biggest shad, so that they dangled, two on a side; then I rode home, down Main Street, very proudly, very slowly, leaving in my wake a trail of blood, scales, and friends heading for the Western Auto Store's fishing tackle department. That was in late April 1959, the formation of one man's very personal "base-line data" on the American shad, a benchmark against which he would inevitably measure the quality of all succeeding Maryland springs.

The notion of base lines arises often in the conversations of the bay's environmental managers. Is there too much pollution? Is the water dirtier than it used to be? Have the fish gotten too scarce to allow more fishing? You cannot know with enough certainty to take what often are controversial corrective measures unless you have established an accepted base line, a prior standard, against which to measure progress or decline. More than that, a base line holds us to account, pushes us to also establish a bottom line, a level of degradation below which the situation simply is unacceptable. Neither mark ever was set for the shad, or for most bay species for that matter. The peril in such cases is that each succeeding generation ends up accepting a new, lower base line, as matters keep edging nearer the ultimate bottom line, extinction.

The long, sad *dégringolade* of the American shad was effectively checked only three times since records of commercial fisheries landings began; first by the tremendous disruption of normal commerce created by the Civil War, then again by World War I, and by World War II. These were blunt instruments for conservation to say the least; nor is it certain that starting another global conflagration would do the trick again, so complete has been the shad's depletion. It is almost as if, having been pushed so hard for more than a century, the species just gave up, fell off the edge.

In 1876 T. B. Ferguson, the state fish commissioner, noted the annual shad catch was hovering at a "worrisome" four million pounds, and lamented the ill effects of overfishing, sediment from farmland, and the blockages of dams. He started a shad hatchery movement that during the following century would, operating sporadically, pump out at least two billion fingerlings with no noticeable effect on catches, except to provide plenty of choice bait for the multitude of other species that preyed on the tiny hatchery shad. Ferguson also suggested building fish ladders on the Gunpowder River, where new dams had cut off spawning runs of shad and rockfish so copious that upstream residents had been able to spear them from horseback.

By 1890, bay watermen had responded to the relative scarcity in the same, time-honored fashion that they still often follow—they redoubled harvesting efforts and developed more efficient catching methods. The catches of shad, also bolstered by more people entering the fishery, rose to their all-time high of seven million pounds a year. There probably never was a time when the bay, even at its most pristine, could have long sustained that level of exploitation. Within a decade the catch had dropped to about three million pounds. In 1909 this "perceptible decline in our fishery" caused the Maryland Conservation Commission to devote part of its annual report to the evils of dams that blocked spawning fish, and to chastise the populace for overfishing.

By 1922 the catch was fluctuating between one million and two million pounds a year, and a *Baltimore Sun* headline intoned "Shad near doom as nets bar river" in May of that year. The article, written from Betterton, reported that a giant net had been set up from Locust Point on Spesutie Island to the Eastern Shore in Cecil County, above Turkey Point Lighthouse, "with only a narrow opening for ships to pass . . . No mother fish shall reach the rapids above Port Deposit, where her mission is wont to be accomplished," the article concluded. From Crisfield, another of the newspaper's far-flung shad correspondents told readers that nets strung virtually the width of the bay were resulting in record catches: "hour after hour, 100 buy boats enter the harbor loaded to the waterline with shad." Between 17 March and 9 April 1922, 150 freight-car loads of shad had left Crisfield, the paper reported. That year, Harrison W. Vickers, Jr., chairman of the state Conservation Commission, was assailed with requests for a ban on such netting. The legislature would never hear of it, he said.

In 1925 Herbert Hoover, then the secretary of commerce, called a special fisheries conservation conference to deplore the falling catch of shad in the bay. He noted that California, where shad had been transplanted from the East Coast, currently was shipping two million pounds a year back East to fill the demand for "fresh, Atlantic shad." The conference suggested an elaborate, and fatally voluntary, plan for conservation of the shad. By 1943 the catch had sunk to 600,000 pounds, and a state fisheries administrator called for a fishing ban, proclaiming "too much has been said, and too little done." The *Richmond Times Dispatch* took up the cry, for Virginia's part of the bay had been undergoing similar exploitation: "The shad is another example of the unhappy truth that Americans are too prone to delay conservation until ruinous depletion assumes shocking proportions." By 1950, catches had rebounded to about one and one-half million pounds, thanks mainly to the respite given the shad when the attention of most able-bodied Maryland men was turned elswhere during World War II. A Maryland legislative committee, perhaps lulled by the improving state of the fishery, decided not to press for a fish ladder then proposed for Conowingo Dam, to reopen hundreds of miles of historic spawning waters upstream of it. "Bay shad called too dumb to use fish ladders," a newspaper headline on the story said. That prompted Van Reynolds, a reader and fisherman from Elkton, to reply in a letter that the only hope for the shad was "to get rid of the legislature."

In 1953 a study by the Chesapeake Biological Laboratory of the University of Maryland concluded that the base line had shifted permanently to a lower level. The shad never would be restored to its former glory. "Shad and civilization are not compatible," the report said.

Annual commercial catches of shad in the Maryland bay adhered to this level—between one million and two million pounds a year—from the late 1940s through 1972; then catches plummetted to almost a half-million pounds in 1973; then to half that in 1974. By the nation's bicentennial in 1976, baywide catches of the species that George Washington had loved to net by the ton off the shores of Mount Vernon stood at 109,173 pounds. In 1978 the Izaak Walton League canceled its spring shad tournament on the Susquehanna River for the first time in thirty years. There just weren't enough shad left to make it worthwhile, the league said. Commercial landings of shad fell to 53,818 pounds. Pleas from sport-fishing interests for a ban on netting met an all too familiar response from fisheries officials: the legislature would never hear of it.

The following year, an internal memo at the Department of Natural Resources acknowledged that the shad had experienced a "catastrophic demise" in reproduction since 1973, when only a single young shad was caught in samples taken in the upper Chesapeake Bay. "Recruitment into the adult stock since 1973 is nonexistent," the memo concluded; and in 1979 the landings of shad fell to 20,660 pounds. In 1980 the state, under threat of a lawsuit by a fisherman, placed a total moratorium on sport and commercial fishing for shad, boldly closing the barn door after the horse had gone. There was scarcely any outcry. Those who knew the shad had virtually stopped bothering to fish for it; and already there was a generation of young anglers coming on whose personal base lines did not even include the species.

Maryland's last shad harvest in 1979 was about 1 percent of the catch in 1959, the year that memorable shad on a Caroline County creek chose to establish my own standard. It is ironic and perplexing that the final, great plummet of the species in the bay came during the decade that began with Earth Day in 1970, when the nation made great strides to restore environmental quality, and when shad runs picked up on the Hudson, Delaware, and Connecticut rivers. Even the filthy old Schuylkill cleaned up its act sufficiently to allow a spring spawning run through the heart of Philadelphia, where underwater cameras now record it on a large movie screen at the city zoo. It is further a mystery how the Chesapeake's decline seems to have occurred so uniformly across all its many spawning rivers, each of which, salmon-fashion, presumably has its own separate stock of shad returning uncannily to the waters of their birth.

Only one thing is clear. At each downturn in the fishery, although there was never a lack of expressed concern, there was effectively no level at which anyone had the mandate or the will to say, "Enough!" In recent years, there have been attempts to recoup. The state expressed its intentions to build shad hatcheries to augment the stocks artificially;

and in 1977 began a legal battle to require fish ladders over the great power dams lining the Susquehanna River, which had blocked the shad from its historic spawning grounds for a century. Some hasty attempts were made to improve sewage treatment, although no one had the slightest idea whether that was a problem in the shad's decline. We knew surprisingly little about a fish that had been a mainstay of our sport and commerce through most of the preceding century—except for how to catch it. We were adept at that. In the 1980s, a state fisheries biologist would offer a modern version of the conclusion reached in 1953 when the Chesapeake Biological Laboratory called shad and civilization incompatible: "We have looked at land use changes, agricultural chemicals, sediment, urban runoff, sewage discharges, overfishing. . . . All these things probably never will be sorted out, except to say that they all happened at the same time the shad declined."

The bankruptcy of a species is sad enough in itself, but the loss of shad impoverishes April in Maryland well beyond the loss of its economic value, which was 38.8 cents a pound, dockside, in May 1979, the last year you could catch one legally. The lives of Maryland's river dwellers have been nudged for generations by the cosmic rhythms that impel the fish each spring from the deep oceans to their natal streams. On the river that becomes the creek that became my base line for shad, the time for the shad's return each spring is marked by the waxy buds of swamp maples emerging, garbing the banks a royal, deep maroon. In the little river towns "shad barges" are readied—slender, graceful little craft unique to the Nanticoke's spring shad industry for nearly two centuries, a lapidary fit of stylish form with the functional demands of commercial netting.

Their length, 22–24 feet, was just right for two men, one in each end, to handle the stretched-out width of the deep mesh nets used to catch shad. Wide washboards, sloping low to the water at the barge's center, accommodated the rolled-up net, and also made for ease of paying it out, taking it in, and grappling fish over the side. Even with the low freeboard, "a ton of shad wouldn't tell her nothin'," Jake Windsor, one of the last of the living shad-barge builders, told me in 1978. "It was just something built for that kind of work and they wa'nt nothing else would give satisfaction," said Powell Horseman, another retired builder.

John Edward Goslee, of Sharptown, on the Nanticoke, is the only active builder left, and most of the shad barges he makes anymore are for collectors. To make one right, he said, you need a board wide enough to make the sides from a single plank. He does his own logging and sawing, and he still owns three virgin pines that soar one hundred feet before branching and will measure several feet in diameter. The last one he cut had overlooked the Nanticoke for nearly three hundred years, and it made several nice shad barges. The fishermen would unfurl their nets across the low, wide washboards of their barges, on the slack crest of an early morning high tide, the time, they would say, "when the net fishes best." To watch them, casting their nets into the river, casting their hopes into nature's hands, was to watch the reenactment of something incredibly special and ancient. I have watched strikingly similar rituals on the Nile at Khartoum and on the Amazon at Belem, and from the U.S. Route 50 Bridge on the Nanticoke at Vienna.

If the shad does not return, perhaps it is because we do not love it enough. L. Eugene Cronin, a bay scientist and a native of the Susquehanna who is steeped in the lore of the old-time shad fishermen, notes that "the decline of the tasty, but bony shad as a favorite edible" may have presaged its slipping away. Who can say at what point of the shad's decline it was that the decline in people who had enjoyed it, whether on a plate or on the hook, became a telling factor. Certainly there is room to imagine that the present paucity of the species never would have been tolerated as recently as 1949, the year when the Great Shad War erupted among readers of the *Baltimore Sun*.

It was not uncommon in those days for a letter to the editor to extoll the virtues of the bay's seafood, occasioned by nothing more than its being in season. For example, the spring of 1944 brought the news that shad roe "fried and accompanied with a bit of lemon and a strip or two of bacon is so eminently edible that to undertake an investigation of its further possibilities seems almost irreverent." No one disagreed with that; but fireworks were touched off in 1949 when a local columnist recommended a way around the tedious process of boning shad, which have at least two extra sets of bones running the length of their bodies. This curiosity of the shad family means about six minutes' work for an expert shad deboner, and about a week's worth for the average citizen.

The columnist told of a new method, by which the bones could be dissolved by cooking the shad six hours in a young red wine, with a sprig of thyme, bayleaf, sliced onion, garlic clove, and salt and pepper. "If ever this method becomes widespread, the populace would demand conservation above all else. Baltimore's finest square would be renamed 'Shad Place', . . . and catching shad out of season would be a hanging crime," the columnist wrote. It was not to be. A Monsieur Vellegant, chef at the Sheraton Belvedere hotel, wrote of his own experience with dissolving shad bones: "This used to be a shad . . . what is it now? I will tell you. It is a pickle. The flesh is still there, but the spirit has departed."

There was a lot of sentiment for the "bone-dissolve method." Letters flowed in subsequent weeks with more bone-dissolve recipes from the likes of Ferdinand C. Latrobe and M. Jules Smucker, who signed himself a "Fenchurch road piscator." There were recipes entitled "Alose sans os" and "Alose l'Avignonnaise."

If there was ever a recipe to bring back the shad, however, it might be the one attributed to Harry Lyons, of Edgewater, New York, the riverman in Joseph Mitchell's classic on shad netting in *The New Yorker* in 1959: "Harry has a shad boner come up from Fulton Fish Market and bone them . . . he nails them to white-oak planks . . . two or three strips of bacon across each fish. He props the planks up, fish-side foremost, in a ring around a bed of charcoal that has been burning on the ground for hours and is red-hot and radiant . . . gradually moving them farther back, so that the fish will broil slowly and pick up the flavors of the bacon and the oak. The shad is crusty on the outside and tender and rich and juicy on the inside (but not too rich since a good deal of the oil has been broiled out of it), and fully justifies its scientific name, Alosa sapidissima."

The Caroline County creek has benefited, as have most of our waterways, from the nation's environmental cleanup. No tomato peels or chicken offal clogs it now, and a modern sewage-treatment plant hums away efficiently on its banks. Bass fishermen from around the state come to angle for large-mouths there. Although its shad swim mostly in memory, a spring seldom passes that I do not stop for a token cast, hoping, I suppose, to hook into even a remnant of the power that surged in those channels a quarter century ago. Having chosen one's base line, the important thing is to stick to it; how else is one to measure quality amid so much change?

The fight to effect fish ladders over the Susquehanna dams to restore the shad there was rekindled in the late 1970s and still drags on between the state and the power companies, and it easily could last another decade. New studies indicate that polluted rain may be turning the once great bay spawning and nursery rivers of the shad into areas of lethal acidity each spring. In the Bay of Fundy, where the Canadians are preparing to build a mammoth string of turbines to take advantage of the tides' huge ebb and flow there, scientists have just discovered the summering place for most of the shad on the Atlantic coast. It is doubtful that many would escape being hashed in the turbines, if they are built as proposed.

In 1984 another species, the rockfish, was placed under a state moratorium on fishing. Natural-resources managers noted that the shad were allowed to decline to just 1 percent of their traditional numbers before a fishing ban came. The rockfish, they further noted, were still at 10 percent of previous harvests when action came. In decimation is progress, one is left to suppose.

State biologists still sample the bay each spring and summer for young shad, but they find so few that they can offer no evidence of any uptrend. Finally the base line and the bottom line have been determined.

The Passion of Eels

*A*round *the* Chesapeake Bay, our attention to autumn's migrations tends to be monopolized by wild geese returning. We scarcely notice the concurrent exodus of another creature from every rivulet in the estuary's 41-million-acre drainage basin, a journey that is still tinged with mystery more than twenty-three centuries after humanity began to wonder at it. It begins as it probably has begun for seventy million years, on October and November nights, always in the dark quarter of the moon, usually in the wake of a storm. Throughout the bay and throughout half the globe, the eels' hour has come. Only a few Marylanders anymore are attentive to the great departure for the spawning grounds. A handful of the bay's commercial watermen harvest the ocean-bound hordes of eels, chasing them down the bay until, miles off the Virginia capes, the migration drops over the lip of the continental shelf, a point beyond which no one has ever seen a spawning eel.

Even before the watermen, Tony Robucci has seen the migration coming. Robucci, of Hagerstown, is superintendent of Minor Power Stations for the Potomac Edison Power Company. Each fall the eels, moving down from Appalachian and Piedmont creeks high in the drainage of the Shennandoah and Potomac rivers, must be cleaned from the turbines in the utility's old but cost-efficient hydropower dams in Western Maryland. "I have seen 'em four-foot long and they can clog the water intakes some years," Robucci says. An eel that big may have spent nearly twenty years maturing, much of it in a stream no wider than you can jump across. Camouflaged by their grayish and muddy yellow coloration, and nocturnal in their activities, eels are such unobtrusive residents that people are surprised to find how abundant they are. With the possible exception of man, no species ever has colonized the bay's watershed more ubiquitously. A five-year study of sixteen streams across Maryland found eels the most abundant species in all cases—up to fifteen hundred per acre of water. In the bay proper, eels by the early 1980s had become the second-biggest commercial fin fishery in Maryland, at about one million and a half pounds, behind menhaden and ahead of rockfish. The record eel ever caught here was 42.2 inches long and weighed 5 pounds, 10 ounces.

No one knows what compels the eels' fall migration. Not all of them go in any given year, nor does their departure come at any particular age or size; but those chosen have been undergoing dramatic changes for some months to ready for the long—and presumably final—journey. Their digestive tracts have shrunk and, to facilitate navigation through the darkness and the intense pressures of ocean channels one hundred times deeper than the bay's, their eyes have grown to twice normal size and their swim bladders have toughened. The shape of their skulls has altered, and their coating of slime has thickened, armoring them against dehydration from the extreme salinities they will soon encounter. And such fine-looking armor! Gone are the drab colors matching the eel to its stream-bottom home; now it shimmers olive and bronze and metallic silver that glints pink, and almost purple in certain lights. The late Gilbert Klingel was the only person I have known to describe such an eel in its full glory. He wrote in *The Bay* of a dive one night, several decades ago, beneath the bay's surface: "In the depths of the Chesapeake, in its own environment, this great eel was a thing of exceeding grace . . . but its real beauty was in the hitherto unsuspected iridesence of its soft, silken skin . . . of a soft lustrous glow, leaf green above and pearl pink below. This pink altered in tone as the eel moved its coils. One moment it flashed pale-lavender fire, next delicate and evanescent yellows." Alas, when taken from the water, the eel's glory fades as quickly as that of tropical fish.

What triggers the great change is as much a mystery as what guides the eel—which all its life in the bay never ranges more than a few miles—to rendezvous unerringly across half an ocean with every other migrating eel in North America and Europe. Eels do not appear to rely on odors, orientation to the sun and stars, salinity and temperature differences, or any other of the underwater guideposts that are thought to guide salmon, herring, and other anadromous (upstream) spawners from the oceans to the streams of their birth. The eel, whose migration goes just in reverse, is the bay's only catadromous spawner of any note. It may well be using subtle electrical fields created by water currents to navigate from its home streams to the continental edges, scientists think; but that is still a long way from where the eel must go, and, despite the considerable amount of fishing that has gone on for centuries in the Atlantic Ocean, no one has ever caught a migrating adult eel once it leaves the continental shelf. A few eels were found in the belly of a sperm whale harpooned off the Azores years ago; and a television camera lowered into the Straits of Florida once showed a silvery female snaking along the bottom nearly a half-mile below the surface. But that is all.

Apparently, their spawn (eggs) and milt (sperm) do not develop until the eels are well at sea. Thus, outside of laboratory experiments, it is still true what Aristotle, the first person to establish that eels moved downstream to the sea, wrote twenty-three centuries ago: "Nor was an eel ever found with either milt or spawn." (Wouldn't that be a gift for the person with everything, for the most jaded gourmet—caviar produced from eel roe, a dish no king has ever tasted?) This uncertainty about eels' spawning led to some wild versions of how they reproduced, including spontaneous generation from slime, or from horsehairs thrown into water. Oppian of Cilicia in A.D. 2 gave poetic expression to what until recent times remained the most widely held theory—that the eel mated with snakes:

> [the eel] glowing with uncommon fires,
> the Earth-bred Serpent's purfled curls admires;
> He, no less kind, makes amorous returns.
> With equal love the grateful serpent burns.
> . . . His mate he calls with softly hissing sounds.
> She joyful hears and from the ocean bounds.

Seamier details of this slimy affair abound in Oppian's *Aleuticon*. By 1684, a Tuscan nobleman, Francesco Redi, had confirmed that adult eels spawned in the sea. But no one had a clue as to where until just before the Civil War, when German scientists first identified as European eel larvae some transparent organisms the shape and size of willow leaves, found floating in the Strait of Messina. Nearly half a century more passed before the detective hunt for the birthing place of the eel began in earnest. A young Danish biologist and oceanographer, Johannes Schmidt, was charged by his government to crisscross the Atlantic, dragging a fine mesh net behind his ship, the *Thor,* until he found where the little willow leaves originated. For years the search spread—to the North Sea, the English Channel, the Faero Islands, the Azores, across to Newfoundland and down to the Antilles—twenty-three Danish ships were involved by now. Ever smaller *Leptocephali*, as the larval eels were called, kept turning up as Schmidt closed in on the location, finally announced in 1920. It turned out to be a place of supersaline, stagnant water where an estimated ten million pounds of seaweed in great clumps drifted timelessly in an area nearly the size of the continental United States.

"It might very well be," wrote Rachel Carson, "that some of the very weeds you would see if you visited the place today were seen by

Columbus and his men." The place she spoke of, the birthplace and universal spawning ground of all the eels of two continents, was in the depths of the Sargasso Sea. The helpless, free-floating larvae, the little willow leaves, scientists would later show, are seized by great, slow, clockwise currents that many months, even years, later deliver the American and European eels near their respective seacoasts (their spawning areas are in slightly different parts of the Sargasso).

By the time they reach the coastal fringes, the eels have reached the "elver" stage, a few inches long, looking quite eel-like, and are able to swim on their own. And how. Up and up they go, up the bay, up the rivers, up the creeks, up the sheer walls of high concrete dams, up sewer pipes, even overland to ponds and wells more than a mile from flowing water. What urge impels them so toward fresh water, to bodies of water they could not possibly have prior knowledge of, is not understood, save that it is one of the more powerful motive forces on the planet. They surmount Great Falls on the Potomac in Washington, D.C., a barrier that historically has stopped even the great leaping spawners like the shad. Richard St. Pierre, a fisheries biologist with the federal government on the Susquehanna River, says he routinely gets reports of eels crushed as they slither across U.S. Route 1 where it traverses the top of the Conowingo Dam. Built in the 1920s, Conowingo is more than one hundred feet straight up.

Because the eel breathes quite nicely through its skin as long as it is moist, it can travel over land some distance if there is so much as a heavy dew on the ground. Sometimes, if it cannot climb a dam, it just goes around it. Eels returning from the Sargasso appear to have crossed even the eastern continental divide which runs through the far western third of Garrett County in Maryland. Traveling, perhaps, through inland waterways of the Potomac system, eels have somehow gotten into the Youghiogheny, the only river in Maryland that flows toward the Gulf of Mexico rather than the bay. Charles J. Hassel, Jr., a thirty-five-year plumbing veteran of New York City, tells of the time the water supply was cut off for an entire building at Third Avenue and Sixty-third Street. Blocking the main pipe was a healthy, thrashing, two-foot eel.

It is mostly female eels that seem to have the urge to push as far upstream as the water lasts, say John Foster and Robert Brody, the state biologists who have made a study of Maryland's eel population. Males, which never grow more than about 18 inches long, stay in brackish water and in the creeks along the ocean coast. Chincoteague National Wildlife Refuge takes advantage of the seaside elver run each spring by opening floodgates connecting fresh-water ponds with the ocean. The millions of elvers thus trapped in the ponds provide food for migrating wading birds and, indirectly, hearty fare for the tens of thousands of bird-watchers who flock to Chincoteague each spring. As you might expect of eels, they don't all follow the rules. I know one big old female that, for whatever reasons, never pushed farther upstream than Smith Island, where she has lived for years under the crab shanty of a man in Rhodes Point, who feeds her royally on dead soft crabs.

Foster and Brody know as much as most scientists about the habits of eels, but even they, in talking about where eels go to spawn and die, at depths far below our scrutiny, must always hedge. To recall Aristotle's writings, "nor was an eel ever found with either milt or spawn." Scientists have, however, calculated the calories of energy in the body of an adult eel and then estimated the energy that eel would have to expend on its spawning run to the Sargasso. It looks like they have a one-way ticket. It is easy to imagine their arrival on the spawning grounds, based on such one-way trips documented in some salmon species—flesh literally rotting, bones demineralized and spongy, all systems irreversibly shutting down, remaining energies all channeled into the organs of reproduction, a sad, ruined version of Klingel's glorious encounter beneath the Chesapeake. But what a way to end it all. Imagine billions of eels, each female bearing millions of eggs, silvery projectiles all converging on the dark, warm Sargassan womb (also tomb), literally disintegrating in a blast of superfecundation that covers thousands of square miles, only then sinking slowly into the cold abysses, even as a galaxy of tiny willow leaves starts drifting gently back toward the Chesapeake Bay.

Short, Important Trips of Oysters

If these biology fellers are right, there's a lot to learn about an arster.
—the late John Larrimore, a skipjack captain for forty years

It's a hot, drowsy day in late June. The crabbers out here on the Tred Avon River have called it an afternoon. Not a cloud moves in the blue sky. Not a ripple kisses the hull of our research vessel, the *Ridgley Warfield*, which is anchored over the oyster bar known as Double Mills. Several feet below, however, on thousands of acres around us, the molluscan equivalent of a moonshot is in full swing. A great journey is beginning; an annual migration mysterious as the convergence of the world's eels on the Sargasso, as epic for its tiny voyagers as the flight of the monarch butterfly from North America to the mountains of Mexico. Its successful conclusion, far from assured, is as salutary to us bay dwellers as the arrival of wild geese in the fall.

Never mind that the critical passage made by the larval oysters being spawned here and throughout the bay this month will measure only feet, even inches; or that it will be mostly bobbing up and down. Dominated all our lives by gravity, we are creatures of the horizontal. It is the salmon's mounting one thousand miles of river and stream to spawn that catches our fancy; or the spring herring that once ran from the Chesapeake's mouth to Binghamton, New York, on the Susquehanna. The voyage of the oyster reminds us that there are dimensions in nature nonetheless wondrous for our inability to identify with them.

For weeks the oysters that appear to lie so quietly at the river's bottom have been furiously converting their winter stores of glycogen, a starch, to the business of reproduction. Water temperatures, reaching the mid to high seventies, trigger the release of sperm into the water by male oysters, and eggs by the females. What an event it must be! Paul Galtsoff, author in 1964 of what remains the definitive work on the American oyster (*Fishery Bulletin of the United States*, vol. 64), once attached a device called a Kymograph to the shell edge of female oysters, producing a tracing on a graph of the minutest openings and closings of the oysters. Then he released sperm into the surrounding water to excite them. In minutes, the shells began to heave excitedly up and down; the tracings on the graph paper went from foothills to Himalayas. I have several pages of those tracings, probably as close to erotic literature as a mollusk ever will produce. Galtsoff might think it unscientific, but I like to imagine, on warm June days, the bottom of the bay all a-clatter, the tawny, olive waters of its shallows fogged, from Gibson Island to Crisfield, from Swan Point to Great Rock, with the Vesuvian eruptions of sperm and eggs from three billion oysters bent on making more of themselves with a fury not to be denied.

It is one measure of the pollution we have caused, and the overexploitation of the shellfishery we have allowed, that the fecund Chesapeake oyster's numbers have been reduced an estimated 95 percent in the last century. There was panic at one point in bay oyster circles at the suggestion there might no longer be enough male oysters to fertilize all the females' eggs. Oysters are alternative hermaphrodites, starting off all as males, then switching their sex to females after a couple years. Several years of mysteriously poor survival of young that began in the 1970s and continues today had left the bay floor covered with mostly aging, unfulfilled females, the thinking went.

A subsequent survey found the sex ratio in good balance, however—and something equally interesting—it appears that oysters on a bar can somehow sense if there is an imbalance in sex ratios and convert back from females to males, as needed. Because a female releases up to ten million eggs, and because there are at least one billion females at any given time in the Maryland bay, the reproductive problems that have been plaguing the oyster in the last decade do not seem to be with initial blast-off. But the heady promise of June fades quickly. Life gets tougher immediately as the new oysters hatch, microscopic particles cast far and wide from their home beds by the vagaries of tide and wind. Lacking any powers to swim, they have from fifteen to twenty days to find a place to *set*—attach permanently to the bottom to form a shell—or they will die. Of an oyster's life span, which may exceed a dozen years, these few weeks are the most critical and the least understood. What goes on between the trillions of eggs, the billions of larvae, and the millions of *spat*—the larval oysters that manage to set and encrust themselves in a protective shell?

For decades, watermen and state fisheries managers have annually spread thousands, sometimes millions, of bushels of oyster shells in areas where it is hoped the presence of clean, hard substrate, or *cultch*, will encourage a spat set. Shelling the bay bottom and moving *seed*, or young oysters, from bottoms thick with them to leaner ones have become almost as much part of oyster season as tongers and skipjacks. "Goin' spattin'," hiring their boats to the state to plant seed and shell, has become part of the waterman's seasonal cycle, a welcome source of income in April and May, the months between oyster season and the onset of crabbing.

Like much else in bay fisheries management, this planting is a good biological concept that frequently is driven by purest politics. "Oistuhs here!" say the St. Mary's watermen. "No, put the arysters over here!" rejoins the Tangier Sound contingent. Around every tidewater county of the bay region each spring, local accents ring like hammer against anvil as the tongers and dredgers committees from each subdivision clamor for their share of the state's shell and seed, regardless of where the most likely setting might occur. And frankly, even the best biologists in many years might just as well be trying to catch stardust as young oysters on their carpets of shell, so capricious has been the success of the bay's spat set.

For several winters I have made the annual winter oyster cruise on which a host of state and university biologists pull up cultch from oyster bars throughout the bay, to assign success or disaster to last summer's spawn by counting the number of spat that have set. They have advanced degrees and are as knowledgeable about the oyster as anyone; yet, watching them huddling over piles of muddy shell, holding each piece up to the light, twisting it to count the little dime-sized bumps of new oysters and make their forecasts, they remind me of nothing so much as ancient Roman haruspices, trying to divine the future by poking in the entrails of a sacrificial beast.

Only in the mid-1980s, in the face of the lowest oyster harvests on the Chesapeake since the 1840s, when serious oystering was just beginning, have serious research efforts like the one here aboard the *Ridgley Warfield* been assembled, to try to unravel where the oyster goes and what it does in that brief and momentous migration, after which it must establish itself for life or vanish. The picture that has emerged is quite unlike the sedentary, gray, dull old oyster of popular conception. What we seem to have here is a creature that represents as much a peak of evolutionary adaptation in its world as we do in ours; an organism capable of the utmost discriminating taste in food, employing in its search for a home the refined olfaction of a homing salmon, and possessing an exquisite sensitivity to its environment beyond anything science had assumed.

To envision what happens during the brief migratory life of the larval oyster, which is too small ever to be physically tracked on its journey, the scientists looked instead at the bay's circulatory system. It would seem to present the larvae, whose swimming powers are feeble at best, with an insurmountable problem from the very instant they are born and drift toward the bay's surface. The net movement of water at the surface—that is, after allowing for the back and forth movements of the tides—is strongly in one direction, toward the sea. The lighter, fresher water from the bay's rivers is always slipping out over the denser, saltier tongue of the ocean that extends up from the bay mouth. All this coming and going, salt upstream and fresh downstream, ultimately balance out, of course, or the estuary would overflow—or drain dry; but the fact remains that anything which rises will inexorably be washed to sea.

The fact that oysters are not, that spat sets from an oyster bar can even occur miles *upstream* from the bar, indicates that the "helpless" little oysters somehow have learned to harness both the coming and the going of the mighty estuarine transport system. They do it by migrating vertically. It need not be far. The salinity of the bay's layered water can double in the space of as little as eight inches (going from top to bottom). For creatures as attuned to salinity as those in an estuary, a vertical trip of a couple feet can bring a change in circumstance equivalent to a goose's two-thousand-mile flight from summer to winter.

How neat for the larval oyster. If it wants to head toward Baltimore, it sinks just a bit in the water column; rise a bit and it is Norfolk-bound. It is probable that many of the bay's tiny zooplankton, little shrimplike copepods and the like, which cannot swim much, ride the comings and goings of the bay this way. It is their way of staying in roughly the same place, where habitat is optimal for their survival, within a system that is always trying to wash them away. But for the little oyster, this still begs the question of how a microscopic blob of flesh can *know* to ride the system, not to mention knowing when, and to where. Some of the University of Maryland scientists here on the *Ridgley Warfield* were astounded one day in the lab when they put some oyster larvae into a new tank, with water from a nearby river that was virtually identical to the water in which the larvae had been swimming near the surface. Almost instantly the larvae sank to the bottom of their tank. It appeared they were unbelievably sensitive to a difference in salinity. The salt content of the new water was perhaps .0005 percent greater than that of the old water. What it means, the scientists think, is that the larval oyster can fine-tune its position vertically, using salinity, with incredible precision. For example, heavy rains occurring in the bay's watershed can send torrents of fresh water barreling down the estuary, sweeping everything in its path oceanward: but at the first infinitesimal signal of such an event in the freshening of the water layer around it, a migrating oyster could immediately drop down to saltier currents moving up the bay.

This still is a relatively gross mechanism for delivering the tiny larvae to where they can profitably settle down on the bay bottom. Out of millions of acres, how can the oyster find a spot that combines a firm, hard surface to which it can attach, and also a place where currents will be adequate to bring by plenty of plankton for it to feed on? It must choose well, because the oyster will never move another inch in its life. The fact that the bay, for all its problems with pollution and overfishing, remains the greatest natural oyster bed in the world is proof that the larval oysters pick good spots to set more often than bad. The secret is akin to, though not so romantic as, the apparent capacities of spawning salmon and herring to pick up the organic bouquet of their natal streams and follow them home.

The oyster's goal is to sniff out a good, thick slime. A lot of the life in the Chesapeake Bay derives from the organic matter, the slimes, that form on hard surfaces on the bottom. Nutrients, dissolved in the water at levels too low to do a hungry critter much good, concentrate in the slimes at levels thousands of times greater. Where such a slime exists, it is not only a rich source of food for a little oyster to use in building its protective shell but also proof that here is a location where a good supply of food can be gleaned from the water. The slimes beckon to the larvae, which now, late in their race to set before they starve, have extended a soft little foot and begun descending close to the bottom, touching, probing, sampling. The little oyster homes in on a highly specific chemical odor exuded by the slime. Home sweet slime. University researchers who have isolated the substance find it may be commercially marketable in aquaculture and have patented the stuff.

Impressive as the journey of the oyster has been so far, if there were no more than that to a salutary spat set, you and I would be able to buy Chincoteagues on the half shell at a dime a dozen, so abundant would oysters be. To arrive at its chosen slimy home in good enough health to begin the energy-consuming task of shell-building, our little oyster has to eat well on its migration. It appears to have been well enough equipped for that by nature. It is a relative "Jaws" among the microscopic algae, the floating plant life on which oysters feed; although given its overall size, that translates to a mouth that gapes about .0004 inches, or 10 microns. Nowadays, the bay would seem, if anything, overfull of oyster food. In recent decades, by our sewage discharges and our heavy use of farm fertilizers, we have flushed into the bay so much nitrogen and phosphorus, the primary food of algae, that the water has become soupy with them.

But the scientists on the *Ridgely Warfield* think that less and less of the algae that the bay is growing these days is to the liking of oysters. It has puzzled them for years why the river here grows fine, fat adult oysters, but virtually never produces a good set of young ones. But algae, like us and oysters, are what they eat. Under natural water-quality conditions, algae tend to get a diet of about 15 parts nitrogen for every 1 part phosphorus. Nature tends so strongly toward this 15:1 mix that it has a name, the Redfield ratio. The Tred Avon, it turns out—and quite likely a lot of the bay—has been forced far out of synch with the Redfield ratio by injections of excess phosphorus and nitrogen in sewage and fertilizers running off farmland.

This appears to have caused algae to predominate there that simply are too big to fit in even the mouths of larval oysters, which may be starving to death in the midst of plenty. Adult oysters, with their larger mouths, continue to flourish in the Tred Avon. Adults are not necessarily immune, however. In other areas of the bay there may be a problem for them, not with the size of the type of algae growing under the bay's changed conditions, but with its digestibility, the scientists say. It may seem a bit much, talking as if the oyster had such a discriminating palate. After all, this is a creature that feeds by simply pumping bay water and all it contains continuously through its gills at rates that can exceed two gallons an hour—hardly a gourmet diner, it would seem.

But the oyster is able to sample for size, digestibility, and, for lack of a better word, *taste,* virtually every one of the millions of particles of sediment and algae entering its mouth every hour it is feeding. Everything not to its liking is rejected out one side of its shell before digestion. Its digestive apparatus, too, is one of the marvels of the living world. Called a crystalline stile, it is a pale olive rod about an inch long and the diameter of no. 11 spaghetti, which works by rotating at 60–70 RPM. It is the only rotating organ known to biology, the closest nature ever came to inventing the wheel.

The day is drawing to a close and a boat has come to take me back to shore. The *Ridgely Warfield* will remain here on station for another two days. Perhaps these scientists will turn the trick, will be able to divine enough about the oyster to help us save it. All day they have kept our conversations largely within the bounds of scientific observation and hypothesis. Now they share a couple other thoughts. It can be estimated that the three billion or so oysters that are now left on the bay's floor in Maryland would have been dwarfed by the numbers there as recently as a century ago. Seventy billion, perhaps one hundred billion, oysters covered the bottom then. Imagine each of those, pumping dozens of gallons of water a day, filtering its sediment and algae. Such a shellfish population could have filtered the entire volume of the bay every five days, as opposed to about every four months with today's reduced stocks. Much as the Amazonian rain forest, by its very vastness, maintains a microclimate of moist conditions ideal for its own perpetuation, so might the great oyster populations of the bay have controlled water quality throughout much of the estuary's history. It is further possible that the great solid reefs, in which oysters grew before dredging broke them up, created enough turbulence as the tides rolled over them to mix the bays waters, helping to keep them more oxygenated than they are now.

The extent to which the bay's oysters and other biota controlled their environment is mostly educated speculation, but increasingly those who study natural systems are learning that their workings can best be comprehended in terms of an ongoing give and take, a dialogue, among all their parts—and well before modern times people were a major part of these conversations. When the settlers arrived, the "primeval" forests of New England were already being managed by Indians, who burned the understory to facilitate hunting. Oyster dredging in the bay more than a century ago broke up the oyster reefs, spreading them out across the bay bottom; and that alteration, in turn, altered the harvesting methods and life styles of the watermen.

So it is that a troubling consideration sometimes presses on the scientists aboard the *Ridgley Warfield*. Once a week, a tug drags a big oil barge up the Tred Avon. The river's channel is not deep, and each week the barge churns up, it seems, half the river bottom in its passage. The scientists watch it and wonder: Of all their careful measurements of nitrogen, phosphorus, algal sizes, water clarity, and other factors critical to their developing theories of spat set—how much is it really measuring nature? How much might it be measuring what they half-jokingly call "a barge-driven ecosystem"? It would be ironic: even as we advance toward understanding the workings of the natural world, other facets of our advance already have so intruded as to become the dominant factor in those workings; we peer, expectantly, into the secrets of the bay's behavior, and see only ourselves.

The Caprice of Crabs

Aboard the Linwood Holton, *August*

O*ut here, forty miles* off the mouth of the Chesapeake Bay, and maybe beyond, a process improbable as alchemy is generating the blue crabs that two years hence will make work for ten thousand watermen and gladden a million palates from Norfolk to Havre de Grace. For as long as we have harvested crabs from the bay, their annual comings and goings have been recognized as the most capricious of all creatures in the estuary. In Maryland waters alone the catch can soar close to a record high of thirty-six million pounds one summer, as it did in 1965, only to drop to ten million pounds in 1968, the lowest catch in recorded history; and then bounce back the very next year to a respectable twenty-seven million pounds.

All that was known for sure about the mysterious life cycle of *Callinectes sapidus* was that toward the end of their second year of life, the females, having mated all over the bay, migrated in the fall to the waters near the bay's mouth. There, after wintering in the mud of the deep channels, they would release their eggs in a hatching period lasting from June through September, and peaking in August. Where the newborn crabs went or what they did between then and a year or so later, when they began scuttling, nearly grown, into every artery and capillary of the bay's system, was less understood than the dark side of the moon. The public—to answer each spring its recurrent question, Will it be a good crabbing year?—had to rely about equally on the pronouncements of the press, crab scientists, and sage watermen. All of these enjoyed about the same level of predictive success as tribal shamans throughout the ages.

The key to divining the caprice of crabs, scientists were fairly certain, was in what happened to the crab during its most vulnerable stage, the month or two of larval development after hatching. That was when the millions of eggs produced by each female were reduced to only a couple of survivors, just enough to maintain a stable population (if even three eggs per female regularly survived, crabs would then be increasing their population at a rate of 50 percent a year and would jam the bay's rivers carapace-to-carapace in short order). Whatever's going on during that period, there's no doubt it must be something very quirky, Steve Sulkin, a University of Maryland crab researcher, would say. Just how quirky was first revealed to a group of Sulkin's colleagues from Old Dominion University as they bobbed on a flood tide in small boats near the bridge tunnel that crosses the Chesapeake near its mouth. Here, during the humid, predawn hours of an August morning in 1980, the scientists witnessed for the first time the full strength of procreation in the greatest nursery in all crabdom.

The zoea, the crab's gnatlike, cyclopean early larval stage, were popping to the surface by the zillions, washing onto beaches, rocks, everywhere around them, recalled John R. McConaugha. The scientists' nets caught up to 100,000 zoea per cubic meter of water. The hatch, it would turn out, always occurred just as the tide began its ebb seaward, virtually guaranteeing that the tiny, helpless zoea would soon be adrift miles out on the open ocean. Worse than that, to the amazement of the scientists, the tiny crabs all remained packed into the top four inches of the water's surface, precisely where they would be most vulnerable to every whim of storm winds and currents during the next several weeks of development. This was a radical twist on what the larvae should have done according to classical theories of survival in an estuary like the bay. It was Sulkin's "something very quirky."

Classically, free-drifting larvae of any species in an estuary face a common, immediate survival problem—how to keep from getting flushed out of the nursery. The inflow from fresh-water rivers creates a net motion seaward, the back-and-forth motions of the tides notwithstanding, so the larvae are always threatened with expulsion, to be lost forever in the ocean. An escape hatch exists in the underlying wedge of heavier, saltier ocean water, whose net movement is constantly into the estuary. The larvae of many species, including oysters, have adaptations that are often astounding in their complexity to let them move downward in the water column, where they can use the salt wedge as free transportation, in effect, to travel back up the bay. The blue crab alone seems wont to gamble its existence, to forsake the "classical mechanism of retention," as the scientists call the salt-wedge transport. The baby crabs, afloat and exposed on the surface, bet the whole shooting match each August on the mercies of wind and wave; and one has to wonder, as swells toss the sixty-five-foot *Linwood Holton*, Old Dominion's research vessel, how the little critters the size of a fingernail clipping which we are finding out here plan ever to make it the two hundred–plus miles back up the bay.

As it turns out, the crab has no choice but to send its young initially seaward. Although it is often considered a prime estuarine species, because it flourishes so brilliantly in the Chesapeake, *Callinectes* remains in its genes a creature of the oceans whence it evolved. In its adult form it is what the scientists call an osmo-regulator, able to pass from the saltiest water to the freshest with impunity by internally regulating its bodily fluids. But in the larval stages it is an osmo-conformer, assuming the salinity of the surrounding waters; and it is only in the high salinities of the bay's mouth and the ocean that it can survive at this tender stage. That it does survive is not in doubt. As attested by the average crab harvests of sixty-five million pounds a year, Maryland and Virginia combined, a few do make it back in from the sea. But how many make it back each year—and when—are supremely determined by the vagaries of offshore winds and the equally variable flows of river water coming out of the bay.

Several years ago Donald Pritchard, a pioneer oceanographer of the Chesapeake, strung current meters across the mouth of the bay and found something, he said, that just couldn't be. There was ten times more water flowing out of the bay than was flowing into it. As it turned out, the bay was not on its way to emptying. It was a short-term, if dramatic, quirk caused by a combination of wind and atmospheric pressure which had forced excess water into the bay, no doubt causing flood tides at its upper end. What Pritchard measured was the bay relaxing from this condition. Just think about what such an event can do to future crab catches if that huge flow comes blasting out of the bay's mouth just as the larvae were all floating offshore. Similarly, if the Atlantic winds that normally blow toward the bay's mouth in August and September should peter out or reverse—and they sometimes do—how many million pounds of crab cakes, crab imperial, and soft-crab sandwiches are we the poorer? There is a spinoff from the developing theory of offshore crab development which, if proven, could burst the balloon of chauvinists who claim the taste of a Chesapeake Bay crab superior to that from any other estuary. It just may be that each estaurine crab spawning ground along the Atlantic coast feeds at least part of its larvae to the estuary below it—Cape Cod to New York, Delaware Bay to the Chesapeake, Chesapeake to North Carolina, and so forth. Periodic reversals in winds and currents would explain how the northernmost estuary gets its fair share in this scenario.

It is just dusk as the *Linwood Holton* chugs back to its berth in Little Creek, laden with samples of crab larvae taken far out past where the olive Chesapeake waters dissolve in the deep, clear blue of the Atlantic. We have been sixty miles offshore, finding larvae all the way. The tide is ebbing slowly, about to turn. Around 3:00 A.M., at a time when human body rhythms have sunk to their lowest, the flood tide will start to run seaward, triggering a silent barrage of hatching that may, if the winds hold fair and the rivers do not rise, someday send welcome armies of blue crabs trooping the length of the bay.

The Tribs

Like an Arab fingers his prayer beads reciting the Koran, I love to run through the names of the bay's rivers in my head. They conjure powerful images, the ghosts of Indians and the legacy of English settlement; the graceful meander of slow water and the sibilance of the wind in the marshes. "SUSSS-que-HANna, WI-com-i-CO . . . and the YORK, Rap-a-HAN-nock, and James," sings the Patuxent River poet, Tom Wisner. He captures a lot of the delight of the "tribs," short for tributaries, in his music. But there are more tribs to the bay than one song can encompass—nearly fifty major ones. That number may strike you as high, but don't forget the Piankatank and its northern neck of Virginia neighbor, the Corotoman; or the Bird and the Bush, the Bohemia and the Corsica, all in Maryland's upper bay; or the lonely, sinuous Transquaking, Chicamacomico, and Blackwater, all merging into Fishing Bay in lower Dorchester County.

The names of the tribs are merely remarkable. Their most wondrous aspect we take for granted, seldom thinking how profound are its implications. The tribs branch, and branch again and again, extending the relative impersonality of the bay deep into the creases of the Maryland landscape, and into the familiar consciousness of all who live in it. The incredible ecosystem we call "the bay" is for most of us more correctly limited to a branch or a twig of the main tree. Long before we know the bay, most of us know a trib.

My first trib was so many times branched from the bay, you would not even think it connected to where it debouches into upper Tangier Sound and is known as the Nanticoke River. There, it is big, lusty, salty water, open to gales romping up through Hooper Straits, a place where rugged men in big workboats from towns like Bivalve and Wetipquin tong for oysters off places named Roaring Point and Nigger Gut. Miles upstream from there, if you looked left crossing the U.S. Route 50 bridge at Vienna on your way to Ocean City, you would see where a slight rise in the land and a little drop in the water's salinity work a miraculous transformation on the Nanticoke's personality. The river sloughs off like a molted skin the measureless tidal marsh that has embraced its either bank most of the way from the bay and wraps itself in forested swamps. But the greater marvel of this reach is not vegetational, but chemical and biological. Here, where the salt of the ocean and the fresh water coming downstream strike a balance that seems to encourage fecundity, begins one of the bay's great, invisible nursery areas, where rockfish and shad and herring and white perch all come to spawn and to pass their most fragile, early life stages. Like most of us, the bay's fishes know a trib before they know the bay.

The men who work the river here are close kin to the tongers of Roaring Point, but they float on calmer waters in smaller, graceful craft, deftly setting fragile skeins of net to drifting through the river channels, to fill its folds with bright silver. It is a lovely, primitive sight, this annual ritual of man and net and river, which takes place as the bottomland forests are profligately minting fresh, tender greens, currency to atone for skinflint winter's poor wages. But this is not yet my trib.

Now the river narrows again, and the banks are higher, the forest thicker; black ducks wheel over wild-rice beds and the irrigation pipes of farmers stick into the water, here where the influence of salt falls away completely. The little crossroad settlements have names like Brookview and Harrison's Ferry; and the trib, having branched, is here known as Marshyhope Creek. Dubbed thus by some early settler, the name persists despite sporadic attempts by garden clubs and historical society ladies to turn it back to its more proper title, Northwest Fork of the Nanticoke. Near head of tide and navigation is the town of Federalsburg, a solid little community of the Eastern Shore's scantily touristed agricultural interior.

Most residents are only aware of their connection to the bay, which is sixty river miles away, when the herring run gluts Mowbray's and Jimmy's creeks and sometimes tries to mount the dam at Chambers Lake during a few weeks of each year. The herring are one of early spring's great enthusiasms, on a par with the blossoming of forsythia, and in their spawning throes they will press to the uttermost capillary ends of the bay's drainage system; but even those exuberant voyagers ignored my first trib. My trib began life as a two-foot-wide ditch, draining waste oil and grease from a Federalsburg trucking company. It trickled, nameless, for half a mile to the Marshyhope near M&L Trucking through a shrubby ravine known only as "the branch." It was polluted, it was fishless, it was obstructed with brush and junk—and it was a source of more hours of childhood joy and fantasy than I can recount.

Never mind its biological shortcomings—it was flowing water, falling, pooling, racing, freezing, rippling, reflecting all the moods of the sky and the day and the breeze and the seasons. It made an otherwise ordinary depression in the land unique, lent it focus and character; and its size seemed just right for kids. We felt it our own—dammed it, channeled it, splashed in it, raced wood chips down it, swung across it on vines, just like generations of Federalsburgians before us and afterward. Such a humble thread of water, a minor glimmer in the grand web of the bay's drainage; but what human perceptions, memories, emotions are attached to it. You begin to see the implications of this branching we call the tribs, of which there are an estimated eighteen thousand miles in Maryland alone.

The bay, by the classic definition, is a mixing bowl where rivers meet the ocean, and the resultant tussle between salt and fresh water creates what we call an estuary. To the estuary and most of its creatures, the ocean part is at least as important as the tribs; but for us land dwellers, the tribs are where the action is. This brings us to another list of names I often go over in my head—Mattawoman, Patuxent, Cox's Creek, Western Branch . . . These are not from any Tom Wisner song. They are all sewage plants, all on the tribs whose names they share, and whose water quality they have in most cases come to dominate. You could run through the same exercise with most of the dams, power plants, and many major industries. If the tribs are where we first grow to love the bay, they are also where we first begin to kill it. It is a simple lesson that we have only begun to heed. To examine the bay's health, you don't look just at the bay. By the time many of the ills show up there, it will be too late, requiring massive surgery at the least. If we are to save the bay, ultimately it will have to start with respect for the tiniest of tribs.

Susquehanna: The Biggest River

I drain a thousand streams, yet still I seek
To lose myself within the Chesapeake
In reedy inlets of the Indian bay.
—*"We Heard the River Singing,"*
a Susquehanna sonnet

If we were honest about it, there would be no Chesapeake Bay in Maryland, only the Susquehanna River. It is the biggest flowing river on the East Coast. Its drainage basin, 1 percent of which lies below the

Mason-Dixon line, sprawls through more than a third of Pennsylvania and into New York State as far north as the latitude of Vermont. On the very droughtiest of days it carries one billion gallons of water past its mouth at Havre de Grace; but when engorged with rains, its mammoth watershed has hurled 650 times that much down channel—a flood equal to the average daily discharges of the Mississippi and Yukon rivers combined, with the Nile thrown in for good measure. The Maryland map does not do it justice, showing only a thin, blue line poking in from the top of the state, splitting Harford and Cecil counties for twelve miles before losing itself in the broad Chesapeake. By contrast the Potomac, where its meeting with tidewater slows and widens it from below Mount Vernon to its mouth, seems an altogether more impressive river. Similarly, the Choptank, Patapsco, Chester, Patuxent, and Pocomoke impress the eye more than the Susquehanna. But the Susquehanna also has a broad, impressive tidal portion. On a map of Maryland, place your finger from Solomons, at the end of Calvert County, across the bay toward Hoopers Island on the Eastern Shore. Down to about there, at least 90 percent of the fresh water comes from a single river, the Susquehanna, and this is more nearly its rightful mouth.

Born from a tiny spring a mile above baseball's Hall of Fame in Cooperstown, New York, the river had already carved the deep channels of the present Chesapeake more than ten thousand years ago, when melting polar icecaps began to raise the sea to its present level. Three thousand years ago this had flooded the Susquehanna's valley through the soft sediments of the Atlantic coastal plain to the present extent of the Chesapeake Bay. Above Havre de Grace, the change in the geology of the river's valley is dramatic, and arguably serendipitous for the environment of our modern bay.

For much of the 440 miles from Conowingo, near the Pennsylvania line, to Lake Otsego, near its source, the river has been cutting away at some of the ruggedest terrain in the East for 250 million years. Its channel there is plaited with bedrock and shallow across its entire breadth for long stretches. The Susquehanna consequently is the longest nonnavigable river in America. That has denied it, for all the river's mighty flow, its Henry Hudsons and Mark Twains, its stern-wheel river boats, and its status as a highway of commerce and exploration. It has also meant that the bay in Maryland never was plagued with the untreated sewage and industrial toxins from the Baltimores, Philadelphias, or New Yorks that surely would have arisen on a deepwater river extending into the rich coal fields and fertile farming valleys of central Pennsylvania and New York.

To say the Susquehanna is nonnavigable is to speak only of human commerce. It was the greatest fish highway that ever existed in the East, perhaps on the continent. To every rivulet that paid tribute to the bay throughout the vast watershed, the Chesapeake each spring sent back a king's ransom of silver shad. Because it is a supremely tasty fish, weighing up to nine pounds and prized for its delicately flavored, fine-grained roe, the April–May spawning run of the American shad has been an event eagerly awaited on every East Coast river from Florida to New England since humanity first inhabited their edges. Nowhere did the annual run surpass the Susquehanna's. It seems likely that the shad were making their way up the river from the Atlantic Ocean even before the bay began to form in its valley one hundred centuries ago. Like the West Coast's salmon, they appear to be drawn back to their natal rivers and streams by forces still not well understood, but probably involving a homing-in on organic odors peculiar to each stream, at least in the final stages of their journey.

Just as mysterious is what compelled the Susquehanna's shad up and up the bay, past the James, the York, the Potomac, and the Chesapeake's forty-odd other spawning rivers; and what continued to draw them, once in their home river, past the prime spawning waters of Harford County's Deer Creek and the Octoraro Creek from Cecil County; past the Juniata above Harrisburg, past Sunbury, Wilkes-Barre, Scranton, ever higher into the watershed, past the Wyalusing and dozens of other creeks, the sleek fish now wasting rapidly, having swum more than five hundred miles from the bay's mouth, a journey on which they did not eat. And still they pressed on, reaching as far as Binghamton, New York, more than six hundred miles from the sea—the longest fish migration known in the eastern United States.

Charles Miner's *History of Wyoming* (Wyoming being a Pennsylvania county near the New York border) tells how the annual pulse of migrants up from the Chesapeake Bay brought a happy conclusion to a lean February 1773, for the settlers at Wilkes-Barre: "Never was an opening spring or the coming of the shad looked for with more anxiety or hailed with more cordial delight. The fishing season . . . dissipated all fears, and the dim eye was soon exchanged for the glance of joy and the dry, sunken cheek of want assumed the plump appearance of health and plenty."

J. B. Wilkinson's 1840 *Annals of Binghamton* says the best fishing was at night, when the shad "would run up on the riffles to sport. The shad seemed never to find either a place or time at which to turn and go back. Even after depositing their eggs, they would continue to urge their way upstream until they had exhausted their entire strength . . . the shores would be strewed with their dead bodies. Their young fry would pass down the stream in the fall, in such numbers as to choke up the eel-weirs." That last observation is one that modern fisheries biologists find fascinating, because shad, unlike many species of salmon, are not known to expire at the end of their migrations. Usually they return for several years. Perhaps those fish of the upper Susquehanna represented a genetically distinct race, now lost forever. In fact, by the mid-1800s, the building of dams for mills and canal transportation was already making the most extreme excursions of shad no more than a wistful memory.

"Their coming was the principal food for all the inhabitants . . . no farmer, or man with a family was without his barrel or barrels of shad the whole year round," Gilbert Fowler, a resident of the upper Susquehanna, recalled in a letter to the *Berwick Independent* in 1881. He concluded that although he was eighty-nine, "I still hope to live long enough to see all the obstructions removed from one end of the noble Susquehanna river to the other, that the old stream may yet furnish cheap food . . . and pleasure to two millions of Pennsylvanians along its banks."

As late as 1891 there still were commercial seines operating as far above the Chesapeake as Tunkhannock, near Scranton, but the era of the big dam was upon the river. The first to span the main Susquehanna was at Columbia, between York and Lancaster, forty-three miles above the bay. It was built in 1835, and periodic damage from ice and floods permitted intermittent passage of fish upstream. In 1904 the first hydropower dam spanned the river at York Haven, and it endures to this day. Three more hydro dams would plug the Susquehanna's channel in the next two decades. The giant, hundred-foot dam at Conowingo in Maryland, only a few miles upstream from the bay, was the capstone in 1928. Federal fisheries experts deemed it impossible at the time to construct a fish ladder for the shad over so high an edifice, and the state of Maryland agreed to accept annual payments of about $4,000 annually as reparation.

Finally, cheered the engineers and the power companies and the politicians, all that wasted water that used to roar down the channel was being put to work, disciplined by huge turbines that would feed on the power of the river to light and heat and cool homes up and down the valley. Forgotten was the migrant tide that used to flow upriver on the "wasted" waters of the spring freshets. By the 1920s, the river could lay claim to being nonnavigable in the fullest sense of the word. A special part of the Pennsylvania spring had become a fading memory. An anthology of the river published in 1899 had carried this lament, dedicated to the dam at Columbia that was the beginning of the end:

When April comes on the shadfly's wing
'Tis a sign that shad are ripe and Spring,
The luscious creature, has bared her arms
To show the world voluptuous charms,
 . . . She hears the fisherman's tale of woe
From Havre de Grace to Otsego,
For the savory shad is seen no more
Above Columbia's smoke-wrapt shore.
 . . . Through centuries we'll sing the psalm—
"O dam Columbia! Columbia dam!"

Conowingo Dam began generating power in 1932. It had already been half a century since the last great shad runs pushed far up the Susquehanna. Nearly another half a century would pass before consciousness of the great bay that was their river's legacy would return to Pennsylvanians; it would not be anything so sweet as shad that would come calling from downstream. As for most Marylanders, if they were taught anything regarding Pennsylvania, it was usually about what separated the two states—the historic line surveyed in 1767 by Charles Mason and Jeremiah Dixon. That a mighty waterway connected them, and that events unfolding on the lands of its drainage basin hundreds of miles above Baltimore could be shaping the future of their beloved bay—those were notions as remote from the thinking of Marylanders as sunspot theories of climate change.

The collective consciousness of bay dwellers got a jolt from the big river above them in June 1972, when rainfall the likes of which had not been seen in the recorded history of the Susquehanna came crashing down into Maryland. For weeks the swollen bay was opaque with mud to well below the Virginia line. The debris made boating unsafe. The Susquehanna, the scientists who assessed the impact said, normally carried a million tons of sediment into the bay in a year, an inevitable aging process that in another ten thousand years or so may turn it into a marsh. During one week in June, the rains of Tropical Storm Agnes had carried forty times the annual amount of sediment bayward. The river that we hardly knew existed had aged our bay by decades in a few days.

In March 1979, a small island in the Susquehanna not far above the old Columbia Dam erupted into international notoriety when its nuclear power plant seemed for a time to be out of control and threatening a catastrophic meltdown. Catastrophe was averted at Three Mile Island, but as cleanup of millions of gallons of radioactive water contained in the facility proceeded, Pennsylvania proposed to discharge it to the river. It was relatively low-level radiation, and the huge dilutive capacity of the river would render it quickly harmless. Perhaps they were right in a technical sense; but *radioactivity*, even in very small amounts, is a word that captures our attention. The specter of even slightly radioactive oysters downstream in the Chesapeake Bay was enough to scotch any plans for discharge of the water. Suddenly every fisherman and waterman and seafood lover in Maryland, and their elected representatives, had become quite well-informed that what Pennsylvania did with its river could matter to them, too.

Three years later, that budding realization was hammered home with the release of a massive, long-range federal study of the Chesapeake Bay's most pressing environmental problems. The late 1960s and early 1970s had seen steadily worsening water quality in many areas of the bay. The Susquehanna Flats off Havre de Grace had lost their luxuriant underwater celery beds. Once these had supported wild ducks by the hundreds of thousands. At one point there were an estimated forty thousand duck decoys in use by hunters on the flats.

This lower Susquehanna had been an even more prodigious shad producer than the Pennsylvania reaches. In 1827, a gigantic seine on the Cecil County side, which could not be hauled for four days because of weather, produced a catch estimated at some fifteen million shad, herring, and rockfish. As late as the 1960s the lower river still produced annual shad catches in the hundreds of thousands of pounds; but by the 1970s it had fallen to the tens of thousands, and to nineteen thousand in 1977. That year the Izaak Walton League announced it was shutting down its traditional spring sport-fishing tournament for shad on the river. There just were not enough fish left to make it worthwhile. And by 1980 Maryland had banned all fishing for the American shad.

The federal pollution study filled hundreds of pages and grew fairly arcane at times with its discussions of toxic chemicals and nonpoint source pollution; but in a nutshell, it said that sewage plants and farmers fertilizing their fields had been overwhelming the bay with two plant nutrients, phosphorus and nitrogen. Both were essential to growth of everything from corn on the land to algae that formed the base of the food web in the bay; but too much nutrient was causing the algae to grow explosively. It was turning the water opaque, shading out the light needed by the underwater celery and other grasses, as well as consuming oxygen from the bay that was vital to the health of its other organisms. The study's identification of the source of the pollution sent reverberations up and down the length of the Susquehanna watershed. Of more than a dozen major rivers carrying pollutants to the Maryland bay, the Susquehanna was responsible for about half of all the phosphorus and three-quarters of all the nitrogen. Unless Pennsylvania's river could be controlled, Maryland's bay never would be cleaned up, the results indicated.

Pennsylvanians were somewhat shocked and bewildered at their new status as the biggest polluters of North America's largest and most productive estuary. The Susquehanna basin bore hardly any resemblance to the sooty, industrialized, overpopulated places associated with environmental degradation. Of its twenty-seven thousand square miles (three-quarters in Pennsylvania, the rest in New York), almost 80 percent remained in forest and pasture, and a mere 2.4 percent was settled more than sparsely. Furthermore, Pennsylvania had fairly aggressively controlled the discharges from what industry and sewage plants it did have in the basin. If the shad no longer ran there, fishing was generally excellent. Smallmouth bass had made a comeback; the muskellenge, a species needing fine water quality, was flourishing. Mile after mile of acid-polluted river, victim of drainage leaching from abandoned coal mines, had been restored. The state spent millions in Harrisburg to combat hordes of stinging black flies, which had not hatched on the river there for years because of pollution. If you heard one overall assessment when you talked to experts on the Susquehanna in Pennsylvania it was that "the river is pretty clean."

But what is clean enough for a flowing river is not necessarily clean enough for the Chesapeake Bay. A river is in constant motion, all in one direction. The entrance of nitrogen and phosphorus into the Susquehanna was like dumping manure on a conveyor belt—it kept on carrying them off, so within some very broad limits, no matter how much you dumped, you never had a dangerous accumulation. In an estuary like the bay, the collision of fresh water flowing downstream with salty ocean water flowing upstream exerts powerful chemical and physical forces that settle out, onto its bottom, pollutants entering from the rivers. Very little is just "flushed away" into the oceans. The bay is the end of the conveyor belt for a watershed extending sixty-four thousand square miles.

As for the origin of those tremendous loads of nutrients coming down the Susquehanna, it had relatively little to do with either the industries or the sewage plants across the drainage basin. It had to do with the rich agriculture that had come to replace nearly 20 percent of the forest that once covered the watershed. Lancaster County, perched only a few dozen miles upriver from the bay, typified the problem. It was famous for its Pennsylvania Dutch and for its thousands of small farms, which produced, the Chamber of Commerce would proudly tell you, enough milk for two million people, enough eggs for five million, and enough chickens for three and a one-half million. Lancaster County contained one million chickens, steers, cows, heifers, and hogs; each year, altogether they produced ten *billion* pounds of manure, which is of course quite steeped with nitrogen and phosphorus. Soil scientists said that Lancaster County spread so much manure on its fields—the only way farmers knew to dispose of it—that it did not even need to buy commercial fertilizers. Nonetheless, figuring you can't have too much of a good thing, farmers there were still applying close to twenty thousand tons of excess nitrogen and phosphorus annually; when it rained, a lot of this found its way to the Chesapeake.

It all could have made for a nasty confrontation. Pennsylvanians could have said the river looked just fine from where they sat. They could have expressed outrage at Maryland's expectation that they spend millions to begin controlling the polluted runoff from their farms; and of course there was some of that. But it almost seemed as if the rediscovery of the river as connected to something greater, to the bay, lent a welcome focus to a lot of Pennsylvanians. Agricultural scientists who had been trying for years to tell farmers that they were wastefully over-fertilizing seized on the bay issue to make their case. Environmentalists sponsored a conference on the bay and—in a state that does not own an acre of it—nearly one thousand people, many of them farmers, paid admission and braved icy roads on a January morning to attend. The Pennsylvania secretary of natural resources took a boat trip on the bay and was gratified to learn that crabs, not oysters, shed their shells. Those with experience in such massive, long-term projects as the current bay cleanup know it is too early to get optimistic, but meanwhile the two states seem to have found that even nonnavigable rivers can carry a lot of good will.

It seems almost too much to hope, but perhaps the Susquehanna will once again carry something else precious. In an office outside of Harrisburg, a blunt-spoken, white-haired man named Ralph Abele sits beneath a huge "Don't Tread on Me" flag. He is the Pennsylvania fish commissioner, and he is in the midst of a battle with utilities that own the four hydropower dams on the river to make them build state-of-the-art fish ladders for migrating shad. "The Pennsylvania Fish Commission was established by the governor in 1866 for one purpose only: its mandate was simple . . . to restore migrating fish runs to the Susquehanna River. We haven't yet, but we don't give up that easily," Abele said. Not long ago he ordered tough Mayor Rizzo of Philadelphia to install fish passageways at a dam on the Schuylkill River where it runs through town. Closed-circuit television cameras were installed underwater to flash pictures of the triumphal homecoming to delighted visitors at the Philadelphia Zoo.

Abele's agency, in conjunction with the U.S. Fish and Wildlife Service, has been gathering viable eggs from shad all over the United

States to hatch on the Susquehanna. Released in the river, the young will, it is hoped, be imprinted to return there from the sea a few years later when they mature. Some of the eggs come from Columbia River shad—the Fish Commission wanted to get fish that are genetically disposed to making the kind of long migration that the native Susquehanna species once made to Binghamton, New York, from the sea. The far-migrating shad on the Columbia have, in a sense, come full circle. The run on that river was begun in 1875 when the first American shad ever to be seen on the West Coast were shipped there in milk cans from the Susquehanna.

In a few years, if the millions of young shad that Abele is releasing make it through the slashing turbines of four dams and survive to maturity in the oceans, they may travel back to the base of Conowingo, the first dam on the river, and try futilely to mount its spillway. It will, fisheries officials hope, make a compelling case for the installation of fish passageways, which now are resisted by the utility company. If all is right in God's heaven, by the time the shad are restored to Pennsylvania, Maryland's upstream neighbors will have cooperated magnificently in helping to cleanse the Chesapeake. It would be occasion for quite a homecoming party.

Patuxent: Bernie's Toes

> Will the people on this river
> Ever see clear water once again?
> —from a Southern Maryland
> river song by Tom Wisner

You could argue that Mrs. Dixie Buck, a soft-crabber of Broomes Island on the Patuxent River in Calvert County, was the first to notice it—what a six-year, $28 million federal study would conclude in 1983 was the widespread and worsening decline of the Chesapeake Bay. It was in 1956, and it was nothing that you'd tell the world about, but in the river—she was almost sure of it—the water was getting a little cloudy. Dixie is seventy-four now, in her sixty-seventh summer of poling her little skiff from the bow, dip net poised, intently peering into the waters of Nan's Cove, where she lives on the island. She is still the one people around the county will send you to for soft crabs. "If Dixie Buck doesn't have 'em, you know there aren't any," they say. But if she catches two dozen in a day now, "that'd be a glut of 'em. I used to get, just me alone, as much as fifteen dozen in a day. There was seaweed on the bottom then for 'em to hide in, to shed. Clear water? I used to nipper oysters out there in twelve feet of water. You could see every one lying on the bottom before you picked it up. You could still see through the water some" until about 1964, she said. In 1970 the seaweed vanished. "Now, you can't see bottom three feet from shore. Will it get better again? I doubt it. But Bernie is trying, bless his heart."

State Senator Bernard Fowler's mother is from Nan's Cove. He grew up on Broomes Island, and the old-timers will recall that he was a boy who always loved to run, even though the school never had a track team. Few of them are aware that, at age sixty, the boy has run the hundred meters in around 13.2 seconds, the four hundred meters in just over 1 minute, and cleans up in gold medals every year in Maryland's Senior Olympics. He entered a regional meet in Florida recently and won five golds. He'd like to try the nationals, where the gold last year in the hundred was taken by a time of 13.1. Bernie is a lean, angular man who looks three inches taller than his six feet. His easy, almost courtly, manner and mellifluous Southern Maryland accent do not hint at the explosiveness of the sprinter. He talks very little about himself, even on the campaign trail. Mostly he talks about things like preserving Southern Maryland's rural way of life, and always about the Patuxent River. He has seen the river and the bay at their very best.

"The cycle of the year at Broomes Island was the oyster in the winter—a highlight of my childhood was the oyster fleet coming in off the river, forty or sixty boats, all jockeying for position to unload in the sunset. There were 135 shuckers at Warren Denton's oyster house, blacks, and they would sing, sing more as they got tired, solid harmony . . . you can't know how enriching that was. In early spring, before fishing got started, the men gigged eels and progged for turtles in the mud of the bottom. The water was so clear they could spot eel holes in eight to ten feet of water. Turtles, you'd use a long iron rod . . . feel that shell under the mud like an empty drum, then hook 'em out with the rod. Shad were the first of the fish, then rockfish and hardhead. The netters would set enormous seines out from shore several hundred yards—'laying around' they would call it—then let the tide help pull 'em back in to shore to make a half-circle around a school of fish. I remember them letting a whole seine full of hardhead go, the market for them was so low. In 1956 I took a friend sport fishing . . . I recall choosing among breaking schools of rock for just the size we wanted to catch."

But it was the summers, and soft-crabbing, that formed his single most vivid memory. It did not seem remarkable at the time, but it would become a touchstone for Bernie, and ultimately for the whole state, in the struggle that would climax nearly forty years later over the fate of the Chesapeake Bay. After finishing high school at sixteen and serving in the navy during World War II, Bernie used a $4,000 G.I. bill loan to buy a rowboat business on Broomes Island. He had a little snack bar, trotlined for hard crabs, kept peelers in floats to let them shed to become soft crabs, and met his wife, who came down with her family from Washington for holidays on the river. "She would crab out of the boat, while I would wade out along the flats with a dip net after soft crabs. I'd see one on the bottom and follow after it . . . wade out to where I'd be up to my shoulders—I'm six feet and one-quarter inch tall—and I could still see that crab on the bottom. I could see my feet in shoulder-deep water, and that's something I've not been able to do for many years on this river."

It seemed so rich, so valued by the people who lived along it, one wonders in retrospect how the river could have declined so far. But it just slipped away, a piece at a time, all through the 1950s and 1960s and into the 1970s; and some years it even would seem like things were coming back a little, just enough to fool you, Bernie says. "You would hear people say, 'The water seems cloudy,' or 'Doggone, oysters don't seems as plentiful as last year,' and 'Wonder what's happened to the hardhead?'. Then the fishermen began saying, 'Gonna put 'er on the bank this year and she ain't coming off no more'—they meant they would haul their big seines up; and sometimes they would, and sometimes they wouldn't, but that's how it began. Then you'd look around and say, hey, Parks's crew isn't out there fishing any more. Once there were twelve crews on Broomes Island, and by the mid-60s they were down to around three. Then the old boats would die. They'd run 'em up in a muskrat lead and that would be the end of them. In the early 1970s the DNR (Department of Natural Resources) ran a derelict boat program where they paid for barges and cranes to clean out the marshes of old boats. They sure got their share off Broomes Island. It surprised some people how many, I think. You noticed all these things, but it comes so slow, I guess its like sitting in a room and the oxygen being consumed . . . you don't notice until most of it's gone. That's how a river dies."

At its other end, the Patuxent's watershed had begun to boom with development during the late 1950s and early 1960s. It is a long river for Maryland, 110 miles, the only major bay tributary lying entirely within the state's borders. It rises on some ridges of the Piedmont Plateau and wanders, more stream than river, through Montgomery, Howard, Anne Arundel, and Prince Georges counties—the heart of the Baltimore-Washington corridor. Around Benedict it broadens and mixes with the bay to create the rich seafood river known to the three

Southern Maryland counties of Charles, Calvert, and St. Mary's. Broomes Island, at river mile 100, seemed a world apart from the heralded New Americas that were being bulldozed upstream out of farmland and forest at places like Columbia and Crofton. New urban and suburban development would soon consume a greater percentage of land in the Patuxent basin than in any other river system of the Chesapeake's sprawling drainage, from New York State to West Virginia. Every new person settling in the Patuxent watershed meant approximately another 100 gallons of sewage a day to be treated—36,500 gallons per year per person, and people were moving in by the tens of thousands. It would all be flushed away from upstream by the dutiful old Patuxent. By the late 1960s the downstream communities on the river were beginning to realize that, like it or not, they were more connected to what was happening upstream than they had dreamed.

In 1970, Bernie ran for county commissioner and was elected on a platform of better schools and preserving the heritage of the lower Patuxent River. That was the year the grass beds, a vital link in the aquatic ecosystem, began to disappear from the bottoms of the coves, victims of dirty water, although it would be another decade before cause and effect began to be linked scientifically. Campaigning, Bernie mentioned often how he could wade out after crabs shoulder-deep, years before, and still see his feet on the river bottom. Sometimes now, he could not see his hand even a foot beneath the surface.

In Maryland and the rest of the nation, those days were the dawning of a new era of optimism about the environment, even as the country admitted it had used many of its waterways unconscionably as receptacles for wastes. Americans would not ignore the challenge. Congress had authorized $40 billion, the largest public-works project in history, to bring every sewage-treatment plant to new heights of technological improvement. Maryland, its Baltimore-Washington corridor by then in the midst of one of the most frantic development booms the country had ever seen, was determined it would have both growth and a clean environment. It rapidly became a national leader in passing laws to protect wetlands, control siltation of rivers, and build modern sewage plants.

After a sweeping reorganization of all its outdated environmental agencies into a modern Department of Natural Resources, the state appointed as secretary its first environmental professional, a Harvard-trained sanitary engineer named James B. Coulter. He was hailed in the press as bringing a new era of expertise to the environmental battles that were ahead. Bernie, as almost everyone who knew Coulter, found him to be an intelligent man of the highest integrity, and a thoroughly pleasant individual. He also had an engineer's implicit trust that technology could handle whatever pollution problems development threw at it; and he was not much impressed that the Patuxent River truly was in decline. So much of the evidence was, he would complain, "anecdotal." The bay system, meanwhile, was well-documented as having gone through huge natural cycles of abundance and scarcity in its living resources long before pollution was much of a factor. Coulter was unconvinced that anything especially different than that was happening on the Patuxent.

"Meanwhile we were losing our way of life," Bernie says. He recalls a meeting of the downstream counties in 1973, after he had tried unsuccessfully to get help from Governor Marvin Mandel and Attorney General Francis B. Burch. An old-time politician from St. Mary's County, Senator Paul Bailey told Bernie: "If you want their attention, you're going to have to sue the bastards." Bernie and his colleagues were not environmental activists by nature. They believed deeply in good-faith negotiation and the power of government to peacefully resolve issues. For four more years they plugged away in hopes of getting action to save their river. By 1976, there were less than a dozen oystermen left on Broomes Island, and only Dixie Buck and a few other softcrabbers. Just upriver at Benedict, and even at Solomons down at the river's mouth, similar declines had occurred. Nearly half of all the fresh water flowing past Broomes Island in the summertime now had passed through an upstream sewage-treatment plant first.

Events of the several months that followed would prove among the most seminal in the environmental history of the Chesapeake Bay. The state of Maryland and the U.S. Environmental Protection Agency (EPA) endorsed a new water-quality plan that would govern the Patuxent River for the next twenty years. It would allow the river's freshwater flow, in dry summer months, to consist of nearly 80 percent treated sewage from expanded upstream plants by the year 2000. It would also finish off the Patuxent River, in the opinion of a man Bernie had talked to the year before at a PTA meeting in Calvert County. That was Dr. Donald Heinle, one of a group of bright young marine biologists from the University of Maryland's Chesapeake Biological Laboratory, located at the river's mouth. The scientists had become increasingly skeptical about Coulter's assurances that simply cranking up the existing sewage-treatment technology another few notches was all the river needed.

Their skepticism was based on cutting-edge science, they told Bernie. There were no guarantees; but after analyzing decades of old water-quality data, it looked like the lower river for several years had been suffering from an overdose of nitrogen, a constituent of sewage that no existing or planned treatment processes would remove. The nitrogen was causing the explosive growth of microscopic algae in the water; and the algae in turn were clouding the water, cutting off light needed by the aquatic grasses, and consuming the oxygen needed by oysters. The scientists estimated this all had begun to happen around the same time that Dixie Buck began having trouble hunting for soft crabs on the bottom of Nan's Cove. It was a ticklish position for the biologists at Solomons, being a state laboratory in opposition to official state policy, but the scientists would do what they could if push came to shove, Heinle had told Bernie—it would be at the very least ironic, he said, if the state's major Chesapeake Bay laboratory let a whole river die on its doorstep.

It was around that time that Bernie invited Coulter to speak about the Patuxent before a crowd of some 450 people at the Rod and Reel restaurant in Chesapeake Beach. It was the local sportsmen's club's annual wild-game dinner, featuring all the bounty of the Patuxent region—muskrat, deer, possum, coon, ducks, geese, oysters, and soft crabs. Coulter rambled personably about the environment in general for awhile before closing with this: The Patuxent River, he said, was a healthy body of water. Bernie, he knew, liked to tell the story about wading out after crabs up to his shoulders and seeing his toes on the bottom. Well, there was absolutely no scientific documentation to show that estuaries like the Chesapeake Bay hadn't always been cloudy. Bernie had just forgotten that he was only eighteen months old when he chased that crab, and the toes he saw were just six inches below the surface.

Retelling that incident is the closest Bernie ever comes to open anger. "What he said was not an enlightened remark. I knew right then that the man was either ignorant about water quality or didn't give a damn, or both." Shortly afterward, the three counties of Southern Maryland took old Paul Bailey's advice and sued the bastards. Attached to the court proceedings in full support of the counties' suit against Maryland and the EPA was an affadavit signed by several very nervous scientists from the university's lab on the river.

Bernie had successfully urged the suit to the region's elected officials in a short speech he made at Shorter's Wharf restaurant on the river. He did not understand much, he told them, about the technicalities of one kind of sewage treatment versus another, or about the highly complex debates sure to ensue over nitrogen's role in the river's ecology. "Indeed I don't expect judges and juries will care too much about that either," he said, "but I bet you one thing they do understand. They can understand there's slimy river bottoms where there used to be clear water."

By 1979 there were signs the tide might turn for the Patuxent. A federal judge had found the state's water-quality plan for the river faulty in eleven of its fifteen major assumptions. The same year, Coulter's department was stripped of virtually all its authority over water quality, and a new agency was set up in the health department to administer it. In December, Harry Hughes, the new governor, accepted Bernie's invitation to spend a day on the river. He talked to the university scientists and the watermen and he saw the dying oysters. Most of all, he would say years later, he was struck by the resolve of the Southern Marylanders to save their river. That day, twenty-three years after Dixie Buck thought she saw the water getting a little cloudy, the governor officially pronounced the Patuxent River to have an environmental problem. He also said it was worth saving.

In 1981, the state health department organized an extraordinary summit meeting on the Patuxent River. Bureaucrats, environmentalists, local, state, and federal politicians, developers, and representatives of any other interests with a stake in the river, all were sequestered at a retreat center until they could agree on a strategy to save the river. Three days later, they emerged with an unprecedented decision. The state would commit itself to restoring the Patuxent River to water-quality levels that existed in 1950.

Doing that would not be easy or quick, even the most optimistic participant in the meeting knew. Long and complex negotiations lay ahead with seven counties, and intricate pollution control problems had to be thrashed out. It was becoming apparent that the pollutants destroying the river came not only from the modern upsurge in sewage but also from soil and fertilizers washing off the tobacco fields and cornfields that were a tradition in the Patuxent region. To have any chance of keeping the cleanup program moving on target, to weld public support, a clear and simple goal was needed, one that anyone could understand. This is what the conference came up with: The job, they said, would be done on the summer day when Bernie Fowler could walk out on the river, up to his shoulders, and look down through the clear water and see his toes.

Epilogue

On a hot summer day, forty years after Bernie chased those crabs across the Patuxent flats, thirty years after Dixie Buck saw the water turning cloudy, I have to skirt a parade and walk nearly a mile after parking my car to get close to the river. The little town of Solomons, at its mouth, is hosting the annual Patuxent River Appreciation Day; and the festival, begun only a few years ago, seems to draw more crowds each time. The old river is moving in some pretty good company these days. Bernie is on the state senate's most powerful committee, a plum of an appointment for a first-term legislator. Governor Hughes, who scarcely knew one bay river from another until a few years ago, now seems likely to be most remembered for his attention to water quality during his two terms. There are more Patuxent River commissions, committees, ad hoc task forces, and such meeting around the state these days than you can keep track of. The health department has targeted $16 million for the first attempt to remove nitrogen from sewage in Maryland at a big treatment plant upriver from here.

The year 1984 was declared by the governor and legislature the Year of the Bay. Instrumental in that turn of events was a U.S. senator, Charles McC. Mathias, who had been scouting for ideas to help the bay several years before, when Bernie made his passionate speech at Shorter's Wharf about the Patuxent's dying. Find out what's causing the sickness down here, because it's spreading, the Southern Marylanders told him. The senator played a key role in organizing and financing the massive, six-year federal study of the bay that concluded in 1983. It lent critical official recognition, for the first time, to the fact that the Patuxent's problems were the problems of the whole bay. The Patuxent began to be mentioned more and more as a "microcosm" of what faced the bay. If the river could be turned around, then there was hope for the Chesapeake. If the river were lost, then what reason was there to think the whole bay would not ultimately follow? The state embarked on a program to spend approximately $100 million a year for an indefinite number of years to avert the latter scenario.

There are never tidy endings to dealing with the environments of big, complex systems like rivers. At the festival here, environmental groups are handing out leaflets announcing legal action they are bringing against the state health department. Upstream counties are continuing to grow, and some of the biggest sewage plants on the river still are not required to remove their polluting nitrogen, the groups charge. The Baltimore-Washington region, meanwhile, is expanding south with a vengeance. Charles County, one of the three Southern Maryland jurisdictions that battled to save the river, now has the fastest growth rate in Maryland. A new bridge over the river here at Solomons has ended the historic isolation from development of both lower Calvert and St. Mary's counties; and all through the lower river's drainage basin, "For Sale" signs are sprouting, forests are being bulldozed, and farms are being subdivided. Solomons is being talked about as the state's next Annapolis. Sometimes, a state water-quality official tells me at the festival, he is no longer sure for whom "we are busting our ass to preserve this fabled rural way of existence on the Patuxent."

Tom Wisner, the bay poet, singer, and storyteller who lives near the Patuxent, has boycotted the appreciation day festival. He thinks saving the river is going to take something a good deal more profound than the have-our-cake-and-eat-it-too philosophy, which combines improved pollution controls with continued growth and development. That is just continuing what Tom says is the "user myth" that has dominated Western civilization for centuries—the bay, and nature, are meant primarily to be used by humanity. He has been thinking the antidote is not going to be wholly found in nitrogen-removal contraptions bolted onto sewage plants, or in less polluting farming practices. No, the place needs a new myth, a counterlegend to the prevailing-use ethic, he says; he thinks the Patuxent region may have spawned a dandy.

The story of Bernie seeing his toes through the water is being told and retold around the watershed to the point it is becoming part of the region's oral tradition, with potential to influence events far beyond the Patuxent, Tom says. It is the raw stuff of which folk legend may evolve. Tom says he intends to make the story of Bernie a part of his performances, to share with others across the bay country. Next summer he is going to invite Bernie and everyone else who cares about the river to wade out in the river and look for their feet. It will become an annual Bernie Fowler Day, open to anyone, anywhere along the Patuxent's 110 miles—no admission, no parades, no balloons, no commercialized festivals to accompany it. To kick off the new legend, Tom has written a poem, "Bernie Fowler Day—A Guide to Wading in the Southern Maryland Waters":

All the politicians gathered.
They'd come from miles around
To talk about the river
That flows by Solomons town.

Seems they had a problem.
Things were looking bad.
They'd looked at all resources
And used everything they had.

The scientists had told them
Everything they knew,
Still—the folks were puzzled
And they didn't know what to do.

It came 'round to Bernie Fowler
And he stood among the best.
He said, "folks, if you'll bear with me.
I think I got a test."

"I think I have a measure
That can't be beat
You just wade out in the river
And look down to see your feet."

If you can't see your cloppers
There'll be trouble in this town
We oughta sue those upper counties
For the junk they're sending down."

It's Bernie's measure!
It's simple—yet profound.
We got a treasure!
You can't buy it by the pound.

It's Bernie's measure,
And it ain't hard to do.
It's a pleasure!
And it will soothe you too.

You just wade out in the river,
Give it all you got . . .
Right up to your chest.
And then you pick your spot.

Next you take your peepers
And cast them slowly down
On the day we see our feet again
There'll be celebration in this town.

Well—we should do this yearly
On Bernie Fowler Day.
Dress up fit to kill
And wade out all the way.

And somewhere in the future,
That day is coming sure,
We'll look and see our feet again;
Could we ask for more?

'Cause I ask you what's the profit
If we gain these worldly things
And foul the air and water
And all the life that brings?

Creek Music

Baltimore, Winter

*T*he stream, *known* as Herring Run, has been the recipient of extraordinary attention in recent years. One of the three major watersheds of Baltimore City, its drainage basin holds 61,253 urban households with an estimated disposable annual income of $521 million. By an act of the Maryland legislature, Herring Run became one of the nation's first metropolitan stream valleys where state, local, and regional resources were targeted to improve every aspect of the environment, from sewage overflows to preservation of open space. Hundreds of citizens have lavished thousands of volunteer hours in the cause along its 11.69-mile course through Baltimore's northeast quadrant. The stream's new sightliness is striking and has been extolled in a slick color brochure published by the Mayor's Advisory Committee on Herring Run. A symbolic stocking of trout, complete with a famous fly fisherman who demonstrated his prowess casting for them, capped the success.

But this is also a stream that is diseased in its very bones, sick beyond the ministrations of litter patrols, and beyond even the whole range of water-quality improvements as they are normally understood. Herring Run is a watercourse wrenched horribly out of synchrony with the drainage basin that spawns it, victim of an unnatural pulse that yaws between delirium and coma. The mechanics of its wild, fatal disequilibrium are evident during a few days of visits to the stream where it passes Morgan State University at Cold Spring Lane. A gentle rain had fallen, but it was more than enough to infuriate the stream's channel. The rain had fallen too much onto straight, smooth surfaces—impervious rooftops, parking lots, sidewalks, driveways. These shot the raindrops, moving in solid sheets now, into gutters and storm drains, more straight lines, narrowing, focusing the diffuse energy of acres of rainfall like sunlight through a lens, to a sudden, sharp peak of destructive velocity.

And now, only hours later, the stream lies gaunt and spent, the ribs of metamorphic rock in its scoured bed poking through scant remaining pools and trickles. Too much rain has left the watershed too fast for much of it to soak into the ground, to seep back out into the stream bed through its banks and bottom over hours, days, weeks, recharging what the hydrologists call its *base flow*. That is a principal reason why the stocked trout lasted only a few weeks. The impoverished base flow, coupled with the eroded, wider, shallower channel so characteristic of the urban stream, could never have maintained cool enough water temperatures for their survival.

One need not wonder what Herring Run might have been like when its pulse was steadier, its heartbeat more regular. A model exists in the Green Spring Valley of Baltimore County, just north of the Beltway. Dipping Pond Run, a rushing, rock-girt stream, has miraculously retained its watershed almost wholly in forest, with a ground cover of dense vines and deep leaf duff. The rain falls about equally each year on the watersheds of Dipping Pond Run and Herring Run—about one million gallons per acre. A lot of that, as much as 40 percent, is intercepted by the forest canopy of the former stream before it ever strikes earth. The rest filters slowly through the dense ground cover, evaporating to the air or seeping into the ground. More than a quarter of all Herring Run's rainfall spurts immediately into the stream channel. About .25 percent of the same rain enters Dipping Pond Run as surface runoff. Its base flow, as a consequence, is very close to its peak flow during all but major rain events. It is a superbly stable situation, the polar opposite of Herring Run's wild gyrations. It translates, ultimately, into trout. Conversely, this is why trout in a stream represent so much more than just an effete form of perch. Above all fish, they signify a watershed in harmony with nature.

All this is explained in a matter-of-fact monotone by Richard Klein as he bends over his work in the middle of Dipping Pond Run. He is rooting deep in its gravel bed with a device called a Surber Sampler, which gives a measure of aquatic life on a stream's bottom which is accurate enough to have been used in criminal court cases involving water pollution. Klein is a low-level state natural-resources employee who has been told he will never advance far without a college degree. That says more about bureaucracies than about Klein, who is one of the most skilled interpreters and effective protectors of small streams the state has ever seen. He has been known to jump out of bed and dart from the house with a rack of water-sampling bottles during a midnight thunderstorm, because that is the ideal time to gather evidence that sediment from a local development site is washing illegally into a stream, choking aquatic life there.

Sediment washes from a watershed like Dipping Pond Run at about twenty-four tons an acre each year, he says. Where the topsoil has been scalped for a new townhouse development, the rate can be as high as forty-eight thousand tons a year, and it can take a stream decades to recover fully from it. Additionally, the pollutants washed in the first minutes of a rainstorm off urban pavements—from dog and cat feces to toxic metals deposited by auto exhausts—can be more foul than untreated discharges from a sewage plant. From his dripping Surber Sampler Klein is plucking fat stone fly nymphs, mayflies, caddis flies—all excellent trout food, and all indicative of an undisturbed watershed. The aquatic insects that most people never see, which spend their lives on the underside of rocks and buried deep in the sediments, can tell volumes about the health of streams if you learn how to read them, he says. The runoff characteristics of streams like Dipping Pond Run have remained stable during most of the time since the retreat of the last ice age, about ten thousand years ago. Organisms like these— he holds up a stone fly—have become acclimatized to very little fluctuation in sediment, oxygen level, stream velocities, and pollutants over all that time. When the forest cover is felled and development occurs, they cannot handle the drastic variations that result. There is nothing in one hundred centuries of their experience to prepare them for conditions such as those that exist in Herring Run now.

Klein has done some Surber Sampling on a dozen small streams around Baltimore County, reading the story of what has happened in their watersheds as if it were tea-leaves in the bottom of a cup. From his samples of aquatic insects, he compiled for each stream what biologists call a Species Diversity Index. Generally, the more diverse the species it hosts, the healthier is a body of water. If the array of life in a Dipping Pond Run could be translated to notes on a musical score, the stream would play a symphony. Conversely, Klein found the diversity, and ultimately the quantity, of aquatic life declined in a given stream almost in direct proportion to how much of its watershed was paved over. At about the level of watershed imperviousness associated with half-acre residential lots, he found, you are talking about a stream that is dying, the range of life there restricted to something approximating a drear monotone, and finally no song at all.

His own home stream was destroyed that way, he told me. Its name these days calls to most peoples' minds only the galaxy's largest shopping mall; but growing up around Parkville during the 1950s and 1960s, White Marsh Run was still a pretty, lively little stream as it wandered north and east to join the Gunpowder River. By the early 1970s it had no aquatic life at all. The mall, I am told, has a superb diversity of stores, including more than a dozen that just sell shoes. Klein, typically, describes the demise of his boyhood stream unemotionally; but his devotion to the cause of small streams since then can only be described as passionate. He has, almost single-handedly, built a successful statewide organization called Save Our Streams (SOS). It is predicated on the fact that, although most people may be put off by the technical aspects of water quality, virtually no one in Maryland lives more than a half-mile from a stream; and after a session with Klein, many seem inclined to join the "adopt a stream" program that is the core of SOS. The capstone to the stream-saving efforts of Klein and other environmentalists was a state law that aims, for the first time, to manage new development so that the runoff to streams afterward is identical to what it was before the land was disturbed. It holds promise for avoiding more White Marsh Runs and Herring Runs in the future, and many think it was the most far-reaching water-quality law to pass the legislature in a decade.

Meanwhile, Klein and SOS are moving onto more ambitious projects. They are trying to prove to residents along an urban watershed not far from Herring Run that they can someday have trout—if not on a par with Dipping Pond Run, then at least close enough to merit the effort. There is a detailed plan for installing infiltration pits, rooftop dams, rain barrels, and a host of other low-cost, innovative devices to slow the runoff of rain to something near natural levels, to give the soil time to soak it up, stopping destructive storm surges and building base flows. With luck, Klein thinks, in a few years the place could have some of its best fishing since Baltimore was settled. It could become a model for other areas of the state. If it does, if the waterways all across Maryland ever achieve parity with growth and development, it will be in large part because the same forces that produce large shopping malls also occasionally spin off a Richard Klein.

Potomac: The Nation's Sewage Plant

Potomac River, September

In the way a space buff would thrill to strap into the command capsule of a moon rocket, and a horse-racing fan dreams of saddling the Derby winner for a gallop, I like to use the throne room here at the Blue Plains Regional Wastewater Treatment Plant. I like to hear the toilets flush, reverberating through the capacious tile and porcelain and chrome chambers with all the authority one would expect of the sewage plant that serves the capital of a world power and safeguards the health of the nation's river into which it discharges. No other sewage plant on earth combines the size and sophistication of Blue Plains. This is the Apollo Mission of water-pollution control, our thoroughbred champion in the high-stakes race to reclaim our rivers.

Now, if there are two things we nature lovers generally revile as the answers to environmental concerns, they are bigness and technological fixes. Both tend to ignore natural limits to growth and are all too capable of creating problems as bad as the ones they solve. Both reach perhaps their ultimate synthesis in Blue Plains on the Potomac. If there is anyplace where society's pursuit of progress at the peril of natural systems should be bumping up hard against the limits of big high-tech to prevent disaster, it ought to be here at Blue Plains.

It ought to be, but you won't find evidence of it in the definitive report on the state of the Chesapeake Bay and its tributaries that was issued by the EPA after six years of studying the region's most pressing water-quality problems. Almost lost in the EPA's overall message of system-wide decline was this: "parts of the Potomac River . . . currently exhibit improving water quality." So dramatically had some types of aquatic life rebounded that professional bass guides had begun working out of marinas within the District of Columbia. The Potomac's condition was a clear testament to better sewage treatment undertaken after pollution turned the national river into a national embarrassment by the late 1960s. With marvelous understatement, the EPA report of 1983 concluded: "This policy, costing about a billion dollars, seems to have worked."

At the heart of the policy, having absorbed the lion's share of the billion in federal and state tax dollars, stands Blue Plains, the final defense interposed between the wastes from two million people and the Potomac, a Maginot line that works, that seems to say, for enough money, we *can* have our cake (rapid development) and eat it too (enjoy healthy rivers). There is a flaw in such comfortable assumptions, but environmentalists who hope to expose it by waiting for Blue Plains to reach its limits do not understand the nature and history of how our society controls its pollution. Blue Plains collects sewage from an area as large as the drainage basins of many bay rivers. Wastes that enter its arteries on a Tuesday evening out around Leesburg, Virginia, or in Damascus, almost in Frederick County, may not receive final processing at the main plant until the weekend. Sewage moves through Blue Plains at the rate of a third of a billion gallons a day, a capacity that virtually equals all the other sewage plants in Maryland combined. Of the nearly thirteen million people who live in the five-state watershed of the Chesapeake Bay, an area sprawling nearly from Vermont to North Carolina, around 15 percent are hooked to a single sewage-treatment works, Blue Plains.

The plant's beginnings—construction was completed in 1938 on a parcel of land originally called Blew Playne—did not bespeak the current, high level of faith in technology to overcome any sewage problem that might arise. Its location, on the Potomac's east shore below Bolling Air Force Base and not far above the Woodrow Wilson Bridge, was chosen on the simple premise that it could cast its effluent downstream beyond the ability of the tides to bring it back into sniffing distance of the District. Those early years were relatively quiet ones for Blue Plains, which only removed about 40 percent of the gross pollutants in the sewage then. "It looked like a college campus . . . beautifully landscaped," an old-time plant engineer recalled recently.

Now the plant, approaching its fiftieth anniversary, has become a small city, with its own quarterly news magazine. Scarcely a corner of the 154-acre site remains which is not devoted wholeheartedly to concrete and steel, working furiously to process the unrelenting river hurtling down upon Blue Plains from its 725-square-mile catchment area. Rail spurs shuttle in the chemicals that Blue Plains gulps by the 55-ton tanker-car load in purifying its sewage, and a continuous stream of trucks flows in and out of the grounds to carry off the four million pounds of solid residues, or sludge, extracted every day from the waste water. The sizeable technocracy required to maintain the quality of the effluent that enters the Potomac is housed in a soaring, pyramid-like headquarters building, elegantly sheathed in bronze-gold reflecting glass. This last, along with the plant's near-billion-dollar price tag, have earned Blue Plains the sobriquet the "Craphouse Taj Mahal" in national sewer circles.

Blue Plains' state-of-the-art manipulation of sewage begins straightforwardly enough, where twin pipes, large enough to drive through in an eighteen-wheeler, feed the plant through a set of *bar screens*, mammoth grates of steel with inch-square openings. These pluck the grossest matter—tennis shoes, beer cans, condoms, small trees—from the raw sewage, which does not look so gross as you might imagine, because even at this point it is around 97 percent water, 3 percent solids. Visitors to sewage plants always have to make their quota of bad jokes and tasteless questions. I ask Ray Brown, a veteran of twenty-five years in the "primary treatment" section of Blue Plains, do they ever get dead or dismembered bodies off the bar screens? Oh, he says, he recalls a limb or two, probably amputated at hospitals; then, almost as an afterthought, "of course we used to get them . . . ah, them feces . . . " What does he mean, "feces"? What else would a sewage treatment plant get? "No, I mean . . . you know," he gropes for another word . . . "they mostly stopped after the Supreme Court"— he points vaguely uptown across the river—"after they made that abortion ruling. When we would used to get the little things on the bar screens we'd call the cops, give 'em a little burial."

Past the bar screens, the sewage races turbulently through deep, concrete header channels, where grit, sand, and gravel settles out. At this point, the color of the water is a dense, slatey, gray-green. At no point through the plant does it smell all that foul. Emerging into the sunlight, the sewage lingers in a series of placid, circular ponds, one hundred feet in diameter, where further settling of solid matter occurs. Great flocks of seagulls ride the arms of mechanical grease skimmers which revolve around the surface of each pond; frequently, a bird will hover and pluck something gray and rubbery-looking from the water. A cool autumn breeze whisks away odors, and a warm sun spangles the Potomac in the background and glances off the headquarters pyramid, set in golden splendor against a sky of bright, blue enamel. The ponds and seagulls are the final stages in the physical cleansing processes known as primary sewage treatment, which Blue Plains was doing by 1938, and which was as far as the big Patapsco treatment plant on Baltimore's harbor had advanced by 1983.

Next, biology and chemistry are unleashed on the sewage, by this point slightly more translucent than it looked in primary. Giant aerating pumps bring it to a rolling boil in dozens of long, narrow channels that cover several acres. This is where microbes that feed on oxygen and waste attack the subtler stuff, like coffee and other dissolved solids that remain after primary treatment. It sounds simpler than it is. Much care and thought are devoted here to the proper care and feeding of "the bugs," as the microbes are called. Keep them hungry, but don't starve them, and watch so that heavy rainstorm flows entering the plant don't wash them away.

Don't fall into the secondary treatment ponds, workers warn you. If you did, I joke, you'd smell for a week, huh? No, you'd be dead, they say. The sewage at this point is blown so full of air that, although it looks like water, it has the consistency of whipped cream. Even a champion swimmer would go to the bottom of those deep, murky channels like a stone. Next, the "bugs" having had their go at the sewage, it is treated by adding chemicals, ferric chloride and pickle liquor, to flocculate, or precipitate out, whatever escaped the gnawing bugs. Ferric gives you better "flocc," but pickle liquor, a by-product of steelmaking, is cheaper, a technician says. Blue Plains' use of pickle liquor represents a happy partnership between the treatment plant and Bethlehem Steel's giant Sparrows Point works. Blue Plains, whose growing needs at one point were straining Dupont's entire U.S. production capability for flocculating agents, was tickled to take it off Bethlehem's hands, and out of the steel company's polluted discharges to Baltimore's outer harbor.

To all this treatment, Blue Plains also adds chlorine, a disinfectant, in quantities that demand a rail car of the chemical every week. At this point, the sewage has been detoxified to a degree equaling, and usually exceeding, almost any large treatment plant in the world; but Blue Plains is only getting cranked up. Next the waste water flows into a section of the plant where it undergoes *nitrification*. Nitrification does not actually remove waste; rather it converts elements of it to more stable chemical forms, so that they will remain essentially inert and harmless to water quality after entering the Potomac. It is a term I have heard environmental officials toss around fairly glibly at meetings called to express concerns about putting more sewage into various rivers of the bay. Don't worry, they say, if it should turn out that the river can't take the additional pollution, they have left space to expand, they will just install nitrification. You should see what "just adding nitrification" means.

At Blue Plains the sewage to be nitrified is led through a dozen concrete ponds, each nearly the length of a football field, each divided into fifty-nine separate stages for treatment. To provide sufficient aeration so that special, nitrifying bacteria may do their work, the plant is underlain by tunnels containing miles of piping, eight feet in diameter. They carry oxygen pushed by five blowers of 4,000 horsepower each. It takes $500 of electricity to flick one on and off. To control precisely the oxygen, pH (acidity), and numerous other factors so that proper nitrification occurs, Blue Plains maintains a water-quality laboratory on a concrete island amid the acres of treatment ponds which would be the envy of many a state environmental health department. Nitrification takes up about half the space of all the treatment that has preceded it, and it costs more to operate than both primary and secondary.

After hours amid the churning of sewage and the howling of blower pumps, it is a relief to enter the cool serenity of the MultiMedia Filtration building, where sewage gets a final filip and polish before it meets the river. The waste water entering here looks clear as tap water, even before it is forced through the massive filters of two-foot-thick crushed anthracite, a foot of fine sand, and a layer of almanite. After each batch of waste water has been filtered, the filters are backwashed, and clouds of the purest black mud erupt from their every square inch. They remove nearly eight tons of additional solids here each day. Plant officials, I was told, occasionally drink the final product, although my guide said he wouldn't, possibly because he works back in primary. The discharge of water from Blue Plains adds about 4 percent to the Potomac's average flow at this point although, in the very driest of times, Blue Plains may amount to half of all the fresh water coming down from the river's 9-million-acre drainage basin. EPA officials sometimes get heated calls about the quality of the plant's discharge from congressmen flying into National Airport, just upstream and across the river. They call to report what looks like an oil slick emerging from the plant. There is nothing that can be done, they are informed. The old Potomac's waters will always form a turbid contrast to the glassy clear stuff coming out of Blue Plains.

Through the gray-tinted glass of the filtration building, which is constructed just like an airport control tower, except quieter and roomier, you have a fine view back over the whole of Blue Plains, and you begin to appreciate what the water-quality engineers mean when they explain their "linear approach" to problem solving. They proceed stepwise, solving the major or most pressing problem, then turning their attention to the problems that may arise from the solution, and so on. One problem at a time, the engineers like to say. And you realize—looking back over the bar screens, grit chambers, grease-skimmers, "bug" tanks, "flocc" tanks, nitrification, filtration—that for all its sophistication, Blue Plains arose from no grand design or vision, but from decades of adding-on, usually in response to crisis in the river. It is a testament to linear problem solving; and if it seems there is never a problem that Blue Plains cannot solve, then there also seems never to be a time without a problem in need of solution. The chlorination process, for example, has raised concerns about the effects on spring spawning runs of fish from the chlorine that does not get used up in disinfection; so Blue Plains is adding another chemical process to dechlorinate its discharge; and to take care of possibly undesirable by-products of dechlorination, the engineers may tack on yet another chemical addition of sulfur dioxide. Then there is the space reserved at the plant for denitrification, which in a nutshell is what you do if it turns out that even nitrification is not enough to maintain river quality. Some people are not even sure denitrification can be done, but it is generally agreed it would cost $600 million to try it. Ironically, nitrogen is not even a problem in the Potomac River around Blue Plains; but there is mounting evidence that it acts as a major pollutant when it reaches the different chemistry of the water in the open bay at the river's mouth.

If there is a single accomplishment of which the engineers at Blue Plains are justifiably proud, it is the big plant's supreme efficiency at removing phosphorus, the "candy" in sewage on which noxious algae that can choke the river's other life depend for growth. Blue Plains removes phosphorus at an efficiency that often approaches fifty times that of conventional modern plants. Thus, in the summer of 1983, the engineers were shocked when a massive algae bloom, reminiscent of the 1960s, covered portions of the river. After two years of study, scientists hypothesized that somehow Blue Plains may have altered the pH of the river enough to liberate extra phosphorus that had been locked up in the sediments of the Potomac's bottom. The likely solution will be to add another step in the treatment process to increase the alkalinity of the waste water.

Soon, Blue Plains is going to embark on a mammoth expansion, adding capacity to send another sixty-four million gallons daily into the Potomac. Can you really do that and maintain the quality of the treated sewage that goes to the river? I asked the engineers. No, they said, they plan to improve on it. If the money—a contemplated third of a billion dollars or so—is there, the technology will not be found wanting in the foreseeable future. Pass the cake and praise the linear approach to pollution problem solving. But before anyone praises it too much, they should look at what else is implied by an extra sixty-four million gallons of sewage besides a given quantity of waste water, and its impact on a certain point in a river. For starters, the added capacity for Blue Plains means that we will be able to accommodate development to house an additional half-million or so people, mostly in the Maryland suburbs of its service area. That amounts to adding about 10 percent to the state's population, which in turn translates to a number of impacts, which spread across the whole watershed like ripples from a stone thrown into the water.

Adding 10 percent to the population, assuming current trends in our demands on the region's resources, should add about 13,000 boats to traffic on the bay each summer weekend, about 30,000 people to the peak crowds that throng Ocean City's beach, an extra 300,000 automobiles to state highways, traveling an extra two billion miles annually; also an extra 90,000 fishermen competing for catches on the bay in an extra 218,000 fishing trips, and an extra 155,000 new dwelling units. The ripples will not stop there, of course. The extra housing should boost the state's usurpation of forest and farmland for development by about three-quarters of a square mile annually for several years; and because more people will want more air-conditioning, the likelihood of having to plunk another massive power plant somewhere around the bay's edge, where it can draw cooling water, will increase dramatically—likewise for the pressure to build a third bay bridge from rural Southern Maryland to the Eastern Shore, and to embark on another round of highway building.

I thought, driving home from Blue Plains, how the rapid growth of the Washington region has already begun to affect my friend Jimmy Hancock, who has lived all his life about twenty-five miles downstream from the plant, on a lovely little capillary of the Potomac system called Mattawoman Creek. On a canoe trip, Jimmy showed me his childhood swimming hole, where the current had scooped out a place near the bank—his father swam there before him; and he took me to the sand-bottomed slough where he brought his wife when they were younger to catch snapping turtles sunning in the clear shallows. We pushed through a dense cluster of giant water lilies, found nowhere else in Maryland. He used to lie on the gravelly creek bottom and breathe through their huge, hollow stalks. He showed me wood duck chicks and wild swamp roses in recesses of the creek, and told me about the ephemeral lilac scent of one special flower that bloomed only one week each year in one tiny pocket of the marsh, "and withers in five minutes if you dare to pick it." He used to spin tales for his young son of a magical community down on the creek, presided over by Old Judge Owl and by Old King Possum, who went about dressed in spats and a silk hat and was always fighting it out for control with Old King Coon. All day long on the creek, we did not see a soul.

Jimmy, a cobbler in LaPlata in Charles County, had gotten so fed up with local efforts to develop the land around the creek that he earned a law degree by correspondence to fight for preserving the Mattawoman. He won, too. The state is acquiring much of the land for a Natural Environment Area; so I was a little shocked to hear him say, recently, that the place had changed so that he didn't go down there nearly so much anymore. It wasn't land development or water quality, per se, he explained. It was all the big powerboats that had begun to throng the creek since they had begun building new marinas up the Potomac for all the people moving into the Washington area. They churned up the shallow bottom, muddied the clear waters, were killing off the aquatic grasses . . . the place just didn't seem to belong anymore to quiet canoers and sniffers of delicate marsh flowers.

I imagine the engineers up at Blue Plains will feel some sense of accomplishment, being able to accommodate even more human waste, while maintaining, maybe even improving, water quality in places like the Mattawoman. But there is a lot more to it than meeting the list of legal requirements on pollutant discharges in the federal permits for a sewage plant. It is a lesson that we are still learning, that there is a vast difference between keeping Maryland pollution-free and keeping it lovely and unique; between keeping it environmentally legal and keeping it eminently livable. Such considerations become more critical as Maryland and its neighbor states continue on a path that will, in the next few to several decades, see twice as many people living on the land in the bay's watershed, twice as many people desiring to enjoy its waters and its shorelines, its natural areas and its aquatic resources.

The linear approach of the sanitary engineer—add on a solution wherever you spot a problem—is the way we still approach a wide range of environmental problems. But you cannot bolt on equipment to redress the loss of a paved-over forest, or add another chemical process to take the powerboats off Mattawoman Creek, or make bay watermen competitive for fish and for dock space with hundreds of thousands of well-heeled sport fishermen and sailboaters. Because the sewer puts such a sharp focus, quantifiable almost to the quart and the pound, on the pollution we all inevitably generate, there is a powerful tendency to use it as the gauge of our success or failure in protecting our environment. Some see it, hopefully, as the bottleneck whose limits ultimately will undercut our abiding faith in big, high-tech solutions to the impacts of continued growth and development. Others look at the marvels already wrought by the engineers at Blue Plains and say it is proof that such faith is justified. Both sides need to realize we may well be seeing clean water in the Potomac long after the ripple effects of an expanding and well-sewered population have degraded natural systems and supplanted traditional cultures the length and breadth of the state.

There is preliminary evidence that such a realization is dawning. Something is happening along the shores of the Potomac and around the bay that has upset the land-development interests in Maryland as nothing has done in a long time, perhaps in part because it is such a nonlinear approach to safeguarding the environment. The state has passed a law designating a thousand-foot strip around the edges of the bay and its tidal tributaries as a Critical Area. It is complex, and its regulations fill a small book, but the heart of the law says that in all the remaining undeveloped areas of the shorefront, where we do not yet have severe environmental problems, we are going to dramatically restrict human activities, to try and insure that we never do have problems to solve there. It is a very, very controversial piece of legislation, and the next decade will undoubtedly see many attempts to repeal or chip away at the concept. However, many people are convinced it is a concept that must be expanded to the whole state, not just left to protect a thin fringe nearest the water, while progress as usual builds to the bursting point behind it. What we end up doing will make a better gauge of where Maryland is headed than any measurements of treated sewage: Will we admit to limits on having our cake and eating it too? Or will it simply prove too seductive to continue as Blue Plains, to just go with the flow?

Patapsco: The Urban Crab

Baltimore Harbor, July

In the society of the Chesapeake Bay's forty-odd tributary rivers, the Patapsco, Baltimore's harbor, has not been well-connected for a long time. Not for decades has springtime here been enlivened with the ocean-born spawning runs of shad and herring and rockfish which charge other rivers with a crackling energy. Not for close on a century have Patapsco autumns seen the Argentine-bound migrations of fat bobolinks, or reedbirds, which brought trolley cars loaded with gunners to the wild-rice marshes of South Baltimore. Now the event is commemorated only by Reedbird Avenue, the Reedbird Landfill, and the Reedbird incinerator. The Patapsco winters have been bereft of their oystermen since the last bar slumped, years ago, into the soft, muddy abyss of the deepened and widened Craighill ship channel. The clouds of wild waterfowl that once fed here on succulent aquatic grasses are remembered only by the famous Audubon print of feeding canvasbacks whose background, if one looks closely, shows the Baltimore harbor skyline, circa 1840.

Summertime is a happier matter though. One creature, the crab, still faithfully completes the natural circuit, maintains a thread of ecological integrity between the clean slosh of the ocean at the bay's mouth and the uttermost, grimy backwaters of the state's most urban river. H. L. Mencken, reminiscing about the Baltimore of his boyhood in the 1880s, captured the phenomenon. Mencken noted that at that time the city on the Patapsco was nationally reputed to have the finest native cuisine, the prettiest women, and the most gracious living imaginable. Of all these, the skeptical sage of Baltimore wrote,

> the one that came closest to meeting scientific tests was the first.
>
> Baltimore lay very near the immense protein factory of Chesapeake Bay, and out of the bay it ate divinely. I well recall the time when prime hard crabs of the channel species, blue in color, at least eight inches in length along the shell, and with snow-white meat almost as firm as soap, were hawked in Hollins street of summer mornings at ten cents a dozen. The supply seemed to be almost unlimited, even in the polluted waters of the Patapsco river, which stretched up fourteen miles from the bay to engulf the slops of the Baltimore canneries and fertilizer factories.
>
> Any poor man could go down to the banks of the river, armed with no more than a length of stout cord, a home-made net on a pole, and a chunk of cat's meat, and come home in a couple of hours with enough crabs to feed his family for two days.

And a century later, this last scene is still almost exactly as Mencken described it. The crabs endure. The three square miles of original wetlands in the harbor, the vast wild-rice marshes that brought the reedbirds to the Spring Garden flats near the Hanover Street Bridge—all have nearly disappeared beneath the dredge and fill of commerce. Within the city limits fifteen acres of marsh remain, and twelve acres of

that is phragmites, an imported reed of great beauty that grows on
ruined land and has little value for wildlife. The harbor itself has
shrunk by a full five square miles from filling, a loss of 15 percent of its
original water surface. Bethlehem Steel alone has taken more than a
square mile of that by pushing overboard from Sparrows Point its constantly accumulating mountains of slag from steelmaking. The last attempt—in the 1970s—to survey fish spawning in the Patapsco found a
few brave herring still mounting the river nineteen miles from the harbor mouth, and other relict populations of rockfish, shad, and perch
still attempting to carry on their tribes in Bullneck Creek, Marley
Creek, and Cabin Branch. White perch and carp were more numerous
in the survey, but showed evidence of fin rot, tumors, and chlordane in
excess of human health standards.

But forget all that and come with me on a circuit of the harbor by
small boat this hot, steamy, late-summer morning. You will see more
fishermen than most people would dream existed within the limits of
a great eastern city. The bottom of the Patapsco is swarming with
Chesapeake blue crabs, and Baltimoreans are there to greet them with
handlines and trotlines, with chicken necks and fish heads, with dip
nets and ring nets and crab traps and crab pots. From the rotting piers
of Canton to the warehouse docks of Fells Point, the city is crabbing;
from the ramparts of Fort McHenry to the gravelly toe of the Ferry bar
at the foot of Light Street, and on around the Middle Branch, to where
Swann Park squeezes up to the water between the General Chemical
Company and Leadenhall Street under Interstate 95. And onward the
crabbing extends, from Cherry Hill to Brooklyn, out to Fairfield and
past it, to Curtis Bay. They are crabbing, even, from the catwalk of the
Patapsco Sewage Treatment Plant, in the shadow and the hydrocarbon
odor of the Exxon oil terminal.

The center of it all, arguably the world's greatest urban-industrial
crabbing complex, is the Hanover Street Bridge. I can't say for sure
whether it is the best spot for crabs in the city, but the combination of a
small park and a large hospital's grounds make it one of the best places
city dwellers still have access to the river around which more than one
million of them live. And there they have strung lines between stakes,
some extending nearly a quarter-mile into the shallow water. Short,
baited lines are tied to these every few feet, a unique, urban variation
on the bay waterman's trotline. From a distance, in the early light, the
crabbers attending their lines appear heronlike in their fluid, measured
stalking, harking back to a more primeval time and place. Ownership
of the crab lines, which sometimes cover several acres, is communal. It
is first come, first served, and at the height of the season they are pa-
trolled around the clock. It is only an estimate, but on a slow circle of

the harbor from Hanover Street to the Key Bridge, poking into all its nooks and crannies, I would put the number of crabbers on some days as high as from five hundred to six hundred people.

It is a pretty nice thing to be able to just come down here and get some crabs whenever he gets a taste for them, says Charles Johnson, a South Baltimorean who has stashed a few big male crabs in his plastic bucket and is taking his ease on the riprap in front of South Baltimore General Hospital. The water is a good place to come and clear your head, he adds. Perhaps the ancients, I am thinking, sought alchemy in the wrong places. Could any transformation of base substance into treasure equal the blue crab's capacity to translate the fare of the harbor bottom into lump back-fin meat? A good and lucky crabber can get as many as four bushels down here in a day, even more with a small boat, says Antonio Richardson, a Cherry Hill regular around the Hanover Street trotlines. He says he probably eats harbor crab meat one hundred days each year. Crab meat builds you up, he declares.

On any other river, who would argue that it doesn't? But the Patapsco has a curious hydrology that has caused it to retain the great bulk of industrial and municipal pollutants it has received for better than two hundred years. The river's 600-square-mile watershed scarcely provides enough water to float a rowboat on the harbor's bottom. Nearly 95 percent of the harbor's fresh water comes from Pennsylvania, not down the Patapsco. The mighty Susquehanna, flowing with the authority of a drainage basin larger than all of Maryland, dominates the whole Chesapeake to well below Baltimore, shoving most of the Patapsco's fresh water in from its mouth. This can set up in the harbor a unique, three-layered flow of water—in on the top, in on the bottom, outward in the middle layers. The result is a truly remarkable trapping mechanism for most of the nastiness that has ever been discharged there.

Because crabs are essentially bottom dwellers, and scavengers of whatever carrion exists there, Mary Jo Garreis, who is chief of shellfish sanitation for the state health department, has begun to think harbor crabs deserve chemical analysis that goes well beyond Antonio Richardson's taste tests. As the state's top official in charge of seafood safety, Garreis often is asked if she would eat a crab out of Baltimore harbor. "God knows how many I have eaten from there," she laughs. "I grew up in Brooklyn and my father still crabs off the Hanover Street Bridge. I cross it every day on my way to work, and, every time I do, I see a lot of people crabbing there. I know from my family and relatives that it is a major form of recreation and diet in the area."

So far her department's testing has found, as expected, a small complement of cadmium, copper, zinc, chromium, arsenic, and lead in the harbor crabs—more than you would find in crabs from Smith Island, but nothing dangerously out of proportion to seafood from other, cleaner parts of the bay and the nation. A Johns Hopkins toxicologist, Al Wiedow, independently has confirmed that the crab has what he describes as "one hell of a detox system." Wiedow captured Chesapeake Bay crabs and placed them in cages on the bottom of the Hudson River near New York City in a spot where the sediments contain more toxic cadmium than perhaps any other place in the world, far more, at any rate, than Baltimore harbor. The crabs died, but that is beside the point, Wiedow says. Even these lethally exposed crabs collected only negligible amounts of cadmium in their edible meat. That is the good news. The bad news is that Marylanders also love to eat the crabs' major organ of detoxification, the gooey, yellowish hepatopancreas, or mustard, as it is better known. I favor it myself, spread thickly on saltines.

Perhaps it is expecting too much that we should be able to have free crab meat at our urban doorstep and eat our mustard too. Nonetheless, the crab has stuck by us here on the Patapsco through the best and worst of environments, and I think harbor dwellers cannot go wrong if we continue to stand by this hardy scavenger. The harbor seems just now to be entering an exciting new era. People are rediscovering the charms of the water's edge as they have not done since commerce and transportation still depended on rivers more than roads. The eating and shopping palaces constructed at Harbor Place have begun drawing millions of people a year to the Inner Harbor. The new aquarium nearby has a line constantly waiting to get in. Condominium-marina developments are sprouting around the harbor's edges in places as unlikely as rundown, industrial Canton.

Citizens groups in East and South Baltimore are awakening to the fact that the public waterways mean little without access, and several new public parks, piers, and waterfront promenades are now on the drawing boards of city planners. It is not far-fetched, the planners say, to think of walking for several miles on public rights of way around the whole harbor in a few years. Someday this will link up with a trail all the way up the Patapsco's valley into Carroll County. Under the new interstate highways that cross the harbor near Russell Street, workmen are planting acres of new marsh. It is the first time that wetlands have gained ground within the city in at least three and a half centuries.

It is sad to see the other side of this renewal, the decline of basic industry for which the river has always been known. This year the Bethlehem Steel shipyard on Key Highway was auctioned off. It is already being eyed for high-priced office and residential development. It is a joke now, but only a partial one, that if American steelmaking continues losing out to foreign competition, the giant Sparrows Point works of Bethlehem Steel in Dundalk, where ore freighters now dock, may be more profitable as the world's biggest deepwater marina. A recent dispatch from Boston said there was no room in the harbor there anymore for lobster boats, which were increasingly getting in the way of the new white collar–oriented development.

A true harbor environmental renaissance, whatever form it takes, will not easily be accomplished. The Patapsco is still very much a third-rate natural environment, and the urban pressures on its water quality are unrelenting. The business of port shipping, with its eternal need to dredge and fill, may always take precedence over the bird-watcher and fisherman here. That is why the crab seems such a fitting mascot. Of all the bay's creatures, it makes the most of whatever opportunities it has. It is in its genes. Like most all bay-dwelling species, the crab evolved in the oceans. Estuaries like the Chesapeake Bay are rather transitory on the geologic scale of time. They appear, vanish, and reappear as the glaciers alternately thaw and freeze, causing the oceans, in turn, to flood and ebb in the coastal river valleys like that of the Susquehanna, which at geologic high water forms the Chesapeake. Most of the creatures that flourish in estuaries are those opportunistic enough to invade the new territory as it opens, and retreat to the oceans in between Chesapeake Bays. I have no doubt that the first animal in, and the last one out, of this and all past and future bays has been, and will be, the crab.

One image in particular sticks in my mind. It was a soft, warm June morning, around 4:00 A.M., as I slipped ashore in a tragically polluted backwater of Curtis Bay in a Zodiac raft, covering a crew of protestors from Greenpeace, the international environmental organization. They were sneaking into a local chemical company's plant to protest the brew of toxics it had been releasing into the creek. Every shift in the breeze brought new, acrid odors from the industrial complexes; oily muck oozed a Technicolor skein around the shore. In the glare of a streetlight, two young boys examined something they had just brought up from the water's edge and placed in a box lined with newspaper. "Have 'im for breakfast," I heard one of them say, as we hastened on toward the toxic-waste pits nearby. I peered in the box. Just molted and silken to the touch, it was a beautiful, glistening, soft crab.

Pleasures of the Islands

South Marsh Island, Fall

The water wakes long before the land. A raucous hen mallard, sassing the dawn, sails from behind a point of marsh, trailing gouts of liquid fire wherever first light catches her ripples on the cove's black, silken surface. A flight of quick-winged teal circles to land, pinions flailing a sound of far-off jingle bells from the chill air. Now the cove mirrors seamlessly the frosty gold thawing into day on the eastern horizon. The teal coming down could as well be flying up through the water's depths, like the ducks imbedded in expensive crystal paperweights. A burst of wind ruffles the illusion, and the breeze chuckles softly as the stiff marsh grass scratches its belly; then it is gone and the stillness of the island is pierced by one of the wildest songs on earth.

The geese are aloft, piping their haunting obbligato to the grander, slower cadence of winter's coming. It is music that sets dogs to frenzied yelping along the great migration routes from Labrador to North Carolina, and makes people on the streets of large cities pause, cock an ear, and look skyward, stirred by a longing so old and deep we cannot articulate it much better than the dogs. Just as an old, popular tune on the radio can activate a hundred associations from one's youth, so does goose music evoke places and times out of some ancestral consciousness, when the flights heralded changing seasons to prehistoric hunters on these same shores—signified the glad prospect of roast goose in a season when the land would be otherwise lean. The tune no longer has survival value, but we still find it thrilling.

The same elemental shifts of season and weather which tug geese southward, and goad fish across whole oceans toward their natal streams, also whisper to something in our genes that it is time to be moving. We needn't heed such atavism, of course, but an impending snowstorm still sends us flocking to the supermarket with an almost delicious anticipation, to lay in stores well beyond any strictly rational need; and who could deny, watching the flow of Florida-bound Mercedes and Cadillacs on Interstate 95 each winter, that as soon as we are able to afford our druthers, we resume migrating?

The pleasure of migration is part of why I try faithfully to return each spring and fall to camp on islands like South Marsh in the Chesapeake Bay. The other reason has to do with the special nature of islands. South Marsh Island is five miles from the Somerset County mainland and consists of about three thousand low acres, owned by the state of Maryland, which with rare wisdom leaves it pretty much alone. Norfolk lies to the south, Wilmington to the north, and Baltimore and Washington to the west. Ocean City's teeming beaches on the east complete the circle. Six million people, conservatively, are busy carrying on the business of modern civilization within a hundred-mile radius of us. It is obscenely satisfying, in the midst of the conurbation, to be foraging for supper with our bare hands on this utterly lonesome, permanently unpeopled sweep of marsh. Not more than ten feet from shore, in the olive water off the camp, lies a trove of plump, salty oysters. To collect a bushel is the work of minutes, and the toughest chore is deciding how to eat them. We bicker, and then settle on steamed, raw, fried, and stewed. A short canoe trip to a nearby point of land yields an equal harvest of striated mussels. Gouged fresh from the peaty shore and steamed, they retain a delicate earthy taste that is the very essence of the tide marsh, a sort of estuarine equivalent of a mushroom. Fresh drinking water bubbles up sweet and pure from a rusting pipe sunk eight hundred feet deep here decades ago by a wealthy duck-hunting club. It taps a mammoth aquifer that runs beneath the bay, sloping west to east. Tonight we will wash down our fresh seafood with swigs of rain that fell on Appalachian slopes thousands of years ago, filtered a few inches a century through the geologic strata of half a state. In truth, we have also ferried over a case of beer to ease our transition to the natural life. Still, there is something heady and fulfilling about even so dilletantist a reversion to hunter-gatherer status.

Perhaps because they physically bound one's experiences and insulate the senses from the mainland's distractions, islands concentrate and render more vivid everything that happens on them. South Marsh and its neighbors, for example, might strike you as plain with their monolithic vegetational stands of needlerush and spartina grasses; but the rich light of a late afternoon sun can charge such places with a purity and strength of color to shame Van Gogh's palette, floating golden as Eldorado between blue blazes of autumn sky and water. On hot summer afternoons I have seen them, backlit before an approaching thunderstorm, glowing like neon emeralds. Without its islands, the bay would lose a vital texture.

Island communities are the original alternative societies, says the author John Fowles, and "that is why so many mainlanders envy them. Some vision of Utopian belonging, of social blessedness, of an independence based on cooperation, haunts them all." Even a cursory review of literature would show that, from the *Odyssey* to *Robinson Crusoe*, through *Misty of Chincoteague*, islands have commanded attention all out of proportion to their tiny share of the earth's land mass. In a complicated world, they seem alluringly defined and comprehensible. Special things, we feel, are bound to happen there. It seems no oddity that two of television's biggest recent hits, insipid though they may have been, were "Fantasy Island" and "The Love Boat" (boats, after all, are the ultimate islands). Mythically, islands are places of origins, which does not surprise me in light of my growing kinship with islands in the bay. Sometimes on still, clear evenings, it is possible to lie supine on South Marsh, cerebral cortex pressed into the damp peat and eyes locked on the starry galaxies, and complete a sort of primal circuit. Lulled by the amnion bay's gentle suck and glut in every indentation of the marshy edge, you may come close to reexperiencing the pleasures of the womb.

The Chesapeake Bay is favored with about fifty of the world's estimated one-half million islands. They range from Garrett in the mouth of the Susquehanna at bay's head, to Watts, a deepwater rendezvous for seventeeth-century pirates in Virginia. Uses of the islands include preserves for ducks, like South Marsh; preserves for the wealthy, like Gibson Island on the Magothy; isolation chambers, like heavily diked Hart-Miller, for the shiploads of polluted spoil that must be dredged constantly from Baltimore harbor's channels; and military bombing ranges, like cratered Bloodsworth Island in Dorchester County. It is from other islands—Smith, Deal, Tilghman, Kent, Hoopers, Tangier—that the watermen who harvest most of our seafood still choose to operate.

On the islands, elements of our human and natural heritage have been able to flourish well past the time they could still exist, unsullied, on the mainland. Water, even in the jet age, remains a surprisingly efficient barrier. If you doubt that, compare the cultures of Crisfield, where they say *aryster,* and St. Mary's County, where they say *oistuh;* or the Eastern Shore fishing community of Rock Hall with Baltimore City. Neither pair is separated by much more than a dozen miles, but they are water miles, and the insulation they provide is blessedly effective. This essential characteristic of islands enforces an interdependence, trust, and cooperation among their residents that we envy. It sometimes confounds me how the word *insular* ever got its slightly pejorative connotation.

I am convinced we are now living in the best of times—and probably the last of times—for appreciating the bay's islands. It is only in the last generation or two that the growth of road and bridge access, and of leisure time for boating and day-tripping, has begun allowing frequent and easy travel there for most of us. Modern bug repellents have also helped a lot, for these are often low and marshy places. At the same time, forces are at work that probably will extinguish, or greatly diminish, the islands' special qualities in many of our lifetimes. A number of bay islands already have vanished or dramatically receded from wind and wave erosion in the last century. That retreat will only accelerate as our profligate incineration of fossil fuels warms the global atmosphere and melts more of the polar icecaps, causing the sea level to rise at a rate unprecedented in many thousands of years. Right now it appears to be coming up at a foot a century, fast enough to doom thousands of precious island acres in a span of a few decades. It will not take until the islands are actually innundated. Long before that happens, storms riding in atop an elevated sea level will cause more erosion and property damage than they ever did in the past.

And perhaps even before physical forces decide the issue, the bay's declining natural-resources base, on which many waterfront communities depend for a living, could depopulate the islands. Already the difficulty of making a living on the water is reinforcing a trend toward gentrification of some islands, as growing numbers of city folks find the low price and availability of second homes there too good to pass up. On Tilghman Island in Talbot County, the man who owns both the biggest oyster company and a burgeoning tourist complex calculates that between 1978 and 1984 the former enterprise declined 40 percent, while the latter grew by 300 percent. So much of what is happening to the bay islands smacks to me of the irreversible. My advice is to revel in our favored-generation status, and celebrate them while we still can.

Smith Island

. . . Summertime, Soft-crab Time, Island Time, Changing Time

Fending off greenhead flies, the Reverend Henry Zollinhoffer was
cheerily scrubbing out community toilets overwhelmed by the annual
Methodist Camp Meeting the July morning I met him. To get to this
point in life, he had left a prosperous business career in Southern
Maryland. He was forty-eight, in the second year of his ministry to the
island's five hundred or so souls. A young son had died tragically and a
marriage had unraveled during his nine-year struggle to become ordained. He was engaged again when he brought his fiancé here on
board the skipjack *Amazing Grace* for their first look at Smith Island.
She promptly broke the engagement. But God, Henry felt certain, had
directed and sustained him through it all to serve this unrelieved,
marshy archipelago, nine miles off Crisfield in Maryland's lower bay.
The Smith Islanders are nearly all direct descendants of the dissenters
from Maryland's first colony in St. Mary's County, who settled here
more than three centuries ago. They like their religion unadulterated,
and tend to dissect the Sunday sermon as thoroughly as a critics' con-
vention at the theater. Camp Meeting, the week-long spiritual highlight of the year, can be a make-or-break time for the preacher. Henry,
placing large cans of Raid around the big wood and screen tabernacle
where meeting is held, said a nationally famous evangelist he had
brought in at some expense last year, "caught a gnat in his throat and
gagged through half the service." This year he was trying to diversify
and to inject more local and regional talent. I shouldn't miss that
night's program, he said.

By dusk, the strains of "That Old Gospel Ship," a local favorite,
rolled from the tabernacle, mingling with the sussurus of evening
breeze out on the marshes. Beneath bare light bulbs at the altar, the
reverend of the toilet brushes and the Ty-D-Bowl and the Ajax cleanser
stood transformed. Henry wore a jaunty white admiral's cap, navy
blue blazer with twin rows of brass buttons, electric-blue clerical shirt
overlain by a striped silk tie, and an ivory triple cross suspended from
his neck; also brilliant creased white cotton trousers and white loafers
("Flamboyant? You wouldn't be the first to say I was," he said). For the
first time in anyone's memory, Henry had persuaded a black choir and
preacher from Ebeneezer United Methodist Church on the Somerset
County mainland to provide the evening's inspirational service. Blacks
are rare enough to turn heads on the island. Most of the group had

never crossed "big water" before and were sustained in the passage from Crisfield on the island's school boat only by fervent prayer. It was 10:00 P.M. before the preacher took the stage. By then, the choir had fairly shivered the old tabernacle with an earthquake rendition of "Amazing Grace." Sister Carlotta, an ample and kinetic soloist, had praised Jesus to the point of ecstatic collapse; and Fulton Holden, a choir member who drove the school bus in Crisfield, had testified how his impossible recovery at Johns Hopkins had "caused one of the greatest orthopedic surgeons in the world to find God through operating on me." Of all this, the Smith Islanders were appreciative, but reserved.

Then came the preacher. He was a big, lithe man, beautiful to watch—moving graceful as a dancer, hands and shoulders of a basketball power forward, take you to the hoop anytime he felt like it, but not just yet . . . He stamped, he strode, he whirled, mesmerizing with fluid arcs of those great, expressive hands; but it was his voice that was remarkable. He preached loud as thunder, and soft as a cat's purring. He spread those arms and hands wide enough, it seemed, to encircle the tabernacle, exhorting, soaring almost off the register, then modulating so quick and smooth to a whispered, simmering "Do you heeaaaaah me now, chillunnn?" that you knew he was never for an instant out of control. Then, laboring audibly from his efforts, yet crooning seductively—"King Jesus . . . ahhhh . . . I'm on the mountain now, ahhhh . . . on the mountain"—he bid the islanders come forward to receive salvation. In the hush that followed you could hear peeper frogs shrilling in the ditches, and the whine of mosquitoes out on the big marsh, and the distant hoot of the foghorn warning ships off Holland Island bar miles up the bay. No one moved. "Take tiiiime to think about it," the big black preacher rumbled reassuringly "Salvation is not like instant mashed potatoes." And one by one, islanders began moving to the altar, to shed their burdens like so many molting hard crabs.

"Are ye religious? Even if not, it's a good, cool place to sit," Jennings Evans had welcomed me earlier to the night's service. Afterward, a delicious breeze sprang up to hold the bugs at bay, and we sat until late in the wooden lawn chairs of Frances Kitching's rooming house and talked about quieter sides of the religion that seems so pervasive here. Jennings is a crab potter in summer and a patent tonger (hydraulic oyster tongs) by winter, and a pleasure in every season. He has an uncommon reflective bent of mind toward the waterman's lot and has occasionally written poetry about it. Jennings said that early the next morning, Sunday, many of the island men would be starting the day's religious observances by going to class meeting. The class meeting as practiced here is probably as old as Methodism and as modern, my social-worker wife observed, as current group-therapy techniques. Even before class meeting, though, the men would be shuffling sleepily down to the waterfront in the predawn grayness to "fish up" their soft crabs from the holding tanks in shanties on stilts that line the island's boat channels. "A combination of Venice and Tobacco Road," a *New York Times* reporter once labeled these main thoroughfares of island commerce. "Fishing up" is about the only labor sanctioned here on the Sabbath, a day when even the highly popular softball games are not played. Until recent years, even children's activities, such as making paper cutouts, were discouraged on Sunday. But the work of soft crabs is another matter.

Throughout this reach of the bay, known as lower Tangier Sound, extend shallow beds of eelgrass, which are one of earth's richest underwater farms. In full swing there every summer is an ecdysiast frenzy, the greatest strip show under the July sun, in the soft-crab center of the universe. Olive and ivory, blue and orange, in most every life stage known to biology, the crabs of the Chesapeake Bay gather in the protection of the eelgrass to shed their shells, a process they will go through several times as they grow to the maximum size that their life span of two to three years permits. As Eskimos have many words for *snow*, and Arab Bedouins for *camel*, so do Smith Islanders for *soft crabs*. Green peelers, red peelers, pink peelers, rank peelers—all are stages prior to shedding the shell. Busters and buckrams, doublers and paper shells, jimmies and sooks, describe other stages of the molt and of sexual difference. As for size, being good businessmen, the islanders do not have the word *small* in their vocabulary. The tiniest legal-sized soft crabs are marketed as mediums, or even hotels, and sizes range on up through primes, jumbos, whales, and slabs, the last a feast that would cover a dinner plate. To the catching of all these, Smith Island each summer gets fully as devoted as Kansas to growing wheat. The bulk of all soft crabs eaten in North America—millions of dozens of them annually—come from here and neighboring communities around Tangier Sound. So much is this the cynosure for shedding crabs that the *Baltimore Sun*, editorializing on establishment of the thirty-eighth Parallel when the two Koreas were created, saw fit to point out that the line bisected the main soft-crab pond on Smith Island.

The island's "scrape fleet" employs beamy, shallow-draft wooden boats to drag heavy iron dredges across literally every square foot of the eelgrass beds. Hauling the dredges, one trailing out either side, is done by hand, and done several dozen times in a day, and is equivalent to pulling in a large garbage can, mouth open, through the water behind a boat moving at several knots. At 6' 6" and 210 semifit pounds, I struggled to pull the dredges twice in succession on my first scraping trip with Barry Bruce, an islander with massive forearms tight as oak logs. "It's an art to it," he said diplomatically, hauling in the dredge as if it were on smooth ice. The dredges procure crabs in every state of molting, from green peelers—farthest away from it—to buckrams, which are already reforming a hard shell. The peelers are taken back to the shanties, to be segregated in aerated tanks according to their readiness to shed. Even thus removed from the bay, the crabs remain governed by tides, temperatures, and other stimuli that much predate Methodism, which means they shed equally on the Sabbath. If they are not fished up and packed in seaweed soon afterward, they will reform their hard shell and be relatively valueless.

Olden Bradshaw, of the village of Rhodes (formerly Rogues) Point on the island, told me his Uncle Theo was one of the last who would not violate the Sabbath even to fish up soft crabs. We talked in the cool of his shanty, as Olden moved among the holding tanks, picking out the crabs that had achieved a silky softness, discarding those that had died in the effort. As Olden threw a chunk of soft crab through the wide cracks in the floorboards, a coil of mercury, thick as a man's wrist, rose from the green water sliding by below us, engorging the tidbit and dissolving back into the depths. "Tame as a old house cat, he is," he said of the eel. "Been living down there for years." Some wild black duck chicks glided out of the marsh to compete for the crab scraps. In a corner of the shanty, Olden's wife tended a kettle of sweetly steaming hard crabs. In a worn easy chair pulled up next to the soft-crab freezer, his elderly mother picked out the back-fin lumps, still smoking, from a bushel of done hard crabs, while Olden's son and granddaughter kept her company. A shaggy black retriever padded in off the dock to stand next to a window fan, and a neighbor on the way back from evening church stopped in to chat.

The Bradshaw family, all or part, spends from 4:00 A.M. until late evening here with the soft crabs during summer harvest season. Long, long hours, "but it is worth right smart to be your own boss," Olden says. "Now Uncle Theo, I recall one Sunday, the crabs were a-sheddin' heavy. Me and my cousin, just boys then, couldn't stand it. We fished up close to two boxes [six to nine dozen crabs] from his floats and packed 'em out. Monday we told Theo. He said, 'I was afraid of that.' He took two boxes, less three or four dozen that might have shedded Saturday night, and tossed 'em overboard. But he had to quit. He was a good man, a Christian, but my God, he warn't making a livin'! Anthing that's your livin', that's no sin."

There were fifty or sixty men at class meeting in the island's main town of Ewell the Sunday I went, and, as they filed in, two class leaders worked the crowd, clapping shoulders, touching, clasping hands, setting out themes for the morning's witness: "Speak on't. Sea nettles! Small crabs! Mosquitoes, greenheads! . . . there's a better world beyond this one. Speak on't, speak on't . . . something beyond this! Sometimes the leaders stopped to take a waterman's witness, murmured too low to overhear. Others would be moved to stand: "I'm here to praise the Lord . . . last week I left off crab-scraping to haul a neighbor's boat off the bar. The next lick I made come up so full of soft crabs I decided to head for home early. And a good thing I did, for the pumps back at my shanty [circulating water over the crabs there] had quit. Pray for me!" And another, a tall husky young waterman, said, "I can handle the nettles and the small crabs and all that mess, but I am alarmed by the amount of alcohol that is being drunk out in the shanties. Pray for me!" And each time, this last, closing statement, "Pray for me!", would be followed by much touching and clasping among the rough-hewn parties to the class meeting. I would guess that in no other place on earth are God and crabs more regularly and sincerely allied than in these Smith Island meetings. "Lord, give me the grace and vision to see opportunity," they might have prayed in the mainland Methodist church in which I was brought up; but here it is "Send more crabs, Lord and, while ye're at it, send 'em close to Ewell." It is old-fashioned stuff, such a personal God, but eminently suited to a place where people and nature still are so closely twined, where the bay shapes us more than we shape it; and where the patterns of daily life are tied less to forty-hour weeks, night shifts, and flexitime than to wind and tide, and the mysterious seasonal comings and goings of certain marketable crustaceans.

"They are still talking to God when the most of us are talking to the government to save us," Henry suggested. "But government won't save you from that big wave, won't make more crabs." Jennings Evans said the way he figures it, "you've got to be thankful to someone. In the water business we never plant anything. We just harvest. Oysters, crabs, fish . . . it is just reap, steady reap. But you know somebody's got to be doing some planting . . . there's got to be some system to it all somewhere."

Now, you would expect the church to play a large role in a place like this, and Smith Island is a theocracy; if not as pure a one as Vatican City, or as absolute as the Ayatollah's Iran, still it is as close as we come in modern America. Here the church has the major role in streetlighting, water supply, medical services, cutting elderly people's lawns, maintenance of public buildings, and half a dozen other traditionally municipal governmental services. That both understates and oversimplifies the role of the church here. "It may even be wrong to call it just 'church,' " says Reuben Becker, perhaps the only true outsider who has ever really stuck here. Reuben, about the same age as Henry, is a talented painter and sculptor who used to manage Baltimore's second largest dental laboratory. "But when they stopped working with gold I didn't much care for the work anymore. Gold was such a pleasurable material to work with." He lives in the part of Ewell called Over the Hill, in a haunted-looking ramshackle house whose weathered exterior gave no indication of human habitation. Lately he has painted it a warm, barn red, as if after about thirteen years he has decided to settle in for a while. Inside, in a comfortable studio Reuben paints pictures—paints pretty much what he pleases, when he pleases, and for whom, except on occasions when his life-support system of barter and handyman jobs and lackadaisical sales of paintings at too-low prices leave him in need of cash. "I feel like my life began here," he says. He only goes off the island once a year, usually on his birthday, usually for a day or two. "About what they call church here, the only way I could explain it to you is with an example of how things work on Smith Island . . . say I'm going to burn off my backyard. Well I'll talk about it for a couple of days before and notice what the neighbors say, how they look . . . do they seem worried I'll burn down their house? The church is an important center for getting feedback, which can be very, very subtle, and if it's negative, you don't do it. We're all in this together and very conscious of the fact we are living in a very small place."

The island has three towns, Ewell, Tylerton, and Rhodes Point, and each fiercely maintains its own identity and its own church. Henry starts his Sunday sermons at Ewell, then he travels by boat a few miles to Tylerton, then across more water to Rhodes Point. There was a plan several years ago, backed by Governor Marvin Mandel, to run a bridge across the marsh from Ewell to Tylerton; but the latter place would have none of it. It would just have brought automobiles down from Ewell, which currently has the island's only real road, a couple miles connecting it to Rhodes Point. Also, many citizens of Drum Point, as old-timers still call Tylerton, felt there was enough godlessness up in Ewell that a few miles of water between the two communities was a good thing. A boat, a zippy fiberglass stern drive of twenty-four feet, came with the Methodist parsonage and its $10,000 annual salary, which is the minimum pay permitted by the Methodist Conference, which includes Smith Island. But maintenance on the boat costs so much that "now I just hitchhike most Sundays," Henry said when I saw him a few years after that first, memorable Camp Meeting.

Islanders had always said of Henry, even before he married Jan Evans, an island girl some twenty years his junior, that he had "right smart of the boy in him." But he seemed wearier than I ever remembered him. Times were tough all over the island, he said. The bay's oyster stocks, on which the winter economy of Smith Island depends almost totally, were badly depleted from several years of mysteriously poor reproduction and from overharvesting. For the first winter in anyone's memory, most of the local stores and the oil company had said they no longer could afford to carry people on credit. "Never seen so many of the tongers so out of heart," people would say; and they would tell you how Otis Ray Tyler, a prominent member of the community, had gotten his fourth ticket from the marine police for attempting to sell undersized oysters.

Henry mentioned more than once that in six years here he had buried nearly 10 percent of his friends and neighbors—53 funerals among a population of 533. He had just completed a door-to-door census of the island, and the population of full-time inhabitants turned out to be markedly lower than the official 1980 census of 600. The census apparently reflected the growing number of part-time residents and outside homeowners who are around in the summer when the count is taken. "And a lot of the full-time ones are so old and so alone," Henry said. "We have a street on the island where every resident but one is seventy or older. 'Preacher,' one old woman told me, 'at night there aren't any lights in the houses around me anymore, and it is so lonely.' And when the old ones have to go off [usually to a mainland nursing home]—they throb so with this island, like a crab with the tides—take 'em out of here, they don't last long."

The earliest available census records show there were close to 800 people here just fifty years ago. That is a loss of fully one-third of the island's people in half a century, most of it coming in the last fifteen years. Henry thought you might have to go back to the early decades of the settlement established here in 1657 to find a lower population. Why is the population dropping so? I never found a simple answer. Smaller families, elderly people with no adequate support system moving off, tough times for watermen; young people who share the belief from class meeting that there must be "something beyond" nettles, mosquitoes and greenhead flies—but believe it is to be found right now, across the Sound and up the road to Salisbury and Ocean City and Baltimore. In sum, there are a lot of forces decreasing the number of people who make a hard-earned living out here, and virtually nothing working to bring new watermen to the island.

That is not to say people aren't coming to Smith Island. They are coming in increasing numbers—day-tripping tourists and retirees or second-home owners lured by the ridiculously cheap prices of property here. They come mostly to savor a culture relatively unsullied by the rapid pace of change in mainstream America. Drawn by the mystique of changelessness, so many are coming that Henry and others here say they fear the island is on the brink of fundamental change.

Some clarifications about change are in order here. First, for all that numerous travel writers have overwallowed in the unspoiled, yesteryear qualities of Smith Island, the place and its denizens scarcely have been mummified. For the record, the island got automobiles in 1923, a paved road in 1937, phones in 1951, and its first major crime (excepting game-law violations) in 1977. That was the winter someone, who had to be a resident—since the whole place was icebound at the time—stole Chelton Evans's safe, containing cash and securities worth $67,000, from his unlocked home. The safe was found in 1985, but never the thief, though everyone has their theories. After the safe job, some people said they began locking their doors, and many people began looking suspiciously to see if neighbors were living better than they ought to be able to afford.

The island also boasts a huge number of outhouses, which in local parlance refer to outbuildings used for crab-picking, making crab pots, carving decoys, storage—every use but bathrooms. Its toilets all are hooked to one of the state's most modern small sewage-treatment plants. Fiberglass is replacing wood in the boats and, lately, even in the shafts of oyster tongs. Recently I caught a ride on a twenty-degree night in an old wooden skiff piloted by Chris Marshall, a young islander. He was on his way from Tylerton to practice with his rock band in Ewell, a Model 1800 Rickenbacker bass guitar resting on the seat. He said the band has $20,000 invested in electronics and can blow the roof off the community hall at half-volume. Smith Island also has a vexing and growing trash-disposal problem, video games in the general store, marijuana, glue-sniffing, and increasingly open drinking, though the church remains adamantly opposed to alcohol. Church attendance among the young is down. Henry said recently he was shocked to "hear a Skilsaw going during sermon." No one, in sum, could accuse the island of not vying to share in the mainland's progress.

Second, about change, the legendary resistance to it among watermen assumes a radically different look in the context of the bay environment in which Smith Island and Smith Islanders have been steeped more than three centuries. It is said that the bay in its ability to handle change is paradoxically both tough and fragile. Creatures of the Chesapeake are survivors because, unlike the watershed it drains, the bay is no "Land of Pleasant Living." It is defined by a constant war for supremacy between its fresh-water rivers and the Atlantic Ocean, which results in frequent and violent swings in salinity, temperature, and turbidity. Nothing that isn't resilient to the point of toughness could survive such dynamism in every parameter of existence. Nothing that wasn't adaptable and opportunistic could have colonized the bay in the first place, because it isn't always here, but winks open and shut for the merest geological instant (twenty thousand years or so) as glaciers retreat and advance, and as sea level rises and falls to flood and drain the valleys cut by the Susquehanna River. Thus, the top-dogs in the estuary are mostly those critters who can hang out in the ocean, biding their time, then zoom in and establish dominance amid a constantly shifting set of environmental conditions. The bay can be fragile, however, if you inject something unnatural, a Kepone spill, or chlorine or another toxic substance for which nothing in the genetic experience of a crab's or an oyster's evolution could possibly have prepared it.

Similar to the species he preys on, the bay waterman has survived down the decades by being flexible enough to switch easily among whatever changing opportunities present themselves, be they eels, crabs, oysters, fish, clams, terrapin, waterfowl, or what-have-you. He has proved most opportunistic in extending his range, winning two landmark legal cases. The first was the 1968 Bruce decision, which first allowed bay watermen to cross inside other counties' waters, effectively opening the whole bay and its tributaries to all watermen. The second was the momentous decision in 1981 nullifying the centuries-old law that kept Maryland watermen from crossing the Virginia state line. Both times, the suit was instigated by the same handful from among the bay's thousands of licensed watermen. Both times, it was the Smith Islanders. As Dr. L. Eugene Cronin, a long-time bay scientist noted at the time of the Virginia line decision: "They're not trying to bust some law; they're just trying to crab." Bill Goldsborough, a biologist who lived on the island in the early 1980s, wrote his master's thesis on the fight over the line. It refuted, he said, the traditional view of watermen as conservative and resistant to change: "They are resistant [only] to changes that would restrict their livelihood and ability to adapt to changes . . . watermen may be the epitome of change."

But Henry said that what was really worrying him was that a shift seemed imminent in something as fundamental to the nature of Smith Island as the very bay that suffuses its marshes and culture. It had to do with insiders and outsiders. The more I went back to Smith Island, the more I became fascinated with watching the outsiders who aspired to live there as my way of trying to understand the insiders. The island seemed sooner or later to reject all outsiders, the good ones and the bad ones, implacably and impartially as Tangier Sound's shoal waters and narrow channels kept the pleasure yachts and cruise ships at a distance. The islanders, I came to feel, could love an outsider and carry deep grudges against one of their own; but if forced to choose, they would almost always choose the latter, as if guided by a collective wisdom that this way led to survival of the culture. The real genius of the place lies in something beyond its crabby picturesqueness and waterborne heritage. It lies in the complex, partly ineffable mechanisms for peacefully coexisting in a small space, which have been refined and reinforced during 325 years. It lies in Smith Island's having one of the highest percentages of people in an American community who know and accept their place in the scheme of things. "They are more solidly anchored than most of us," Henry said. "They have a sense of worth, of belonging. They feel comfortable with their universe, with their community. They can say, 'I'm a Tyler, or an Evans, or a Bradshaw, or a Marshall' [the four names shared by most of the Islanders], and they know that's something of real value." Another factor, of course, is that the options are limited. The place founded by dissenters has had few avenues for further dissent. The island is peopled largely by those who work long, hard hours on the water and those who have left.

Even with this measure of enforced homogeneity, the close circumstances of life require considerable artifice in getting along. One winter I was in Tylerton's only store, a cozy, one-room affair with potbellied stove, benches for conversation, a perpetual domino game, and some of the best crab cakes obtainable. An ominous hand-lettered sign hung from the stovepipe: "We know who took our gas tank full of gas ($11 worth) out of our outboard. Somebody seen them do it. Come tell us and we won't cause you any trouble, but if you don't we are going further." And from a rafter hung another list, boldly proclaiming every waterman who hadn't yet anted up his dues to the watermen's association. Sometimes a fight can flare that seems provoked by a small remark, but that may be rooted in something years, or generations, deep. I know an outsider who intervened in one of these and was knocked unconscious with a pole by the person he sought to help. But there is amazingly little outright violence. People who for whatever reasons prefer not to encounter one another manage it to an extent that you would not believe in a town of 180 people like Tylerton, which can be walked around completely in about fifteen minutes. There are residents there who have not seen neighbors, except across a stretch of water when crabbing and oystering, for up to fifteen years. No one seems to think this is very unusual. There can also be a degree of accommodation and communication on Smith Island that would surprise outsiders who fancy themselves far more liberal and nontraditional than the islanders. I have heard adults and teenagers discuss oral sex quite unashamedly in the general store, and have been told by younger generations of quite frank discussions with their ninety-year-old grandparents about sex.

"Oh, there are people here that probably are certifiably crazy, but the community supports them," said Reuben. A few years ago, a wealthy Pennsylvania businessman lodged his schizophrenic son on Tangier, Smith Island's neighbor across the Virginia line, because somehow the little island accepted him better than the rest of the world. "Living on an island, there are a lot of lines to toe, kind of invisible ones we keep in the back of our heads," said Jennings Evans. "We all know about how far to go here. I don't mean we're all buddy-buddy, but you never let the differences get too wide. We're too dependent."

Lynette ("Schim") Becker, a native of Australia, a nurse, and for seven years Smith Island's only medical resident, said that Smith Islanders "are very, very, very loyal within the family. People from outside sooner or later always end up having to take sides . . . or make some fateful decision here; but people from here can change around, they can cross sides, they can go back from a position. For outsiders, it is tough to fit in. I'm one of the lucky ones who did." She was talking in her modern apartment in York, Pennsylvania, where she works at the regional hospital. It was in the late spring of 1972 that she came to the island, married to Reuben then, full of high hopes and announcing, when asked about salary, "We're not very materialistic." She reflected on her leaving alone, seven years later, fiercely proud that "not an old person had to go off while I was there. But it wore me down. I had gotten too close, tried so hard to carry everyone's medical burdens. I could never bear to charge people, and when I finally sat down and took a look at my last year's salary, it was $6,700 [the island furnished her an apartment] and more than a third of that went for expenses— for boat repair and gas to get around. The island sucked me dry . . . I play the lottery. If I ever won, I'd move back to Smith Island in a minute.

"But even then we'd still all be dying down there, and I'm not just talking about the land eroding" (on the bay side, the island is retreating at seven feet a year, threatening Rhodes Point with evacuation within the next decade or so). It is almost impossible for visitors to realize, Schim explained, how much harder everything is to do on an island several miles away from the mainland. High-school kids travel by boat to and from Crisfield each day, which makes after-school activities untenable. To leave the island to shop, or even to buy a spark plug for an outboard motor, you must plan either to catch the 5:00 P.M. boat back or spend a night away, The boat is $4 each way, $5 round trip. Similarly, carpenters and other tradespeople who come to install anything must leave on the late-afternoon boat, and the first boat of the day bringing them back across does not arrive until about 1 P.M. Cars, lumber, strawberries, milk, dog food—every conceivable item for living except crab meat and oysters—must be imported by boat. And in much of the time since Schim left, there has been no full-time medical person on the island. Taken piecemeal, all this can seem trivial, like the time I woke up craving French toast and walked the few yards to the store, to be told bread "would be comin'" on the afternoon boat; but it adds up and it can grind you down over a lifetime.

Schim said neither local nor state government ever has recognized "the effort these five hundred people go to to maintain themselves. I think constantly about how much Smith Island has to offer, the qualities in those people . . . every one of them to some degree still has the backbone, the pioneer spirit, the nurturing qualities of their ancestors. But it is dying, that's my opinion; the values are changing . . . I see warm, loving, caring people who are finding it harder and harder to maintain their civility, their family support systems, especially with the old people. It is happening to all of us, perhaps. Perhaps it is easier to see on a little island."

Perhaps, as with the creatures in the bay, the marvelously complex and resilient systems for surviving on a small island are going to prove paradoxically fragile as they are increasingly exposed to "unnatural," or outside, forces. One wonders whether the place will be able to acquire the needed adaptational mechanisms fast enough. We may not have to wait long to find out, because increasingly a lot of planning, de facto and otherwise, is being done for Smith Island's future, and most of it involves outsiders. Henry's census found nearly twenty-five of the island's two hundred houses, as well as significant amounts of acreage, were owned by off-islanders. By the early 1980s a retired navy man from Washington had bought one of the two oyster-packing houses. The Chesapeake Bay Foundation, an Annapolis environmental organization with forty thousand members, had bought a house on Tylerton for a nature center, in what seemed to be one of the most successful and natural alliances of outside with inside. The press had thoroughly discovered Smith Island, and it is not unusual now for it to be featured in the *New York Times*, the *Wall Street Journal*, and *National Geoqraphic* all in the same year, not to mention television and movies. It was the setting for an award-winning children's book and for part of William H. Warner's *Beautiful Swimmers*, the best and most successful book written about crabs and watermen. Almost every islander you talk to has the phone number of a tourist who wants to know just as soon as any place becomes available for purchase. A soggy lot in Tylerton has sold to an outsider for the unheard-of price of $7,000. Most young islanders say they couldn't hope to compete with such prices for places of their own.

Such trends chip at the very economic and spiritual foundation of Smith Island. Every Sunday, every door on Smith Island gets knocked on by church members—collecting for the preacher they call it—and it amounts to a major form of taxation there, for the church supports so much that in most places is done by town government. Islanders, even those who don't attend church regularly, give. Outsiders usually don't. Henry said he had written the University of Maryland to get it to explore alternative forms of government, in light of the theocracy's inability to cope with the changes occurring. "They weren't encouraging, because of our small numbers and the fact that we are split into three separate towns" (each, he might have added, with a fierce sense of identity).

"The island's got to change soon; in years to come it'll be sold out to . . . well, to what we call 'em are foreigners," said Barry Bruce, the big, friendly waterman from Ewell who years before had initiated me into the business of crab-scraping. Barry said that with a shrug and a smile and surprisingly little heat, maybe just because he is one of earth's truly good-natured people, but I have noticed that a lot of islanders, when trying to confront outside or unfamiliar forces, seem unwilling or unable to grapple seriously with the consequences. It is a reaction that approaches fatalism. Perhaps it comes inevitably from three centuries of dealing more on nature's terms than on human ones, but community planning is not the islanders' forte. Others, however, seem more than willing to shoulder the burden of Smith Island's future.

For more than a decade, an earnest, walrus-looking man from the Delaware mainland, Clifton Sanford Justice, has been trying, he and his wife, Margaret, said, "to do something for Smith Island." First it was an airport, to be located on or near some of the ninety acres that the Justices own on the northern fringe of Ewell. The notion of an airport had proven powerfully antagonistic. "It's what ruined Tangier" (the heavily touristed Virginia island) and "it would bring in the drugs," seemed to be the two most common opinions. "It was island people that approached me about building it." Sanford Justice would say, always maintaining, "whatever we do here, it's for the people of this island." At the time we first spoke, the Justices had spruced up their property, an ancient home known as Pitchcroft, with the best water view on the island. He was renting the three modest bedrooms there, serving locally cooked meals, taking Visa cards, and distributing brochures:

Visit Ye Olde
PITCHCROFT, Inc.
RESTAURANT
and
LODGE.

He was in the third year of a campaign to get the Army Corps of Engineers and the state Department of Natural Resources to approve, dredge, and build the island's first pleasure-boat marina. He would donate the land next to the Pitchcroft for it. If the initial proposal won approval, Sanford said, he would expand the Pitchcroft and its overnight accommodations, build a swimming pool, tennis courts, and perhaps a four-hole golf course. He thought up to two hundred boat slips could eventually fit into the complex. He said the golf course would be a boon to island youth. "What is there to keep young people here now? Only crabbing and oystering." The island would get the dredged sand from the marina to cover its chief eysore, an open dump. He had already donated, from high ground that he owned, 360 loads of dirt to the island's softball field, dirt being a precious commodity in a place as marshy as this. Eddie Marshall over in Tylerton, with no ground to expand his little house, had to get a state wetlands permit just to add a bedroom for the new baby, he said.

The Justices kept repeating their pious refrain that they were only there to see to the good of the island. "The only way Smith Island will change is if the people here want it to—it surely won't be us," Margaret Justice liked to say. A town meeting on the Justice project in 1978 saw it roundly rejected. A second public vote, called like the first one by the corps, drew 150 people to a meeting in Ewell in 1979. Only 65 voted, and the vote that time was 35–30 in favor of the project. "We live so close together, a lot of people just don't like to vote against one another like that," one islander explained to me. Schim said "he swung people around by giving them fill dirt for their new softball field. Money talks on Smith Island, in a superficial kind of way, and Sanford Justice bought his way in with 360 loads of fill dirt."

By August 1981, Sanford Justice was rolling along. The governor of Maryland and the Somerset County commissioners had just rejected a last-ditch petition signed by 174 islanders who said they feared the project would attract undesirables to the island and increase crime. The allegation about crime, a county official suggested to a *Salisbury Daily Times* reporter, was likely a cover-up for another reason for the petition: "It's an isolated island and they want to keep it that way . . . " Such concerns, the official continued, were not valid for purposes of reaching a decision on the marina permits. By July 1983, the project had surmounted virtually its last regulatory hurdle as the corps gave the final permit needed for dredging to begin. He had also acquired a little land in both Rhodes Point and Tylerton, Sanford told me that year. You never know what you might want to do, he said. One thing he said he would never do, though, would be to serve liquor at his new complex.

Most islanders concede that liquor is an issue that has just been waiting for someone to bring to a head. Faster than almost anything else imaginable, this issue would force the island to confront change head-on, they agree. Henry, eyeing the spot where a new restaurant was going in across the road from the church and parsonage, told me the Supreme Court had recently ruled that liquor could be served within spitting distance of a church. The position of the church here on drinking was clear as ever—total abstinence—Henry said. Of course, he knew that alcohol had long been brought to the island, and that it is consumed these days more openly than even a few years ago. It is still taboo at public places and events, though I have seen it passed out from the back of a pickup during performances by Chris Marshall's band. In relatively few homes would you be offered a drink. More likely, if your host were so inclined, you would go down to his boat, or to his crab shanty.

At the island's oldest and best-known eating establishment, Frances Kitching's rooming house in Ewell, a diner from the mainland asked innocently if she could keep her beer cold in the refrigerator while she ate. "You'd be the first," came the tart and dismissive reply. "I have simply turned down some people who appeared to have been drinking when they came here to eat," says Mrs. Kitching. "They were in no condition to appreciate good cooking." At sixty-seven, and the coauthor of the highly acclaimed *Mrs. Kitching's Smith Island Cookbook*, she comes as close as any islander ever has to achieving celebrity. The National Geographic Society filmed her golden anniversary celebration with Captain Ernest Kitching as part of a movie on the bay, and viewers nationwide remarked warmly on it. I talked with her one night over supper, which consisted, fairly typically, of crab cakes, fried oysters, corn pudding, tomatoes stewed delightfully with allspice and cinnamon, carrot-onion salad, green beans, homemade rolls, tossed salad, homemade coconut meringue pie, and big glasses of lemony sweet iced tea. She loves to experiment, she said. "I'm the type'll try to cook a cucumber . . . I got to thinking about how you'd do that, and I put it with some tomato, some onion, and mixed in some diced ham. Put in a casserole with cheese, it was right good." A crab-meat delight unobtainable perhaps anywhere else is what she does with a buckram, as the islanders call soft crabs that have progressed so far back toward reforming a hard shell that they are unshippable as far as the mainland seafood markets are considered. She french-fries them, and the crunchy, highly edible shell, surrounding steaming, succulent back-fin meat, is worth swimming from Crisfield to get.

She knows the value of a dollar as well as any islander—"when Ernest and me were first married I would see him off November first on a drudge [dredge] boat sailing up the bay to catch oysters, and he would return the first day of Christmas week with $13. That money looked as big as this room when I was about to be cut off at the store for running up a bill of $2.50 for three weeks' supplies." The cookbook has scarcely made her rich, but quality control still comes before money where her reputation is concerned. She got a call recently from Crisfield: Could she feed a tour group of forty-eight coming over on short notice? "Let me study it for fifteen minutes, I told them; then I told them no. I could have called the girls in and got something together, but it would have ruined all the reputation I've made serving meals all these years to do less just once. I'm sixty-seven and I cannot do what I have done. I ask people to tell me if my food's not as good, because then I'll close down." She said Sanford Justice had been around, "talking about that airport again and saying, 'Frances, you are getting some age to you, why not close down and come cook for me.' Not likely." And a man from Nantucket had just called about buying her home and restaurant business: "but you take me out of here and thirty days later I'd be planted in the graveyard."

Just down the street a few dozen yards from Mrs. Kitching's, and across the street from the Methodist church and Henry's parsonage, another restaurant has opened to accommodate the increasing number of tourists. Another that is scheduled to open eventually will include ten "first-class" motel rooms, which will easily double the overnight accommodations available to mainlanders now. Its owner, Alan Tyler, of Rhodes Point, is a force for change unique on Smith Island. He was born and raised here and says he was "kicked out of school in junior high." Until eight years ago he ran a modest general store in Rhodes Point with his wife, Dixie. Since then Alan has acquired the state school-boat contract, the island oil company, and a state contract to plant oyster shells and seed to replenish the bay's oyster bars each spring; also the *Captain Tyler*—which brings about five thousand tourists a year to his restaurant and gift shop in Rhodes Point—and another restaurant in Crisfield. He is the pilot in winter of the school boat, named the *Betty Jo Tyler* for his daughter, who is in college in Salisbury, and in the summers he runs the tourist boat. He splits his life as few islanders do between the fancy marina-restaurant complex in Crisfield, where he keeps a blue Lincoln Continental, and the island, where he maintains a rusting pickup truck and still lives above his restaurant in Rhodes Point. He travels often to Baltimore. One day you may see him at the marina entertaining the smart yachting set at the open bar on the *Captain Tyler*, and the next day, grubbing around the island, unkempt. To the extent it is possible to be both insider and outsider on Smith Island, Alan is. He says sometimes it wears on him, wondering just where he does fit in.

Of the island's future, he told me one evening, "it's going to be tourism. I hope I can really build things up big here." When he first opened his gift shop, he told me, he did not much like the idea, "but the tourists demand it. It is just amazing how they'll buy anything if it has the name 'Smith Island' on it." He said at the time how he was proud that he kept his tourists confined to buses when he showed them the island. A few years later he conceded his new motel-restaurant plans would mean an increase in foot traffic, "but people here will just have to adjust."

Will his new place on the island serve liquor if the tourists demand it? "I'll tell you this; I could get a liquor license whenever I wanted one," Alan said. "When I got one for my restaurant in Crisfield, I had to get twenty-five signatures of residents on a petition. Now I could either get twenty-five signatures over here, or I could show you twenty-five hypocrites." Whatever he does, "I want to do first class," Alan said; and few tourists have anything but praise for his operation. They even seem to like the imitation Mississippi River sternwheeler steamboat that is the latest addition Alan has made to his tourist fleet. Seen coming through the big marshes into Ewell, it makes an extraordinary impression. Recently, Alan scored maybe the PR coup of the decade, when he hosted more than one hundred staff members of the *New York Times* for crab cakes aboard his boat in New York Harbor for the Statue of Liberty rededication.

When the islanders are pressed about the future of Smith Island, there is one nearly universal sentiment they express. They hope they never get like Tangier, a few miles to the south. It was a visit I made to Tangier one recent summer, the first time I had been there since the early 1960s, that got me thinking about change on Smith Island. We flew into the airport, where close to two dozen other small craft were parked. The white picket fences I recalled had all been supplanted by chain link, giving the island's one narrow main street the look of a dog kennel run. We walked three abreast with the horde of close to six hundred other tourists that had disgorged from day-trip boats. The few natives brave enough to buck this tide kept their eyes averted. I felt that a lot more of them must have been waiting behind their doors until we had all cleared out, to venture up and down their own street. I found it an uncomfortable experience, and quite in contrast to Smith Island, where you generally still get a wave and a hello, and conversation if you want it. I can't say that Tangiermen are at heart any less friendly and open than Smith Islanders; simply that they have joined most of the rest of the modern world in no longer having the luxury of being that way to every stranger.

Jennings Evans says he's not really antitourist; he sort of likes them in small doses, especially sailboat people. "I'd like to see 'em have some place to tie up, but I do dread the thought of walking tours. I was working on my diesel one time and a man came up and said, 'Hold it there,' for a picture, like you're some kind of ornament. The water business is getting harder every day and I just am getting to feel like we're going against the grain of things. If we lost the waterman business, though, we'd lose our natural being."

Sanford and Margaret Justices' professed desires of making Smith Island a better place for Smith Islanders finally began to unravel, after state officials became convinced the constant shoaling that occurs around the island made dredging a marina and boat channel too risky a proposition. The Justices blamed "a few jealous islanders" for the reversal of their fortunes. Their relationships with the locals deteriorated, and for a time they were seldom seen on Smith Island. Ye Olde Pitchcroft, Inc., came near falling down after a couple winters of neglect, and then burned, mysteriously. Most recently the Justices have been talking again about an airport, and dickering with county officials about putting a townhouse development next to Ewell that would double the population of the town overnight. Whatever they do would only be for the good of the islanders, they say.

The retired navy man's plans for the oyster-packing house at Rhodes Point also came to naught, and he is said to have moved away for good. "I think he was just one more who comes in here and thinks this is a small pond he can be a big fish in," Reuben remarked. Alan's motel is behind schedule, but the restaurant is almost completed. Mrs. Kitching's son Harry has opened a small motel across from her rooming house. Henry Zollinhoffer is preaching in Berlin, near Ocean City. A group in his congregation that had become increasingly alienated by his outside notions had seized an opportunity to push for his transfer. The island finally got a doctor, but he is already beginning to complain about all the time he spends in the summer treating the minor ailments of the increasing tourist hordes and may soon leave.

I have had my first dispute with an islander, who decided anyone asking so many questions must be up to no good, and accused me of trying to pry into whether he was illegally trapping ducks. I suppose my protestations to the contrary weren't bolstered when, several months later, he was fined $1,200 for duck trapping. Lots of other islanders told me, don't pay it any mind, I was welcome there as far as they were concerned. I never doubted their sincerity; yet I know that it would be a mistake to put most islanders in the position of choosing between me and him.

Schim told me she had been visiting Block Island "to try and make up for leaving my island." She found it more beautiful than she thought an island could be, with "no trash, no rundown buildings . . . the inns were simple and charming and the food was wonderful. I met the most entertaining old salt. He was from Virginia and had never been in a boat. It is all supported by tourism there. There are no watermen left." The struggles and rough edges of Smith Island were pleasantly absent, but tragically, she felt, so was any authenticity of culture.

I told Jennings about her trip. He said he had visited Mystic, Connecticut, the famous old whaling port and historic center. "It was okay, but of course there were no real live whalers. Now that's who I'd have liked to talk to . . . the men who really went out after whales. Smith Island could never get like Mystic, I don't think. I sure hope not."

The last time I was on the island, I visited with Lula Bradshaw, Olden's mother, who was in her eighties and could recall a day when erosion and storms had not taken so much of the high ground, and there were "plenty trees, peach, pear, plum, apple . . . good gardens, lots of chickens and livestock, and, oh my, there were more people." Lula's granddaughter Brenda stopped in from her job shucking oysters to see her, and the two bridged the generation gap with a conversational ease and camaraderie that seems still the rule here. Brenda told me about yet another house that had just been sold to an off-island couple. It brought the number of places now owned by off-islanders to nearly forty, or about 20 percent of the available housing stock.

"But you get used to outsiders," Brenda said brightly, "and they just love it to death here."

The Ultimate Edge

Parramore Island, Virginia, March

Even as we moor on the island's marshy backside, miles from the beach, the Atlantic surf murmurs, a gentle stimulus that urges us forward, beckons on levels remote from our everyday senses. Some birds, more acute receptors of subsonic vibrations than we, are thought to tune in on such surfy mutterings for orientation from hundreds of miles away as they follow age-old migratory flight paths up and down the interior of North America. We feel on no less urgent business this early spring day, eager to be on the edge of things. Edges have always produced phenomena that are among the most interesting in nature— the great migrations of fish and fowl triggered by the intersections of the seasons; the abundance and diversity of wildlife known to any hunter who stalks the junctures of forest and field, and the fantastic habitats of the tide marshes at the merge of land and water. Parramore Island is one of the literal and most unsullied edges of the American landscape, lying five miles off the mainland of Virginia's Eastern Shore and sixty miles south of Salisbury.

At seven thousand longitudinal acres extending about twelve miles between Wachapreague and Ouinby inlets, it is the largest and most magnificently forested in a fifty-one-mile chain of coastal barrier islands preserved from development during the 1970s by the Nature Conservancy. In a third of a century the conservancy has purchased many of the most environmentally precious parts of America. Of the approximately one million acres of marsh, mountain, prairie, forest, bog, and barrens thus protected, the Virginia barrier islands are considered by many of its officials to be the crowning effort, and Parramore Island the jewel in the crown. The Conservancy calls its acquisition the Virginia Coast Reserve, as if it were some uncommon and treasured old spirits; and indeed this is vintage wild seacoast, an unspoiled ecosystem of beach and dune and salt marsh that can only rarify with age as the trend to make more Ocean Cities, Hilton Heads, and Miami Beaches continues to spread throughout the rest of the barrier islands that stretch from Labrador to Corpus Christi.

In the acquisition of Parramore and its sister islands there seems hope for humanity, a hearteningly ironic recycling of capital. The purchases were enabled by substantial grants from the foundation of Mary Flagler Carey, whose grandfather, Henry Morrison Flagler, made the family fortune by pioneering the development of a set of similar coastal islands farther south at a place called Miami. Parramore easily could have met the same fate. "Were it located 100 miles north it would become one of the most famous resorts in the world; Atlantic City, Cape May, Asbury Park, would all sink into insignificance when compared with this favorable isle," trumpeted a history of the region published in 1903. Since that was written, there have been schemes to log the island, to drill it for oil, and to use it as a military bombing range. The only thing that succeeded was goats. Left there by early settlers, their population had grown by the 1940s to where passing ships often remarked on the white-flecked shores of Parramore. The goats met their Waterloo when the island's private owner imported several dozen crack cowhands and sheepdogs from Texas. The roundup was spectacular enough to draw coverage in the 23 January 1950 issue of *Life*. More than three thousand goats were corralled and sold for meat and for the manufacture of antirabies serum.

Last Memorial Day weekend, when a reported half-million people were packing onto a dozen or so miles of sand just north, in Ocean City, Maryland, conservancy officials flew over the chain of beaches in the Coast Reserve, which are open to day use. They counted ninety people in more than fifty miles, and forty-five of those were in one party. That kind of isolation, now assured in perpetuity by the conservancy, still rankles certain development interests and elected officials on the sleepy, lower part of the Delmarva Peninsula. They had dreamed of bridges, with Disney Worlds and a generally unlimited tax base to follow.

The mood of the local boomers was not helped by what happened to Metomkin Island, whose owners had refused to sell it at any price for inclusion in a reserve that would only "lock it up forever." When a company calling itself Offshore Islands, Inc., finally bought Metomkin, more than a few locals cheered to see the nature lovers get their comeuppance—until they found out that Offshore Islands was a dummy corporation created by the conservancy. The Accomack County commissioners, in retaliation, voted not to recognize the Coast Reserve's designation as an "internationally important biosphere" by the United Nations. The United Nations stated that in years to come the reserve would serve as an example against which we may compare the long stretches of overcrowded, despoiled, and ravaged coastlines of our continent.

So it is that there is no hotelier, no marina, no human occupant to welcome us to Parramore, only a great blue heron who startles up from a tide-marsh gut, rasping with all the indignation of a rightful owner. That the herons are the duly appointed sentinels of every edge where land and water effect a marshy interface, I have never had a doubt. From the smallest headwater bogs of the bay's tributary creeks to the eye-stretching sweeps of Atlantic salt marsh, a heron is present in every season. The heron's family, *Ardeidae*, which includes egrets and bitterns, is old even as their fellow birds go, having emerged during the lower Eocene some sixty million years ago. The race has proven astoundingly adaptable. The fossil and historical record shows that of seventy-seven lines along which the heron's clan evolved throughout all its time on earth, sixty-one still survive, and only one of these is considered endangered today. The great blue heron fits better than any creature I know with our region's thousands of miles of shoreline. He is lord of the edge, and we acknowledge his sovereignty: "Other birds have nicknames, glossies for ibis, seaswallows for terns, etc.," writes

Phillip Kopper in his fine book on beaches, *The Wild Edge*, "but some things never get nicknames—Oliver Wendell Holmes, Martin Luther King . . . Great Blue Heron."

We have come from Quinby on the mainland in a sixteen-foot flat-bottomed skiff with a 9.9-horsepower Evinrude, which is laboring to push the four of us with field gear and fifty pounds of lunch (a bushel of oysters). The skiff has many times proven adequate transportation on the bay side of the peninsula, but it seems uncomfortably frail out here, even though the day is calm enough. There simply is more and rawer energy flowing around these sea islands than on the gentler Chesapeake. Tides are several feet greater and currents rip at a fierce pace; and the inlets of the gray-green Atlantic, wracked with shoals and breakers, are never far from sight or mind. We hang the bushel of oysters from an old piling in one fast-running tidal gut. The oysters, tonged that morning near Kent Island from water that was nearly fresh, will have become salty as Chincoteagues from filtering the seawater when we return for them in eight hours. The marshes where we debark on the island are unexpectedly firm footing to one accustomed to sinking thigh-deep into similar-looking terrain on the bay side. Even the bottoms of the tidal guts are swept clean of muck by the amplitude of the tide.

The biotic production here is enormous; the marsh crunches beneath every step of our hip boots. I estimate that in one area covering several acres there is close to a pound of shucked meat from just the mussels and oysters growing on every square foot. Add to that a thick crop of periwinkles and fiddler crabs, the estimated ten tons per acre of organic matter flushed annually into the aquatic food chain, the habitat for nesting black ducks and the nursery provided the young of ninety-six species of fish. Agriculture can yield some pretty impressive production figures too—we raise our chickens to four pounds in eight or nine weeks, in only a square foot or so of space per bird; but those systems take constant inputs of purchased energies like feed, heat, light, medicines, and human labor. The sea island does it all for the price of being let alone; and does it more prettily than any chicken farm I have known.

A second surf, the breeze in the tops of old growth pines that stretch eighty feet or more, rolls far above our heads as we enter the forest of Parramore Island. Spaced well apart, the pines preside over a cinnamon carpet of needles so thick that no seedling, and scarcely even a greenbrier, penetrates their surface for acre after acre. No landscaped and tended English park could be neater, or more ordered, airy, and spacious. Some of the scientists brought here by the conservancy say this is an ecosystem forged by frequent natural fires, which keep all undergrowth from gaining a hold, but cannot damage the mature pines with their inches-thick bark. At least a partial explanation, others say, has to be the foraging on the undergrowth that went on so long by the goats prior to the 1950 roundup. The island's abundant deer herd seems to have taken up the goats' lawn-mower role, as every shoot of greenbrier that has poked through the needles appears to have been browsed. It is an eerily quiet hike for some distance. Footfalls are muffled by the needles, and the cathedral effect of the great forest suppresses conversation; but in the hush, all around us rage the storms of centuries ago, frozen in the fantastic, windsculpted forms of dead and dying giant cedars interspersed among the pines. The cedars, traditional early colonizers of sand dunes on barrier islands, far predate the pines, which themselves are more than a century old. When the cedars were young, the ancient dunes on which Parramore's forest grows were hard by the ocean, rooted in barely stabilized agglomerations of sand and beach grass, bearing the full brunt of waves and storms.

Now they are more than a mile back from the modern beach front. One great old cedar, still living, is buried in the dune up to its first crotch, where it still measures a full twelve feet around. Its limbs and the grain of its trunk have grown corkscrewed in a clockwise direction. To rest in the silent, storm-sculpted forest, beneath the sixty-foot spread of such a tree is like entering a temple; it invites contemplation. How did you come here, old cedar? How many years have you seen? And what furies shaped you like this?

It makes invigorating walking to cut a sinewy cedar staff that will come about nose-high, and inhaling with every step the incredible aromatic essence, a perfume several centuries in the making. It takes a little while longer in the forest to realize why there is something different about this island than any place we have been before. This is not a walked-in place. Unlike the other islands in the reserve, it is closed to the public entirely because of a private owner's retention of recreational rights from the conservancy for several years. You come upon things here you don't find in other outdoor spots—the delicate plumes of a snowy egret hanging from a pine branch; and the skeleton of a red-tailed hawk, complete down to the talons. The bear, wolf, bobcat, and puma that once prowled these sea islands are said to be extirpated here, but it is easy to imagine different. Animal sign from fox, raccoon, and white-tailed deer is all over, not yet confined by human intrusions to narrow trails through the thickets as in most "natural" places.

It might not seem that most forests or parks, even in eastern America, are all that overrun, or disrupted, but consider just one aspect of our expedition to Parramore. The four of us, almost unthinking, broke off perhaps a half-dozen branches from the island's magnifi-

cently gnarled cedars for walking sticks in the space of an hour.
Multiply that by, say, fifty visitors a day, a light usage for a twelve-
square-mile island, and it adds up to thousands of branches stripped
off each year. In a decade or two, the appearance of that forest would be
substantially different from the way we found it, although few new-
comers would think the island much altered. And egret plumes and
hawk skeletons, as well as the delicate sand dollars and lustrous conch
shells that now litter the beaches, would be rare finds indeed. After
talking this over at lunch, we carefully picked up the peanut shells we
tossed away earlier. They would degrade after a while, but one begins
to feel more obligation than that after a short time here.

Some day the Nature Conservancy may face a decision on whether
to allow public use of Parramore, and to what degree. Their current
programs range from the last refuge for a blind salamander in Texas,
from which even most researchers are prohibited, to a tract thirty miles
from Manhattan that is only closed temporarily whenever foot traffic
threatens to wear out the trails. As for Parramore, I, who have already
had the pleasure of it so unspoiled, would prefer it remain just that
way, with, of course, just one visit permitted me every spring. As for
the other ten million or so people within a day's drive of the Coast Reserve, I suspect they would agree—as long as each of them, too, could
visit occasionally . . . "Just me, maybe a couple friends, we'll keep it
quiet; too many people, sure, it would spoil the place in a minute . . . "

It seems strange to talk of preserving anything unchanged on a
coastal barrier island like Parramore, because constant alteration and
everlasting impermanence is the order of the day on these, the most
dynamic land forms known to geology. It is most obvious on the ocean
side, where Atlantic breakers of palest, icy jade pound a broad, firm-
packed beach wide enough to land 747 jets. All this horizontality,
stretching uncluttered as far as the eye can see in either direction, is
fully as pleasing and renewing to the spirit as any snow-capped mountain wilderness.

The wreck of a nineteenth-century schooner, her bones protrud-
ing from the surf, draws our attention. She is built so massively, dou-
ble-planked with foot thick timber, fastened to 14-by-14 inch ribs with
wooden pegs an inch in diameter, surely she must have borne gold or
other heavy treasure (an inspection of the records later downgrades
that somewhat—her cargo was guano fertilizer). During the decades
the wreck has disappeared and reemerged as ocean storms and currents played serve and volley with the island, fattening the beach here,
gnawing at it there, breaching the entire island in a single storm, closing the inlet back up in the next one.

The emerging specialty of coastal geology is documenting in

places like Parramore how the barrier islands actually depend on storms, and on their own instability, to survive. The periodic overwash of the islands by storm tides carries sand to the islands' backsides, providing the marshes there enough substrate to keep ahead of a sea level that has been rising, trying to submerge them, since the glaciers of the last ice age began to melt. In a time when the seas were lower, and miles more of the continental shelf was high and dry land, the barriers existed, in much the same shape as they do now, miles offshore of their present location. They have survived by literally rolling over themselves, migrating ever landward as the mainland submerges. Ecological banana peels, they have been called. Someday, if sea level continues to rise, the Atlantic rollers may lap at the shores of the Appalachians; and there, a few miles offshore, will likely be a version of Parramore Island and its sisters in the coast reserve. The current island, with its unusually extensive forests, seems more secure than that; but Hog Island just to the south once was similarly forested and seemingly just as secure. Now uninhabited, it held four hundred people as recently as 1933. Since 1871 parts of Hog retreated toward the mainland nearly a half-mile, even as other portions of the island advanced seaward by 3,300 feet. Dunes there that towered an impregnable 80 feet, sheltering a forest behind them, have been reduced to nubs.

Parramore has not exactly stood still either. Although the long-term net movement, driven by rising sea level, has been landward, the islands tend to wander widely in both directions, controlled by shorter shifts in the currents, which bring them the sand that is their lifeblood. In 1852 Parramore was nearly a mile further seaward at its southern tip than it is now; and from 1852 to 1911 it accreted 600 feet in its midsection. In a film shot in geologic time, the barrier islands would flicker back and forth across the screen like Keystone Kops, or a cancan line. What the Nature Conservancy has acquired out here on the continent's wildest edge goes well beyond the usual plants and animals. It is preserving a natural process of land formation so dynamic as to constitute a living system in its own right. The process is correctly known as migration, because for the most part it does not involve an overall loss of sand, only shifts in its shape and location. It is only when people try to anchor their condo-castles on these, earth's most dynamic land forms, that the barrier islands are said to be "unstable," and natural migration becomes an "erosion problem."

The light is beginning to fall in long, oblique slants across the island now. Up and down the beach the rich, late-afternoon rays pick out auburn little foxes detaching themselves from the shadows of the dunes to forage on whatever the sea has tossed up. Walking back, we notice a small pine forest being enveloped by dunes, cresting over it in slow motion as if transmitting the rawer, faster fury of the ocean combers. The trees are dying, bent toward the mainland, bare branches entreating skyward. Nothing that is too well-rooted can last here, I think, and I think about the billions of dollars poured into stabilizing the barrier islands at Miami, Cape Hatteras, along the Jersey coast, and other places in this lovely, shifting chain of sand that runs intermittently from Labrador to Texas.

During the boat ride back to the mainland, a sea fog begins rolling in through Quinby Inlet. No "little cat feet" to this dreadnaught. It has on seven-league boots, moving lots faster than a 9.9-horsepower Evinrude can push a skiff. By the time we dock, you cannot see the mouth of the harbor one hundred feet away. The next day's forecast is high winds and near freezing. You can't count on late March in these regions; but we have plucked enough blossoms from the Virginia sea islands on this voyage to stead us well into warmer weather.

The Bottom of the Bay

*Broad, beautiful, productive, mysterious, polluted . . . how many are
the adjectives we reach for in trying to describe our beloved Chesapeake.
I would suggest a new one that may lend some perspective to most of
the others. When you think of the bay, think* THIN.

When the Army Corps of Engineers constructed its hydraulic research model of the Chesapeake Bay, visitors from far and wide came
to marvel at the length and breadth of the project. Duplicating the bay's
195-mile length and 30-mile width in concrete, even at a scale of 1,000:1,
made the model a sort of regional eighth wonder of the world. It took a
fourteen-acre building, slightly larger than the base of the Cheops
great pyramid, to house it at Matapeake, on Kent Island. Standing in
Norfolk, you could barely make out Baltimore in the dim recesses of
the building's other side. The model's computer-driven pumps, using
a water supply big enough for a town of five thousand people, could
simulate a year of the bay's tidal cycles in a few days.

But if you asked the engineers who conceived the model what was
its greatest challenge, they seldom mentioned any of the above. Look at
the water in the concrete channels, they would say. *Look how little of it
there was.* The deepest part of the huge model was only a couple feet;
and most of it was only a few inches. Even that represented some
rather large-scale deviation from the scale of the bay model's more
spectacular horizontal dimensions. At a thousandth of life size, had
the engineers scaled the depth truly, the deepest hole in the deepest
channel of this, North America's greatest estuary, would have contained less than a couple inches of water; and the model for most of
its fourteen acres would have been covered by nothing more than a
heavy dew.

So shallow, so thin is our bay that its average depth, across more
than one million acres in Maryland, is substantially less than the
length of most watermen's workboats. More than 10 percent of the bay

in our state has been estimated to be less than a meter in depth. A great blue heron could stalk it without wetting more than its tail feathers. I, who measure precisely two meters, could, with nose held high, traverse nearly a quarter of the bay on foot. This is anything but an idle curiosity. So much of what makes the bay a unique marvel, also much of the reason it is uniquely vulnerable, follows from this simple fact: its bottom is very near its top.

I became intimate with the bay's bottom early on in life. As an apprentice duck hunter, I sacrificed more than one pair of hip boots to the lusty, sucking mud gods that dwell in the bottoms of its creeks. Name the type of boat, and I have probably been aground in it. Where I grew up boating, around Hoopers Island, anytime we could not see bottom under the hull we considered ourselves in a major ship channel. Knowing the slightest deviations in the bottom—that it was a foot or so deeper if you ran closer to some shores, for example—could make the difference between getting somewhere and waiting for the tide to rise. I doubt you could have given a Hooper Islander a cabin cruiser if it took much more than a meter of water to float it. Anyone who has truly explored the bay by boat will know the truth of what the oyster skipjack captains say: "If you ain't been aground, you ain't never been nowhere." Positively the best name I ever heard for a bay boat was *Despot's Heel*, as in *"The despot's heel is on thy shore, Maryland, my Maryland!"* (first stanza).

Our long and close familiarity with the bay bottom has endowed it with a rich variety of names, such as Chinese Muds, Terrapin Sands, and Clay Leaves, to describe its every color and texture. Bay watermen often speak of where they were, not in any mapped coordinates, but thus: "I caught eels on the mud, then I moved down to the hard but didn't do no good"; and, "They was scarce arysters on the rock pile, but we did good on the cinders." I once watched an oyster-dredging captain maneuver his skipjack fruitlessly for an hour in the space of a few acres just to get on what he called "a kind o' oozy, easy bottom, a little cindery, but not exactly"; and when he finally hit the narrow strip, he caught fifty bushels of the biggest oysters I had ever seen.

Other arrangements of the bottom are variously identified as lumps, shoals, rocks, swashes, hollows, hills, holes, and dreens (drains). In most cases these involve departures from the horizontal of a few feet at most. A repertoire of bottom stories has grown up in the folklore of watermen. Many involve variations on an old sailing cap'n who can tell where he is on the darkest night, anywhere in the bay without leaving his bunk, just by sniffing the mud on the anchor when the crew hoists it. In a version of this, well-told by the late Alex Kellam of Crisfield, the crew plays a joke on the captain, smearing the anchor in the droppings of some chickens that were aboard to supply meat and eggs, then passing it below to the skipper. He inhales deeply and says: "If I didn't know we were in sixty foot of water right off the mouth of the Patuxent River, I'd swear I was in my old lady's chicken coop."

If the bay bottom is locally familiar, some of the animals that live there are world-famous. It is unmatched in the known universe for growing immense quantities of the highly edible mollusk known as *Crassostrea virginica*, the American oyster. Ideal conditions for the bivalves include depths from around two to ten meters; and the bay, with an average depth of twenty-seven feet, could not be better situated. As much as a half-million acres, nearly half the total bay bottom in Maryland, is considered suitable for the growth of oysters. An estimated three billion oysters currently populate the bottom now. A century ago as many as seventy-five billion resided there before pollution and overfishing took a heavy toll.

Oysters grow admirably in waters many times deeper than those of the bay, in places like Puget Sound, Nova Scotia, Portugal, and the Far East—but there they are grown in floats, or on ropes suspended from buoys. The difference is that between the corporate aquaculture of those places and the rich subculture of independent bay watermen that has evolved here. Virtually everything we celebrate about our Chesapeake oystermen, from skipjacks to hand-tonging, flows from having an easily accessible bottom, one close to the top. The bay poet Gilbert Byron once wrote of "Hip-booted men, with long tongs," who "rake the bar of oysters bare":

Men who never wrote a line
Are the greatest poets ever.
Verses of love inscribed upon
The bottom of the cove.

On every oyster-bearing patch of bottom in the bay, the waterman has left his colorful stamp in the names he has given them. One of the state's finer little contributions to bay literature was its *Index and Cross Reference to the Common and Official Names of Natural Oyster Bars*, published in 1976. More than one thousand bars are listed, lying in the waters of twelve counties. Windmill Point, Bald Eagle, Pigpen, Sheep Pen, Cantaloupe Field, Watermelon Point, Buzzard Roost, Peach Orchard, Pine Tree, Pear Tree, Cherry Tree, Potato Hill—more faithfully than anything left on land, they portray the bay edge as it must have appeared a century or more ago to watermen on the creeks and rivers. Other names are more esoteric, their origins in many cases lost forever: Chicken Cock, Gibson Girl, Daddie Dare, Butter Pot; and France, Marumsco, Benoni, and Kingcopisico; also Normans Fine Eyes, Hollicutt

Noose (also Hollaga Snooze), Black Beard, and Blue Sow; not to mention Twitch Cove, Whalloper's Gut, Roaring Point, Apes Hole, Bugby, and Bungay. I suspect no other body of water in the world has so evocative a bottom as the Chesapeake Bay.

Nor as provocative. Anyplace encrusted with so much wealth in the form of shellfish was bound to stir strong emotions. During the previous century Maryland was forced to mount an Oyster Navy to combat the heavily armed pirates who were dredging the bay's rich shellfish beds into oblivion. An oyster war of equal intensity was waged in councils of government between 1897 and 1904. A Baltimore City sewage commission had recommended discharging the burgeoning city's raw wastes to the open bay: "There would appear to be but little reason why the City of Baltimore should deny itself the facilities and advantages which nature has vouchsafed to it, namely the diluting effect of the bay . . . May not Baltimore, without offense to others purify herself in the broad waters of this great bay without thereby disturbing or annoying any existing interest?"

Even the medical community in those days was not sure it was such a bad idea; but the oystermen of the Chesapeake felt strongly that it could ruin public perception of oysters as a quality product; and in that era, the rural counties had the votes in the legislature to win such showdowns. The way Baltimore likes to tell it nowadays, its forward thinking made it the first major city in the country to adopt sanitary sewage treatment; but the truth is that it was the oyster that forced the issue.

That was scarcely the last round in the politico-legal history of the bay bottom. Pleasure boaters skimming across the bay's surface may perceive it as gloriously unfenced, a welcome change from the stoplights, one-way streets, and traffic congestion of the land. But just below them, the hills and hollows and dreens and lumps of the bottom are zoned by state regulation as precisely as any dry region of Maryland. This bottom is for clamming, that for oyster dredging; that for hand-tonging, this for oyster diving; no anchored gill nets above this point, no staked pound nets below that island; this area for dredge spoil-disposal, no dumping during spawning season; crab pots in this tributary but not past the mouth; this area closed to all shellfish harvesting by pollution—check the health department for further notices of closures . . . and so forth. There has not been a year since the Civil War when the Maryland legislature did not have before it several bills dealing with modifications in uses of the bay bottom.

The greatest and most controversial of these bay-bottom issues, however, the lawmakers have debated inconclusively for at least one hundred years. Should the bottom remain a common property, open to any citizen of the state who wants to pay the nominal fee to harvest its shellfish? Or should it be parceled out through state leases to private "farmers," a system that probably would lead to more efficient, but considerably less colorful, harvesting of oysters. The watermen say that would result in big companies forcing out the little man. A Frank Perdue of oysters would surely be the result.

But with the unprecedented decline of natural oyster reproduction in recent years, pressure for aquaculture on the bay bottom is building. Imagine the powerful new constituency for water quality a privatized bottom might create. A capitalist system may not always heed the cries of environmentalists or fishermen that the water quality is declining; but you can bet it would react quickly if the Frank Perdue of oysters complained that his multimillion-dollar business and thousands of employees were in jeopardy. Nonetheless, such a scenario would involve nothing less than transforming a hunter-gatherer way of life into an agricultural one—a transition that on land, centuries ago, reshaped the course of humankind. So far, we have been reluctant to take that step with the bay bottom, one of the last places in the developed world that still permits an anachronistic life style like that of the waterman to coexist in the shadow of modern cities. Fewer than ten thousand acres of the million-acre bottom currently are under private leases.

Until quite recently in our involvement with the bay, we have concerned ourselves with its bottom mostly as it related to our bellies and our commerce—maintaining its harvestable edibles and, through perpetual dredging, its suitability for shipping and ports. As it often turns out with natural systems, the bay bottom's most directly useful functions to us are not at all what is most important about it. When H. L. Mencken called the bay an "immense protein factory," he could not have known how apt a phrase he was coining. The productivity of the Chesapeake Bay—that is to say its ability to produce quantities of biological life, from algae on up to oysters and rockfish—is ten to one hundred times the average productivity of the open oceans. New England's Georges Bank, one of the greatest fishing spots on earth, a magnet for the commercial fleets of every fishing nation, yields about three tons of seafood per square mile. The Chesapeake Bay yields about twelve tons. At its peak historic harvest of around fifteen million bushels of oysters a year in the 1880s (a harvest that was not a sustainable one, to be sure), it was estimated that the edible meat of shellfish produced from Maryland's bay alone was equal to the flesh of 160,000 prime head of beef.

Such productivity is not just astounding, it is absolutely improbable. A basic unit of food production in the bay is phytoplankton, or algae—microscopic, floating plants on which most everything else feeds, directly or indirectly. The growth of phytoplankton, in turn, depends on supplies of two vital plant nutrients, nitrogen and phosphorus, which wash into the estuary when rain runs off the surrounding land, and from the discharges of sewage-treatment plants. But when scientists began to measure the inputs of such nutrients, they were surprised to find that even in periods of peak rainfall, when the rivers literally are blasting great cannon pulses of nitrogen and phosphorus into the bay, the amounts are only a small fraction of what it should take to fuel the immense protein production so celebrated by Mencken.

So how does the bay do more with less? An important part of the answer appears to be benthic regeneration, which for all practical purposes means this: each tiny phytoplankter absorbs nutrients from the water as it grows. As it dies, or is eaten and passed through a larger creature's gut, its remains fall to the bay bottom—think of it, baywide, as a never-ending rainfall. There, decomposition of the phytoplankton frees the nutrients for recycling into new phytoplankton, and so on and so on. This is further enhanced by similar processes of nutrient regeneration going on in the water column itself.

Although all bodies of water—oceans, rivers, lakes—do this to an extent, the bay pulls off the recycling trick better and faster than just about anyplace on earth. Perhaps its closest competitor is in the earth's tropical rain forests, where the same rapid recycling of nutrients from the constant fall and decomposition of plant matter enables mighty jungles to maintain themselves atop soils that are the least fertile in the world. And a major reason in the bay's world-class ability to do this? It is, of course, because its bottom, where so much of the recycling occurs, is so close to its top, where the sunlight most favors the growth of phytoplankton. (Remember its average depth of twenty-seven feet? The average distance of the oceans' bottom from the top is about twelve thousand feet. The nutrients that fall to such depths never get back into action in any meaningful time scale.)

Put another way, the bay simply has a higher metabolism than most other bodies of water. Scientists shrink from careless use of terms such as *metabolism*, which relate more to living organisms, in describing something like the bottom of an estuary. Yet the more they come to know about the complex and sophisticated mechanisms through which the bay bottom influences the rest of the system, the thinner the line gets between what is sentient and what is not. Just see how the bottom handles a problem that, by all rights, should thwart even the most sophisticated nutrient-recycling from keeping the bay so incredibly productive. The problem is that, throughout history, nutrients have not entered the bay in anything approximating a constant or predictable flow. They flood the system in the spring, when river runoff from the land is high; but during the winter and in dry summers, the flows of rivers, and the nutrients they carry, may fall to a tiny fraction of the spring cornucopia. Creatures in the system, however, have to live year-round; they need a fairly steady supply of food. What to do, to maximize the efficiency of such a chaotic chow line?

What the bay appears to have done is to evolve some first-rate banking, or storage systems, to harness the pulses of food energy and make them flow more smoothly into the circuits of oysters and rockfish and the like. Again, the secret lies in its bottom—by now, one should have forever stopped thinking of it as so much inert muck. Throughout the shallows of the Chesapeake, which is to say much of the bay, great beds of underwater grasses have flourished during most of its history. Boaters curse them for fouling propellers. Biologists know, however, their immense values as habitat for the young of fish, food for ducks, and shelter for soft crabs until they can reform their hard shells. It is a wondrous experience to watch a Smith Island soft-crabber pull up the dredge he has dragged through the great eelgrass beds of Tangier Sound. The thigh-thick roll of olive grass that the dredge has combed from the bottom will literally throb with all manner of marine life, from baby crabs to sea horses, and grass shrimp to small Norfolk spot. The grass beds of the bay bottom also filter sediment from the water and suppress wave motion, stabilizing shorelines against erosion. But all that is not the most critical role of these bay-bottom meadows, the scientists now realize. Recent evidence shows they are capable of alternately absorbing and releasing large quantities of nitrogen and phosphorus. Their period of maximum growth in the spring coincides with the time of maximum nutrient runoff to the bay. Then, in the late fall, when the bay is getting little nutrient input from the rivers, the grasses die back, releasing vital food supplies to sustain phytoplankton production.

So far, so good, but what about in the summertime, when the rivers may run even drier than in the fall in droughty years? How does the bay stoke its engines of production then? Evidence here is more preliminary, but again, it seems clear that the system depends to a large degree on its bottom. The relatively high river flows into the bay that occur each spring tend to set up a condition known as *stratification*, which for much of the summer can partially seal off the bay's bottom from its top.

The lighter, fresher river water, running seaward, ceases to mix with denser ocean water moving upbay along the bottom. It is sometimes described as if a lid had been clamped over the bottom, although that probably is a little dramatic. Nonetheless, the effect is that the oxygen-rich surface layers do not mix as much as usual with the bottom layers. Bacteria and other life on the bottom rapidly consume the oxygen in the water there. The resulting conditions, in turn, can favor chemical and biological reactions that put back into circulation tremendous quantities of nutrients that the bay has been "banking" in its bottom sediments.

All this is why fantastic productivity literally is the Chesapeake Bay's "bottom line." But just in the last twenty-five years or so, for the first time in the bay's several millennia, we quite literally have changed the bottom line, with ominous results. The elegant and productive interactions of bay bottom with bay top all evolved in a context of relative nutrient scarcity. The heavily forested watershed, largely undisturbed before white settlement of the region, permitted substantially less runoff of nitrogen and phosphorus and thus relatively little growth of the phytoplankton, which today, along with excessive runoff of sediment, makes the water so opaque.

Indeed, many scientists think that for most of the time it has existed, so few nutrients entered the bay that its waters were quite clear—not Caribbean clear, but closer to the transluscence of a mountain lake than the turbid conditions we are familiar with these days. There is plenty of anecdotal evidence that it was normal to see the bay bottom in many areas through twelve or more feet of water as recently as the 1940s. But with the enormous growth of nutrient-rich sewage discharges to the bay in modern times, and the even more rapid growth in agriculture's use of nitrogen and phosphorus fertilizers throughout its watershed, the bay has become glutted with the very stuff its bottom had programed itself to use so efficiently throughout the millennia. The feedback has been akin to what you would get from throwing kerosene onto a fire that already was burning heartily.

The excess nutrient is growing excess phytoplankton. In turn, this algae consumes oxygen as it decays on the bay bottom each summer, causing what appears to be a dramatic historical increase in the volume of water unfit for aquatic life. Lately this foul-smelling, deathly bottom water seems to have been reaching out of the deep channels to devastate the bay's productive shellfish beds. Crabbers tell of pulling their traps from water less than ten-feet deep, only to find the crabs have died from lack of oxygen. Meanwhile, the oxygen depletion liberates more nutrients from the bottom sediments, which grow more phytoplankton, which perpetuate oxygen depletion, which liberates more nutrients . . . If ever there was a time the bay could use the capacity of its submerged grass beds to help absorb excess nutrients, it is now. It has been estimated that the grasses have the potential to soak up fully half of all the nutrients we now discharge into the bay from sewage. But the grasses, just when they are needed most, are in serious decline, covering perhaps 10 percent of the bottom area, where they flourished just a few decades ago. Had devastation of similar magnitude occurred on land, with the state's forests, the outcry would have been intense long before 90 percent of the trees were gone; but for more than a decade, the denuding of the bay bottom was officially ascribed to "natural cycles" or unknown causes. The real answer to the mysterious decline—and with it perhaps the best hope for someday regaining the quality of the Chesapeake waters—did not come until we learned yet another vital lesson about the bottom of the bay.

Because we tended to see it simply as a fluid medium, we routinely underestimated the bay's capacity to remember environmental insults. Surely, we thought, with constant flushing and renewal from the rivers and the ocean, mistakes never would pile up as they did on land. It was a comforting notion, but scientists who have begun learning how to consult the bay's memory are not consoled. With a coring device they extract gray-brown cylinders from the bay's bottom, a distance down through the muck of several feet, but a journey back through time of a thousand years. Grain by grain, layer by layer, a few micrometers a year, the sediments washing off the 64,000-square-mile watershed that extends from New York to West Virginia have compiled a rich natural historical library, awaiting only a generation of readers skilled enough to translate it.

At a depth of two meters, in a layer deposited when Columbus was underway to the Americas, the copious pollen of oaks testifies that the great eastern climax forest was still intact, and the bay's waters, fed by rainfall filtered through a deep, continuous carpet of leaf duff on the forest floor, must have been clearer than any living person has ever known. Just over a meter down in the sediments, the ratio of oak to ragweed pollen shifts significantly toward the latter, telling of the agricultural field-clearing—greater than anything we have today—that marked the nineteenth century. One particularly convenient marker for the scientists comes in the abrupt disappearance from the cores of chestnut pollen at a depth corresponding to the 1920s, when a blight swept North America, annihilating the species.

Pollen is not the only volume available in the bay's archival bottom. Changes found there in the abundance and species composition of diatoms, the skeletal remains of microscopic plankton, reflect the vissicitudes of changing water quality. A learned reading of the muck divulges tales of great storms and droughts, of acid mine drainage down the Susquehanna from the Pennsylvania coal booms, and of the advent of modern sewage treatment. But it is when we get to the topmost couple inches of sediment that perhaps the most dramatic chapters are written.

Until this last moment in the bay's long history, one theme had remained constant throughout the cores, through all the centuries before European settlement, through the massive and rapid transformations of the watershed from forest to field to pavement. In all this time of change, tiny seeds preserved in the sediments revealed a constant presence of the bay's great underwater meadows of grasses. The bay bottom, in the topmost skim of those sediment cores, at long last disclosed the truth, that the widespread disappearance of the grasses, beginning around 1968, was no natural cycle. Something dramatically new was operating in the Chesapeake environment. After a thousand years, something vital in the web of life in the estuary had broken. We have, in studies that fill a couple of good-sized volumes, traced the demise of the grasses to an excess of sediment and chemicals flowing from farm fields, sewage plants, and development; or, as one of the principal scientists in the study succinctly put it, "too much shit and too much dirt." Had he chosen to be a little less scientific, he might have added, "and too little caring about it." We had been pushing the land in the watershed hard, growing more corn, housing more people, and it had begun to backfire into our waters. It is proof that not only are we connected to the bay in our everyday living but also that we have come to dominate its most basic natural systems—and come to dominate them despite spending literally billions of dollars since the 1960s on pollution controls designed to prevent such an occurrence.

"Things fall apart," Yeats said, "the centre cannot hold." It remains an open question whether we will see the denuded, oxygenless bottom brought back into some measure of synchrony with the thin skim of water atop it, and dependent on it, that we know as the Chesapeake Bay. Now public commitment to restoring the bay is running at an all-time high. Throughout the watershed, people and their elected leaders are gabbling excitedly about the prospects, as a flock of geese gets raucous just before lifting off for new feeding grounds. The challenge is infectious, the script outline looks promising; but just as yet, the library at the bottom of the bay reads caution.

Messing About in Boats

There is nothing—absolutely nothing—half so much worth doing as simply messing about in boats," said Rat as he introduced Mole to the river in Kenneth Grahame's wondrous tale *The Wind in the Willows*. Wiser words have seldom been written, but Rat's point, I am convinced, is more subtle than mere advocacy of the waterborne life. There are boats, and then there are boats for messing about, and one should not confuse the two.

I own one of the latter, a messing-about gem of the first water. I could not afford it in 1977 when I bought it, and sometimes I cannot afford it now. Neither could I imagine life without it. It may intrigue nonboaters to know that a boat garaged for want of funds to fix its engine, or to buy reliable tires for its trailer, still is far, far better than no boat; just its potential to take one messing about is endless license to doodle and plan and plot and dream.

My boat, for the record, is a nineteen-footer, fiberglass inside and out. Its motor is a Chrysler outboard of moderate horsepower, with pull-rope starter and tiller steering. The Chrysler, reviled in some quarters for its unsophisticated design, can be virtually disassembled at sea with a Sears adjustable wrench. It has no steering cables to break and no electric starter to die on you. The pull rope will test your cardiovascular capacity severely on a morning cold enough to require more than five heaves on it, but a short breather and hot coffee have so far always recharged the principal starting mechanism. Some say my boat resembles a bathtub; others say that it is too light in the bow, or that its handling is less than crisp. Its builder, the late Francis Klemm, was a banker who late in life quit the Equitable Trust Company in Baltimore, got a Small Business Administration loan, and set to building boats at Eagle Island, in the shadow of the battleship *North Carolina*. He was still learning, he conceded, when he built mine, but he made me a good price—about $1,300, hull only. I have since enhanced the craft's utility with the addition of two large, green canvas and wood beach umbrellas that can be fastened near bow and stern to provide both shade and, unlike commercial Bimini tops, unimpeded scope out either side for fishing rods, oyster and crab dredges, phytoplankton tow nets, and other vital equipment. I also fancy the umbrellas make a rather striking appearance.

Otherwise the boat is utterly simple, which is the next to most important rule of messing about. You cannot enjoy peace of mind in something featuring pleated vinyl and shag carpeting and deeply gleaming gel-coat finish and chrome, the kind of boat that sports a little plaque saying, "Welcome aboard. Remove shoes." Some of my most enjoyable trips, for instance, have been made with Kinga, a potter friend who always makes it a point to bring aboard, in leaky bags and clinging to her shoes and legs, a hundredweight or so of oozing, muddy clay representative of whatever marsh or river of the bay we happen to be messing about. Because of its impurities, most Chesapeake Bay clay is better suited to underpinning salt marsh than for firing in a kiln. But even lousy clay, Kinga figures, can make good memories, preserved in "Wye River coffee mugs" and "Holland Island bowls."

Now I come to the most critical feature of my boat, the very essence of messing about in a system like the Chesapeake Bay. My boat, with the motor down, draws less than eighteen inches and, with propeller cocked up, the whole show floats in about nine inches of water. The bay's shallow nature—average depth, including main channels, around 27 feet—is perhaps its dominant physical characteristic. Consider how much of the estuary's nature and charm is derived from having expanses of bottom accessible to sunlight and to terrestrial creatures, including human beings. The list includes marshes and marsh critters, clams and oysters (and clammers and oystermen); also submerged beds of eelgrass and the soft crabs that shed there, and the Smith and Deal Islanders who scrape them up for a living. And stalking great blue herons, never far from the shallow interface of land and water, dabbling ducks like blacks and mallards, and rockfish taken from the bank on evening flood tides; and the shoal-draft designs of all manner of bay workboats, from skipjacks with their pull-up, centerboard keels, to the classic old Hooper Island draketails. An attribute of the draketail reportedly was its ability to let watermen escape marine policemen by darting across bars too shallow to allow pursuit. A deeper bay, perhaps ringed by high cliffs, would no doubt be aesthetic, and its waters lively enough, biologically speaking; but so much would then be going on out of our depth, so to speak. A less intimate relationship between our race and the bay would be the result.

Just how astoundingly shallow our Chesapeake is has been calculated recently by J. Court Stevenson, a University of Maryland marine researcher. In Maryland alone nearly 10 percent of the bay's area—111,891 acres, or 175 square miles—is a meter deep or less. When the draft of your boat falls below a meter or so, a new country suddenly opens its borders to you. Drop your draft requirements to around a foot and another world of the shoal bay, beyond even one-meter territory, begs to be explored. Plenty of times I have prowled the perimeter of large reaches of the bay, or the mouth of a sinuous creek carrying away to who-knows-where within a marsh, wishing wholeheartedly that my boat drew only six inches instead of nine.

Several winters ago, I found myself in a duck blind with a waterman friend who remarked casually, after we had shot several fowl, that the reason for our success lay in several bags of corn that covered the bottom. I won't claim I was shocked, but I was worried—"SUNPAPERS ENVIRONMENTAL WRITER JAILED FOR DUCK BAITING!!!" I could see the headlines. Not to worry, my friend said. Sweeping his arm in a wide arc indicating the thousands of acres of water surrounding our blind, he explained none of it was more than six inches deep, plenty to float a decoy, but far too little for the game warden's boat or float plane to approach. Indeed, it was well past dark before enough tide came in to let us depart in our tiny, flat-bottomed skiff.

My boat, its design in synch with this essential shallowness of the bay, has transported me to one of the Eastern Shore's loveliest coves, a place of quiet, deep water in which every sailboater on the bay would kill to anchor, only its mouth is far too shallow to admit most of them. In spring and fall I also journey to my "private" three thousand–acre bay island, where you can stay in an abandoned hunting lodge, all paneled in half-inch–thick knotty pine, and dine on the oysters and mussels almost within reach of the shore, but where at low tide any boat that cannot float in substantially less than a foot of water has to flee. I have probed the limits of a couple creeks on the Nanticoke River which harbor some of the state's rarest shrubs and plants in variety beyond all botanical explanation—unless the reason is simply their long isolation from all but diehard messers-about. And I think I have found the bay's most meditative anchorage—a brackish pond off a western shore river where entry is precarious even at high water; but once inside, the ebb and flood of water through the narrow channel forges a tangible link between a viewer and the cosmic respiration of the tides. If someone were to film the procession of life passing in and out of the narrow mouth of the pond in a complete tide cycle, it would make a better documentary of the estuary's incredible life than anything I could write.

Some caution is in order for those who, having acquired a proper craft, are preparing to do some messing about. Its joys are fragile ones and will wilt away in the face of overseriousness and elevation to a major American sport, such as has overtaken bass fishing. You will know the worst has happened should the Chris Craft people ever come to market with a "Messing About Boat." Personally, I find such expeditions best approached obliquely. I can't recall ever mentioning, in preparing for a boat trip, that I am setting out "to mess about." I prefer to mumble something, on departure, about going fishing, camping, or needing to test a new prop or compass. The best messing-about trips may not just happen, but they should seem as if they did.

Because messing about seems connected mostly with the smaller, quiet corners of the bay, you might think: Why bother with something so ungainly as a half-ton, nineteen-foot, motorized boat for such stuff? Why not get a canoe, or a kayak, either of which will float on a heavy dew and fit atop a car? Often I do crowd one or both types of craft into my boat for extended trips. But reaching my favorite marsh island requires a five-mile open-water crossing. It is virtually inaccessible to so frail a vessel as a canoe; and there are even greater expanses of shoal waters, like the coastal bays that lead out to Virginia's beautiful sea islands, where distances, currents, and potential for storms make even small, slow powerboats untenable transport in the best of times. This leads to a final, critical aspect of a true messing-about boat: it must be a compromise. Virtually all boats *are* compromises, of course, and mine is more so than most. It is hopelessly heavy and unmaneuverable by canoe standards, and scandalously lacking in accommodations compared to sailboats of less length and beam; and as a bay-ranging powerboat, though it will take some heavy weather, it offers one of the wetter, pound-the-fillings-out-of-your-teeth rides to be had. Its high sides make it handle just awful in a beam wind, but they are perfect for containing crabbers between the ages of three and six. It is, in short, well-suited for absolutely no single thing, which makes it just right for messing about. As Rat said to Mole, agog to find the latter had never before messed about in boats: "Then what *have* you been doing?!"

Low Tide for a Skipjack

> Come March I'm feelin' weary, and I long to go ashore
> My knees are growin' heels and toes, my back is bent and sore
> I've culled 2,000 bushels and I'm rusted to the bone
> Wind and water whistles where my muscles used to roam.
> —from "Dredgin' Is My Drudgery," a song of skipjacks and
>   oystering by Tom Wisner

*A*board the skipjack *Sigsbee*, it's cold and windy, and the rain has not quit since we headed up the Choptank from Tilghman Island many sodden hours ago. The day began at 4:30 A.M., and it did not begin well for Wadey Murphy, the *Sigsbee's* captain. In the open bay, there is no more graceful sight than skipjacks, North America's last working sail fleet, as they wheel and glide, plowing the oyster beds with twin dredges under full canvas. But in close quarters, sails down and powered only by an ungainly little yawl boat strapped to their stern, the beamy, fifty-foot craft are brontosaurs. Leaving Knapp's Narrows in the slippery, chill predawn with a strong tide running, Wadey's crew failed to hold the *Sigsbee* to the dock until he could point her bow into the channel. Drifting broadside, artless as a flounder, the skipjack came embarrassingly near to crashing against the Narrows draw bridge.

"Christ a-mighty! Think you never been aboard a boat! Modern-day crews don't know, don't care! Twenty years ago there were sail people; now, they just happen to be working on a sailboat . . ." The captain's treatise, hurled into the dark and the wet, continued well out into the Choptank. The sun tried to rise, thought immediately better of it, and tinged the eastern horizon a sickly orange with its sulking. Sunup marks the start of legal dredging. Every time Wadey sent the telephone pole of a boom flying over the deck to come about for another "lick" with his dredges, icy rain water sloshed down on us from the reefs in the *Sigsbee*'s sail. On our first several licks the mighty iron dredges, each of which could hold a grown man, yield four keeping-size oysters. Wadey, wrestling the wheel with his short, wiry frame, says he comes from a "drudgin" (dredging) family. His father, eighty-three and slowed by the death of his wife, has only recently stopped captaining a skipjack; and his grandfather dredged until the day he drowned. Drudgin' is his birthright, but it was days like this, Wadey allows, that almost made him reconsider after quitting school twenty-six years ago to sail-dredge oysters full time.

This is the winding down of the skipjacks' season, the part seldom witnessed by any of the thousands who flock each autumn to Chesapeake Appreciation Days by the Bay Bridges to celebrate the season's start on 1 November. Then the old skipjacks, gathered off Sandy Point to race for the crowd, are freshly painted and the air has a bright, mellow tang, promising pearls of days for the oystermen. The bay bottom is pregnant with a long summer's undisturbed growth of oysters, and the captains and crews are expectant of short workdays in the pleasant air to make their limit of 150 bushels a boat.

But now it is March. Season goes out at sunset tomorrow. The skipjack fleet lies battle-scarred in ports like Cambridge and Tilghman and Wenona and Solomons, decks and sides worn to bare wood, ropes frayed, bilge pumps working round-the-clock. The *Sigsbee*, built in 1901 and named after a ship's officer blown up with the *Maine* in Havana Harbor, is feeling her age. Just one more day of dredging and she will get a rest and a whole lot of new wood she needs in her port side,

Wadey says. I notice he checks his bilge pumps frequently.

The bay bottom also is nearly exhausted, having been scraped and raked and plucked of its marketable shellfish by thousands of dredgers, tongers, and scuba divers, until you wonder how it can ever recover by the next fall. It always seems to, though. Small oysters, those below the minimum, 3-inch harvest size, can grow rapidly over one summer. Nonetheless, in recent years the oysters have been rebounding to lower and lower levels. This year will set a modern record of sorts. The harvest for Maryland's Chesapeake Bay, which a century ago yielded from six million to eight million bushels of oysters a year, will total about one million bushels this year. A paltry quarter-billion or so oysters, this will be the lowest catch since the 1840s, when the bay's richest shellfish beds were just being discovered. Oysters are as scarce as he has seen them in his life, says Wadey, who is forty-two. Fortunately oysters also have been scarce outside the bay. Freakish rains lowered the salinity, killing lots of the beds along the Gulf coast, the bay's main competition. As a result, prices have been extraordinary, as high as $17 a bushel. But in the long run, "I think we are in real trouble," Wadey says.

Where the *Sigsbee* is dredging on this miserable late-winter day is probably the best illustration of how lean the bay's oyster population has grown. We are in shoal water off the mouth of Trappe Creek, where even a small outboard would have to navigate with caution, and where a 47-foot sailing vessel like the *Sigsbee* normally would never go. The skipjack, which began to evolve for dredging oysters in the 1870s, is a monument to the bay's great shallowness. It has an almost flat bottom, with a retractable centerboard instead of a fixed keel, and many a pleasure sailor has run hard aground when blithely following one of the big sail dredgers across a bar, never dreaming it drew as little as three feet of water. Even so, today Wadey is pushing the limits. The depth cannot be more than four feet, and the bottom is strewn with boulders big as pumpkins. We are dredging so close to shore that the tip of the boom sometimes seems almost to touch the bank. With tension plain on his face, the *Sigsbee*'s captain tries to edge in even closer. Mud boils from beneath the wooden hull, and the whole stern lifts as it scrapes over stones. One of the two crewmen manning the starboard dredge looks hard at Wadey, but says nothing. Under full sail, if a dredge were to hang on a solid enough obstruction it could rip the side out of the *Sigsbee*, or snap the rusted dredge cable, with deadly results for anyone in its line of recoil.

Wadey says he knows there are a few "choice spots" of oysters close to the beach among the stone piles. All season he figured to come here if the pickings got really slim. If he could only get at them; but the tide, held out by northerly winds all morning, refuses to rise. Another time, just when he has found a spot with enough depth to make a few serious licks, the wind falls off. He cannot put enough of the center-board down to maneuver as he ought. All the *Sigsbee* can do is prowl, frustrated, up and down the Choptank shore, catching tons of stone in her dredges, waiting for just the right combination of wind and tide and bottom to unlock the last small store of harvestable shellfish Wadey Murphy knows of anywhere in the Chesapeake Bay.

High noon, still low tide, and the decks hold perhaps a dozen bushels of oysters from what has been, so far, eight hard hours of work for the *Sigsbee*'s captain and four crew. At today's market of about $15 a bushel that is $180. The money traditionally is split a third for "the boat" (that is, Murphy), a couple percent taken out to cover the crew's food and gasoline for the yawl, or "push" boat, and the motors that wind the dredges. The rest is split equally among the captain and four crew members. On days when the *Sigsbee* gets its limit of 150 bushels, that is pretty good money for all—enough for the captain to get wealthy, it might seem, until you consider all the iced-up days in January and February, the days with no wind to sail, and the cost of repairs to octogenarian wooden boats. The *Sigsbee* recently needed a new mast, which cost $5,000.

It is 1:00 P.M. and we still seek "the spot." Even in better years, such tiny areas are about all that is left to be harvested by this time of year. Season's end is the time of maximum resourcefulness for the skipjack captains, who must hunt for the little mound overlooked by the rest of the dredge fleet, or the narrow edge of an oyster bar that was too steep for the tongers to harvest with their scissorlike rakes. It does not take much to make a bad day into a good one, Wadey says. He has taken five hundred bushels off a spot no bigger than he could turn the *Sigsbee* about in. Most of the bay's three dozen or so surviving skipjacks have packed it in by this time of year. They simply can't catch enough consistently to keep crews, who work wholly on shares and collect only a hearty lunch and breakfast as fringe benefits. The weather is getting worse, the wind gusting to perhaps twenty-five knots. Russell Dize's *Katherine*, the only other member of the sixteen-boat Tilghman fleet that even put out this morning, has left in disgust, virtually empty-handed. One of the *Sigsbee*'s crew, wrestling another stone of about one hundred pounds from the dredge, looks as if he does not share his captain's conviction that we should wait longer on the tide in hopes of finding more oysters. Wadey says that reminds him of an old captain in the same situation who apologized to his crew this way: "Don't worry, boys. Those other boats may have beaten us in this after-noon, but by *God*, we'll beat 'em out tomorrow morning!"

Of course, had this been Monday or Tuesday, instead of Wednesday, our problems would have been largely solved, Wadey says. Monday and Tuesday are "push days," first legislated in the early 1970s when it seemed as if skipjacks were about to disappear. They allow the boats to drop the little craft they carry lashed across their sterns to power the dredges over the bottom. Power-dredging is to sail-dredging what house painting is to portraiture. There is little art to the former, but you cover lots of territory. It is efficient, if not beautiful. On Tuesday the *Sigsbee* had power-dredged ninety-nine bushels. It might seem ironic that Wadey and other Tilghman Island skipjack captains formed an association this year to convince the state to set aside more areas of the Choptank for "sail-only," with no power-dredging allowed even on Mondays and Tuesdays. The problem, he says, is that power-dredging is too efficient. The only reason there are still oysters here off Trappe Creek is that it is a sail-only area, the only one on the bay, he thinks.

It is hard to think of another industry that ponders how to make itself less efficient; but that has always been the paradox in Maryland's tradition of maintaining a public fishery on its hundreds of square miles of oyster bottoms, open to any resident of the state with the will to have at it. Ecologists call a fishery such as the one that exists on the bottom of the bay a *commons*, and there is a classic essay that describes the tragedy inherent in such an arrangement. A commons shared by all comers means to any individual that it is not in his interest to limit his own use of the commons—it will only be usurped by someone else. Were Wadey to sail-dredge on an airless Monday or Tuesday, in the interests of conserving oysters, the rest of the fleet would have a good laugh as they came in with 150 bushels to his 40 or 50. "More of 'em left for us to drudge," they would say.

Many of Maryland's regulations governing the oyster fishery— and they fill a good-sized book—are attempts to stave off such a tragedy of the commons by keeping the harvesters inefficient; limiting the use of power, the size of dredges, the type of machinery aboard. The very bay bottom in this attempt has been zoned into a bewildering complex of uses and exclusions. There are bottoms for hand-tongers only; bottoms for sail-dredgers only; bottoms for hand-tongers and skipjacks, but not for patent-tongers (who use hydraulically operated tongs raised and lowered by cable). Also bottoms for oystermen but not clammers, and for tongers but not oyster-divers.

The bottom is a source of endless challenge and fascination to those who dredge it. Like a golfer selecting just the right club for each shot, a skipjack captain will switch from mud dredges to shell dredges to edge dredges, and back, to match changes in the contour and texture of the bottom which can never be seen, but are felt through the vibrations of the dredge cables. His father, Wadey says, was one of the best edge-dredgers ever, while his Uncle Buck was perhaps best on mud bottoms.

In other respects, the dredges are undiscriminating. The top of *Sigsbee*'s cabin is piled with old propellers, with bricks from manor houses on islands long since gone beneath the waves; with the vertebra from something a lot bigger than anything presently swimming in the bay, and with a milk bottle from Twilly's Dairy in Cambridge, with a phone number, 574-W, and an oyster growing around its lip. Wadey says he has dredged up prehistoric sharks' teeth big as a man's palm, and still sharp.

But cut the chitchat. The day is wearing heavily on us all, and the tide has not yet turned. Wadey, looking about and seeing we are the only craft on the whole storm-tossed Choptank, is mulling dropping the push boat. Just a few licks under power, at $15 a bushel, could make enough of a payday to help captain and crew forget the last ten wet, bedeviling hours. Can this about-to-be scofflaw and anticonservationist be the same man who, with absolute sincerity, was just advocating that the whole river be declared a sail-only dredging bottom? Would the same Wadey who knows that oysters are scarcer than ever before in his lifetime also do everything in his power to catch the last oyster in the bay? Yes indeed; and the same would go for most of the skipjack captains I have met. This is what the tragedy of the commons is all about. If we don't get those oysters, someone else will someday, maybe tomorrow; so lower the yawl boat, boys. It ain't gettin' any drier out here, and the people I owe money back on the mainland don't want to hear how the tide wouldn't rise. Such is the terrible lure of the engine versus the caprice of the wind.

The truth is, it is hard, and maybe getting close to impossible, for the bay's oystermen to continue being living museum pieces, marvelous anachronisms, a subculture at once celebrated as free and independent yet underpinned by a bookful of legislated inefficiencies and a million-dollar-a-year state program that plants the bay bottom with shells and seed oysters each year (to augment natural oyster reproduction) as if it were the most managed of farms. We want so much more from Wadey Murphy and his kind than just oysters to eat. We expect them, and their boats and their way of life, to nourish something in our souls. The skipjack has taken its place with the Canada goose as a symbol of winter on the bay, an object whose mere sight—or even the knowledge that it is out there—evokes a whole range of good feelings about the Chesapeake region. We who come in ever-increasing numbers once a year to Chesapeake Appreciation Days, and who are willing to legislate and underwrite a host of artificial inefficiencies to maintain the illusion of Natural Man at work on our waters—we should not be shocked on the occasions when our cherished symbols drop the push boat.

The state's entire oyster fleet—tongers, divers, dredgers—all were in the Choptank at the start of the season, Wadey says. Hundreds of boats, working shoulder to shoulder. It made a glorious sight to motorists who saw it from the U.S. 50 bridge over the river at Cambridge, he acknowledges; but it was a bad sign for the commons. It meant, he says, that from Rock Hall to Smith Island there were no oysters left except here in his home river system. A state law used to regulate this, too, preventing oystermen from working outside their own county lines; but it was declared unconstitutional in 1971, and the pressure that now results on the commons is becoming nearly unbearable, Wadey says.

The Choptank can't take that kind of pressure, he says, even as he contemplates dropping the push boat. I can honestly tell you that I have never known Wadey to break the oyster laws of Maryland, because at that moment, around a point of land came the *Tar Bay*, a fast cruiser of the state Natural Resources Police. Whether they could read Wadey's mind, or whether they just did not have a blessed thing else to do, the police hove to in the vicinity of Trappe Creek and made it clear that they were there for the duration. We glared occasionally in their direction, envying the *Tar Bay*'s warm, capacious cabin.

Now it is past 2:30 P.M. and the tide stubbornly refuses to come up. The wind has begun building to what will become a forty-knot winter storm by late evening. We have a very rough two-hour sail back to Tilghman Island ahead of us, in a leaky old wooden boat that has been pounding on rocks all day. Wadey is a picture in frustration, teeth clenched, face raw from the weather, fighting a fierce head cold. "I hate to give up," he bites off each word. Perhaps there is a measure of thwarted greed in his anger, but mostly it is wounded pride, I think. No matter; with about two dozen bushels of oysters aboard, we turn and run before the gale to Tilghman as the light begins to fade. There is a bad moment on the way in. A huge sea wrenches the push boat from its bow shackle. Push boats are little more than floating engines. Separated from a skipjack, they are about as seaworthy as an anvil mounted on a board. Worse, when disconnected as ours was in following seas, they can act as a battering ram, crushing the rudder, even holing the skipjack's stern. Some frantic action keeps everything intact and then, entering Knapps Narrows, comes the crowning blow.

The tide, the same tide that refused to rise, that kept us from Wadey's "spots" since dawn, has now risen to two feet above its normal high. The howling wind makes it clear that no boats will venture out tomorrow, the official last day of dredging season. Dredging is over for the *Sigsbee* and Wadey Murphy until next fall, when once again they will sail up to Sandy Point for Appreciation Days, and the crowds will gawk and remark how romantic it would be, out there dredging oysters under sail in the sublime autumn sunshine, free—or so they think—from the tensions and frustrations of the land.

The Energy Coast

Rockfish and Rockefellers: Is there such a fundamental difference?

S*cientists Cliffs*—someday I'm going to write a pulp thriller set here, I am telling Dr. Joseph Mihursky as we sit on his sun deck overlooking the long, smooth curve of Calvert County bay shore. I'll call it "The Energy Coast." The climax will be built around one of those mammoth tankers that deliver liquid natural gas to the big terminal just down the shore at Cove Point, in quantities so large and so volatile that the Coast Guard buoys off a couple square miles of bay to give them docking room. A mad captain will ram his LNG ship into the twin, 825-megawatt reactors of the Calvert Cliffs nuclear plant, which is nearly adjacent to Cove Point. The megablast, the release in a millisecond of enough energy to power whole cities and heat a million homes for years, will light the bay like another sun, fry the paint off the Capitol dome forty miles away and radiate half the East Coast. I figure it will sell millions and bring a fortune for the movie rights. I am excited.

So is Joe, who has been intently watching an osprey patrolling the bay out in front of us. "Look, there he goes!" says Joe, who is a top ecologist at the University of Maryland's Chesapeake Biological Laboratory at Solomons, just down the shore. The fish hawk, with deadly, swooping grace, has just plunged its talons into the trough of a wave, plucking a rockfish. We have just witnessed a high-energy event of immense proportion, my host explains. The rockfish is a predator relatively high up the food chain of the bay. The pound or so of flesh wriggling in the osprey's grasp has fed on hundreds of pounds of lesser fish. These, in turn, embodied the nourishment captured from feeding on thousands of pounds of barely visible animals that flourish in the bay and are called copepods. The copepods had captured the nutritional energy from tens or hundreds of thousands of pounds of microscopic plant forms, or algae; and the algae represent the photosynthetic processing of millions of B.T.U.s of sunlight falling on the bay, and the absorption of chemical nutrients washed by rainstorms from the 41-million-acre watershed, and delivered to the estuary on the immense currents of its forty-odd tributary rivers. All of this massive machinery of biotic production sustains the osprey and its brood for a few hours until it must refuel, must hunt again or die. It is just a bird doing its thing; no million-seller here, no movie rights, no lights, cameras, action; but clearly, my Energy Coast is energetic in more ways than ever I thought.

To most people, the bay looks kind of quiet, Joe says. He has often thought if there was only some way he could set it to music, to get across the point of just how much work is going on out there—a symphony to capture the furious summertime tempo of photosynthesis, how it sinks back to a low groan in the winter; the din of food production as microbes decompose the luxuriant outpouring of vegetation from the marshes into edible detritus, and springtime's pulsating traffic of a hundred species' migrations and spawning . . . if they could hear it all, it would just blow people's minds, Joe says. "Balls of energy, chasing other balls of energy to make more of themselves, that is what it all comes down to," he says. Ospreys chasing rockfish, rockfish chasing smaller fish, Rockefellers investing heavily in nuclear power, Saudi princes and the Hunts of Texas in oil wells, the Fels financial empire in napthalene . . . balls of energy, capturing more energy, to make more of themselves. The rich and powerful, F. Scott Fitzgerald might have said, *are* different from you and me—they have bigger balls.

Energy, whether derived from the sun and soil, or from the fuels that drive our machines, is both the source and limit of all the world's activities; and scientists are finding it increasingly useful as a common denominator in comparing and evaluating natural and engineered systems. Learning the energy language may tell us some things we don't want to hear. It may also be our eventual salvation. Once you become attuned to it, the world will never seem the same again. The energy language can afford insights that are elegant and delightful, like Buckminster Fuller's answer to a little child who asked him why the logs in a fireplace burned so brightly. It was because the tree was giving up all at once the sunlight it had been storing up every day for a century, he said.

Other times, it can reveal our thinking as narrow and anthropocentric. I heard the manager of a hydropower dam on the Susquehanna River, who thought he knew a lot about energy, speak of all the "wasted" water that used to flow down the river before there were dams to store its power for profitable passage later on through their turbines. It never occurred to him that the river once had the greatest spawning runs of shad and herring of any waterway in the United States, and that these depended on continuous and unobstructed flows for navigation and to keep the water sufficiently oxygenated to support aquatic life.

Professional foresters likewise, when a tract of timber begins to reach its climax state after decades of growth, are quick to warn that the trees are becoming "overmature." Cut them quickly, they say, because the forest is no longer adding new wood at a high rate. What such a forest *is* doing is shifting the energies of sun and rain, which it once translated into growth, into maintenance and long-term stability. It is good for centuries more in such a state, and it affords some of the richest habitat known for nesting birds in the process, not to mention aesthetics and serving as a high-efficiency filter removing pollutants washing from the land into waterways.

We Americans have been reluctant to listen to the scientists who speak the energy language, and why not? Who can have patience with the long, slow flows of energy through the circuits of oaks or even rockfish, when our own species is in possession of the biggest, most dazzling balls of energy in all of evolution. These are the fossil fuels, products of sunlight captured by prehistoric forests and swamps eon after eon, stored and aged long in the earth like fine wines, to become the coal and oil and gas reserves of the planet—such intense distillations of natural energies that they seem, in retrospect, almost a nectar of the gods. Certainly, from the industrial revolution through the present, fossil fuels have propelled us on a binge of growth and expansion that is without precedent. For all the impressive natural energy it takes to make one rockfish, which in turn allows the higher-quality existence of ospreys, how much more luxurious is our own rung on the energy scale, that two people can spend an entire day doing nothing more productive than taking delight in osprey-watching, their drinks and home interiors cooled by the flow of electrons from fossil fuels being consumed in a distant power plant, and their food supplied by an agricultural system that expends seven to ten calories of energy to grow and transport to the markets a single calorie of food?

Godlike it may make us seem, but there is nothing noble about the profligacy with which the most technologically advanced societies spend the energy they control—especially while more than half the world's people cannot afford a big enough ball to satisfy their most basic needs. But to the ecologist there is nothing surprising about it either. From species of competing algae in a test tube, on up to the scale of human civilizations, the systems that "win out" seem always to be those that best use all the energy available to them. And as long as new sources of energy, whether sunlight, oil, or fertile, virgin soils, continue to become available, the ecologically proven strategy for winning is rapid, even fairly wasteful, growth. The weedy vegetation that springs up almost overnight in a plowed field or cutover forest is a good example—poor in structure and quality, but able to colonize the bare soil and its newly turned-up nutrients faster than any other species. Thus have nations like ours sprouted wildly and successfully since gaining large-scale access to uranium and the fossil fuels and to the incredible fertility that resided under the sod of the prairies.

Eventually, the weedy new field succeeds to shrubs, then to small trees, and, finally, if not nipped in the bud by some forester crying "overmature," to a climax forest of giant trees, a system characterized by its ability to maintain its stability long after the original bonanza of nutrients in the soil has been depleted. It is easy for us to shrug off the comparisons to a climax forest, to scoff at the thought that we may be nearing the end of a high-energy existence. Just look at the amounts of oil, coal, natural gas, uranium, and chemical fertilizers left to be extracted from the earth's proven reserves. And who is to say we won't discover more if we just look farther afield, dig deeper, squeeze harder? But such estimates ignore something crucial, the ecologists who speak the energy language tell us. The meaningful calculation is that of *net energy*—how much energy you get from a fuel source after you subtract the energy you must spend to get it out, make it usable, and control its polluting side effects. This question of net energy is much more pertinent than worrying about actually running out of our fuels.

Thus we have found, to our chagrin, that shale oil, because of the huge energies needed to wrest it from rock, costs more to produce than it returns; the same appears to be true for alcohol fuel made from corn, and possibly even for nuclear power, once we subtract the government subsidies it receives and calculate the costs of mothballing old, radioactive plants, as well as disposing of wastes that will remain toxic for thousands of years. Fusion, the type of nuclear energy involved in hydrogen-bomb explosions, is seen by some as a potential source of almost unlimited energy in the next century, but such are the incredibly high temperatures that must be generated and controlled to produce it that there are serious questions about whether it will be much of a "net" producer. Harvesting the abundant, shrimplike krill that abound in thousands of square miles of Antarctic waters was once heralded as the world's next source of cheap protein; but the energy required to send large ships to the end of the earth and maintain them in those hostile climates seems likely to be more than the krill are worth, or at least sure to render them luxury food instead of sustenance for the masses.

Agriculture has shared similar misconceptions. In Africa and South America there are vast tracts of fallow land which are often cited as proof that there will be no trouble producing enough food for any conceivable population there. True perhaps, but food at what price? On closer inspection it turns out that such lands almost always do not have good rainfall; often, too, the soil is not of best quality. Production there can only be wrought with energy-intensive irrigation and large and frequent injections of expensive fertilizers. We have been poking around this world for a while now, and most of the best, most energy-efficient places to grow food on the globe, we have already turned to doing just that. Late in the twentieth century there is no undiscovered gold to be picked up from the surface of the earth, or any new Iowa or Illinois awaiting only the plow.

That we are headed in the direction of the climax forest, of the steady state, pushed by generally declining net energies, there is little doubt, Joe says, as the angle of the sun begins to turn the bay surface in front of us to molten gold. *Conservation, recycling, energy efficiency* . . . all the terms that have become part of our popular vocabulary in the last decade are only recognition of the ecological facts of life; the systems that survive are those that best use the energies available to them. Increasingly that means learning to husband the remaining elixirs of high-quality, nonrenewable energy, and maximizing our living off renewable, natural systems. Harvesting a pound of protein from fish, for example, has been calculated to involve the energy expenditure of about a quart of oil, compared to the thirteen gallons it takes to raise an equivalent amount of protein from grain-fed steers. Similarly, the same acreage of cropland that can feed one person when its grain is first cycled through a steer can feed dozens of vegetarians. In a less energy-rich future, perhaps it will be the meatless who inherit the earth.

The more immediate question, Joe says, is how much by then the Calvert Cliffs and the Cove Points will have impaired the ability of the natural systems to do their undervalued but increasingly vital jobs of water storage and purification, of fisheries production. He isn't talking about my big-bang scenario for the Energy Coast. In fact, the nuclear plant has an enviable safety and reliability record. Furthermore, the burning of natural gas from Cove Point and the nuclear-power generation from Calvert Cliffs produce no air pollution; and careful environmental studies have shown virtually no measurable changes in bay aquatic life off either facility. The taxes paid by both facilities have substantially raised the standard of living in Calvert County, once the second poorest jurisdiction in Maryland. Where, then, is the rub? Is this just the no-growth naysaying of someone who would rather not see any change? It is not change, but the *rate* of change, that is the problem, Joe says. That is the dark side of those marvelous big balls of artificial energy we have got hold of. They accelerate unnaturally the pace at which we develop. They enable our technologies to outpace our ability to deal with the social and environmental consequences; and they make us prideful enough to think we can always correct any imbalances that result. Of the land development in Maryland that currently is overstressing the Chesapeake Bay, nearly a sixth of it occurred in the decade 1970–1980, which is only the last 1/35 of the time since we settled the place.

As Joe and I have talked, the tide has run from full to low, shifting a trillion gallons of water, flushing tons of plant food from the marshes, setting billions of oysters and clams to filtering it through their gills, exposing thousands of acres of bottom to feeding shore birds. The work of the bay has gone on almost beneath our notice. The lines of a song run through my mind as long shadows extend along the Energy Coast:

> . . . knockin' down trees,
> puttin up factories,
> how you gonna tell that old boy,
> how you gonna tell 'im.

It was written by David Norris, a talented young native of the Energy Coast who makes his living working at the nuclear plant. The "old boy" in the song refers to the bones of an Indian that David saw dug up by a back hoe during excavation for another new housing development.

If you look at the stretch of Southern Maryland between contemporary Rome (Washington, D.C.) and Norfolk, Joe says, it is the one region that still has plenty of open space, plenty of water, and plenty of energy. We're plastered with the three major essentials for rapid growth and development, he says; now, you tell me how we're going to stop it. Such development far upstream on the Patuxent, the main river entering the bay along the Energy Coast, has already cost the river much of its fish and oysters and soft crabs, as sewage flows and forest clearing caused an upsurge of pollution. Even as the rural counties of the lower river have mobilized state and federal forces to attack the problem, they in turn are beginning to show all the classic signs of repeating the rapid upstream development, as Joe's contemporary Rome pushes out unerringly along the remaining corridors of open space, water, and energy.

Deforestation along the Energy Coast already is running at one of the highest rates in the northeastern United States; and a baywide moratorium is in effect on the catching of rockfish and shad, which seem not to be able to reproduce in the Patuxent and other rivers so well anymore. Perhaps our calculations of the energy to be netted from the nonrenewable fuels should include more than the energy needed to bring them to market; they should also subtract the value of the natural energies they displace.

When you first learn the energy language, it can be a heady experience; and there is a tendency, like a college freshman home for Thanksgiving after his first exposure to Psych 101, to go around proferring simple solutions to all the world's complex problems. We are not likely ever to make all of society's decisions based solely on which direction will be least demanding of our energy resources. That would be to deny politics, special interests, and legitimate social objectives (health care for handicapped people is an energy drain, for example). It would deny too much, good and bad, that makes us different from rockfish and ospreys. But then we do not study French because we think we should all become French. To learn the energy language can only make us more responsible citizens of the planet. Much more clearly than now, we will see the scope of the trade-offs, the options foreclosed, by our decisions to grow and expand and develop. You may still take another pathway from the one of least energy use, Joe says, but at least you acknowledge it, give reasons why. He doesn't think future generations will condemn us for that nearly so much as if we squander energy blindly.

The prospects of paying more attention to energy in the coming decades are both likely and, Joe thinks, pleasant. "Winning" by growing may be replaced by winning through conservation, recycling, by maintenance of the steady state, by more attention to equitable distribution of resources. Perhaps an ethic will arise that takes more cognizance of the long term than our present allegiance to economists, who in the short history of their profession have known only models of constant expansion. Ecologists know there is life beyond growth; but they also know there is no assurance that it always lies in the elegant austerity of systems like the climax forest. Some ecosystems, such as prairies, go another direction. They are said to "pulse." In the case of the prairie, the pulse is periodic fires, which return the nutrients from the mature growth stage of the plants to the soil so the prairie can start over again. The fires also arrest the growth of young trees that, if unchecked, would have turned the Great Plains into a forest long before the settlers arrived. If one assumes, as some ecologists speculate, that we have become the pulse in the global ecosystem, then we might be fated to consume and compete for the last bits of more and more ex-

pensive fossil fuels, ending in economic collapse or global famine
. . . then the earth could start over again. It is not a pleasant thought;
but here on the Energy Coast, lulled by the bay's slap, slap, slap at
the base of the cliffs and watching the ospreys hunting rockfish, it is a
thought that curiously seems both far away and quite possible.

The Wind Rules

*W*ind-swept, *windblown,* blowin' a gale; zephyrous, wafting; wind
in the pines, *The Wind in the Willows, Gone with the Wind,* wind song,
wind river; the mistral, the typhoon, the Santa Ana, the chinook;
squall, simoom, sirocco, and samiel; sow the wind, reap the whirlwind;
the Windy City; OK!-lahoma, where the wind comes sweepin' down
the plain . . .

Wind—the word, the concept, no matter how you express it, has a
surpassing elemental evocative power. Older races, speaking the
wind's name in other tongues, must have felt it too, to judge from the
many wind gods of the Hindu, the Norse, the Romans, and the American Indians. With all its inspired poetry, the Old Testament repeatedly
can think of no better way to bring God onstage than in the "tempest"
and the "whirlwind." The *aquilo,* or *eagle wind,* the ancient Romans
called the keen, chill air blasting down from the north, just as today the
cruel northerly, when it visits Baltimore, is called "the hawk" by street-
wise blacks. Chariot of the weather, investing the tasteless, colorless,
odorless air with the richest of personalities, the wind is an evolutionary force that shapes our world almost as fundamentally as light and
dark, heat and cold, fire and water. I think no one yet can fully appreciate its influence on the works of human beings and nature, from the
shape of the sphinx to the number of baby rockfish that grow in the
Chesapeake Bay.

"The wind rules from the . . . " is an expression used in assigning
wind direction by bay watermen, who know in their genes how different winds can dictate which shoreline their skipjacks dredge oysters
on that day, make the soft crabs disappear, and scatter the most lucra-
tive schools of fish. The Army Corps of Engineers did not fully appreciate just how much the wind rules in these regions when it constructed,
on Kent Island, a model of the Chesapeake Bay cast in seven acres of
concrete. The model's marvelous, computer-driven hydraulics could
simulate tide and current in every square foot of water from Norfolk to

Havre de Grace, but it turned out not to simulate very well how the bay actually worked.

A major reason was the wind. Scientists only now are realizing that its influence on the bay's ebb and flood of water dominates the cosmic clockwork of the tides as much as 90 percent of the time. Normal tidal rise in Baltimore's harbor is perhaps two feet. A strong southerly wind pushing water up the bay for a few days can add six feet to that. In April 1982, the wind ruled from the other direction. It blew hard from the northwest for two days, in effect "tilting" the whole bay toward its mouth. So much water left the upper portion of the estuary that shipping was hindered in the port of Baltimore for nearly three days.

Even greater is the wind's power over the success and failure of fisheries in the bay, some emerging theories suggest. The blue crab hatches at the estuary's mouth and is washed seaward for many miles by currents there. This contact with oceanic salinities probably is vital for its larval development. But how on earth do the feeble, microscopic larvae buck the mighty currents of the Virginia capes to reenter the bay's circulatory system and fulfill their proper life's goal of becoming succulent eating for one million Maryland crabbers far upstream? The answer is blowin' in the wind. At the crucial time of year, prevailing winds generally shove the larvae back into the bay—and if, as happens sometimes, the winds instead turn offshore, then crabbers all the way to the Susquehanna and Northeast rivers will scratch their heads and blame pollution, or cuss the caprice of the crab.

To enhance the annual reproduction of another premiere bay species, the rockfish, it may take only enough wind to generate a ripple on the water. What scientists think happens is that the wave action, the roughening of the surface layer, vastly increases the amount of contact that occurs between the rockfish larvae and their food supply of tiny plankton, compared to times when the wind does not blow and the water remains slick calm.

> When the wind is in the north, the fishermen go not far;
> When the wind is in the east, it's not fit for man nor beast;
> When the wind is in the south, it blows bait in the fishes' mouth;
> When the wind is in the west, ahhh, then she's at her very best.

So recited the late, lamented Alex Kellam, a Crisfielder who was a regional treasury of bay lore and poetry; but on the man-altered modern bay, some editing of his verse may be in order. These days a west wind can cause polluted water that is low in oxygen to "upwell" from the bay's deep channels onto the Eastern Shore side of the bay, asphyxiat-

ing oysters and sending crabs parading out of the water in what are
called jubilees. An east wind, conversely, may be quite fit for some
beasts. Blowing at the critical time through the big rockfish spawning
area on the Chesapeake and Delaware ship canal, it is thought to keep
the larvae from washing into Delaware Bay, where higher salinities
would hugely reduce their survival.

This is some of what the wind does; but if that were all, it would
remain a dry phenomenon, of penetrating interest only to biologists
and oceanographers. To know the wind in its glory you must seek out
better interpreters than those. There is a precious interlude between
night and morning when, if you sneak up to a quiet cove or pond, its
dark waters just fetchingly rouged by the dawn, the wind as it breezes
up will show you the most extraordinary calligraphy as it etches obsi-
dian strokes across the silken surface. And seldom is the wind's passage more appealing than when it comes shouldering through a big
bay marsh, the reeds bending to outline its every ebullition, rustling
like tafetta as they strain to hold it, sighing as they always fail. Some
trees seem especially talented at lending texture and tongue to the
wind. Aspens and willows pay it shivering, silver tribute as the wind
flutters the blanched undersides of their leaves. Tall Eastern Shore loblolly pines pluck the mournful strains of violas from its passing roar;
and in early winter the rattling snare drum of the wind among sere,
shiny oak leaves can snap a whole forest to attention.

The French author Jean Giono wrote in "Le Cypres" how rural
farmers, in a region too dry to afford them the pleasures of water foun-
tains in their gardens, used always to plant a cypress next to the house,
to catch the wind, "because it's a beautiful singer. They had need of the
company from those things that are not man. He who doesn't feel that
need, make the sign of the cross and go your way; that's a fellow who
has been put together in the wrong way; his mother turned him out a
miser."

In our modern, urban and suburban culture, we don't live so close
to the wind as Giono's peasants but, if anything, extract even more
pleasure from it. Wind chimes hang from half the row-house porches
in my Baltimore City block, and the other half of us are glad to listen.
Kiting is one of our fastest expanding sports—"wrestle with the
wind!", "talk with the wind," "tease the clouds," say the ads that pack
KiteLines, the slick quarterly journal of international kite-flyers. It is
published in Baltimore by—who else—Aeolus Press. And as for anyone in the bay region who does not thrill to the sight of a sail filling its
belly on wind, well . . . "make the sign of the cross and go your
way . . ."

The bay's skipjack captains respect what wind in a sail can do as well as any people on earth. They have a story, told in several versions, about "a penny's worth of wind." Oh, you can buy wind, 'deed you can, the captains will tell you on days everyone is sitting around the deck, becalmed. You can buy it for the price of a penny, even for a pekin' (pecan) nut thrown into the water, along with your wish for a good blow. But only a foolish and arrogant man would seek more than the Lord is willing to give in his own good time, the dredgers say. Those who buy the wind are destined to reap the whirlwind, and some captains would summarily fire any crew member who tossed a penny over the side.

It was a great and fearsome wind that in 1933 helped create Maryland's premiere resort on the coastal barrier island known as Ocean City. The worst hurricane ever recorded cut the inlet that allowed boat access to the safe harbor of the town's back bays, sparking the development that now lines twelve miles of beach with shoulder-to-shoulder hotels and condos. Ironically, this virtually guarantees that the next such wind to hit the city will gain notoriety as causing the worst property disaster in the history of the state.

And all of this is but a smattering of what the wind does. It shapes the very flight of wild geese into the long, pulsating vees that are both aerodynamically efficient and strangely thrilling. Set loose among the clouds, the wind's artifice knows no bounds—flattening, fattening, shredding, kneading, as if engaged in some sort of celestial taffy pull. On superheated, sultry summer afternoons, the wind likes to flash and thunder down the bay's river channels, driving a cold air mass ahead of it, piling up great, glowering thunderheads to either side like snow from a plow. In the clearing, cooling aftermath the world is reinvigorated.

On the wind's currents are borne the pollen and seeds that rejuvenate the forest and revegetate the most barren soils as if by magic. I once watched a strip miner, reclaiming slopes for wildlife habitat high in the West Virginia mountains, bulldoze a few shallow depressions in the earth, to let the wind build him a marsh, he said. A couple months later, "out of thin air," a marsh was flourishing there, with three varieties of wetland plant that did not exist anywhere else for miles around.

Botanists using wind tunnels have shown that pine trees and the wind, conversing through millennia, have evolved a sophisticated partnership between pine cones and the breezes that bear pine pollen. For each species of evergreen, the cone has evolved a geometry that functions like a wind turbine, channeling the right size and shape of pollen through its scales in a way that maximizes its capture. Similarly, the sweet soughing of wind through the boughs of evergreens is doing more than rocking you to sleep in your tent. The needles are assiduously filtering the rushing air for the minerals it bears. The next rain will wash them down into the soil to nourish the tree. Some of the wind's best blowing is not purposeful at all—the occasional pink flamingo pushed by storms far off-course to Chincoteague; the roseate spoonbill that turned up at Smith Island one winter—these chance bits of bright color can energize a region long after the storm that brought them has faded from memory.

And still, this is not all the wind does. I mentioned the sphinx. It has endured for so long that its ability to withstand the ravages of time is a greater mystery than its origin. It seems its shape is supremely aerodynamic, relatively impervious to erosion from desert wind and sand. Were its ancient builders that wise? Perhaps they just observed the wind. Scientists recently have studied huge natural limestone formations in the Egyptian deserts called *yardangs*. Carved by the wind, these formations are so aerodynamic that they exist in near-perfect harmony with their environment—and they look remarkably like the sphinx. It seems quite possible that the sphinx is constructed around a yardang. Other time-tested natural-rock formations that have survived in the harsh, blasting environments of deserts around the world tend to be pyramidal and conical in shape. It takes no great leap of imagination to see in them a wind-authored blueprint for Mongolian yurts, the great pyramids of Giza, the tents of the Bedouin—even the Indian teepee.

That is some of what the wind does; but it does not yet explain the thrill some people get from the slightest breath of wind on the face, or the adrenalin set to flowing by a thunderstorm's approach, or the insane desire—I have heard quite a number of people express it—to stand in the full blast of a hurricane. There is in us, it seems, an affinity with wind that is quite deep-rooted and mysterious. Perhaps the account of the Creation, in the first lines of Genesis, comes closest to an explanation. Readers of modern versions of the Bible know the passage as "The spirit of God moved upon the face of the waters"; but check any good, annotated version of the Bible and you'll find what was the original translation of "spirit."

It was "the wind."

Order!

Chaos! The surf seems to bellow as it explodes rhythmically against the beach here. And the beach whispers back, ever so improbably—*order*.

Something very profound is going on here, and it has to do with order. It has to do with how the raging, random energies of wind and wave and the boiling, unaglommerated sands of the surf zone get organized into beach, dune and thicket, forest and marsh—into a full-fledged coastal barrier island like Assateague. It is a process at once so unlikely yet so inevitable it compels us to reconsider our definitions of *life* and *living*. No other land form on the planet is more provocative of thinking about creation, and the force that binds the universe, than the barrier island.

We have long been drawn to speculate on deeper meanings to the similarities of form that seem to run throughout nature. The meanders of great rivers appear to follow the same lines as the slither of droplets down a thawing, frosted windowpane; and both resemble the sinuous flows of ice on a glacier. This recurrence of pattern moved the English poet Gerard Manley Hopkins to write in "Pied Beauty":

> Glory be to God for dappled things—
> For skies of couple-colour as a brinded cow;
> For rose-moles all in stipple upon trout that swim;
> Fresh-firecoal chestnut-falls, finches wings;
> Landscape plotted and pieced—fold fallow and plow;
> . . . whatever is fickle, freckled (who knows how?).

Indeed, who knows how? Subjecting the phenomena of ordering to powerful, modern computational analyses has only increased the wonder we feel. Striking similarities of pattern keep cropping up in events as disparate as the turbulent flows of air over an airplane wing, the flow of blood through an artery, and the formation of thunderstorms. Peter A. Carruthers, one of the country's leading theoretical physicists, has described curious statistical similarities between the distribution of subatomic particles and the galaxies themselves. Whatever underlies such similarities, he speculates, may hold clues to the differences between order and chaos, between living and nonliving.

"There is a purposiveness of structure which is so characteristic of all living objects without exception and which runs like a red thread through the whole development of life," writes the noted Russian biochemist Alexander Oparin. And Albert Einstein, toward the end of his life, said of the mysteries of order, "I am convinced God does not play dice with the universe."

Or perhaps God just plays with loaded dice. Consider closely what is going on here at Assateague. The waves are booming five-footers, moderate surf for autumn. In a day they will expend the energy of about one thousand pounds of dynamite against each linear foot of beach. Yet even here in the surf zone, the zone of maximum chaos, the powerful march toward order is beginning. Slickly as a croupier at the gaming table, the swash and undertow are sorting sand by size and weight and shape, dealing the coarser stuff to the lower beach, finer grains of quartz up higher on the berm. Even higher up are cast the dark, mineral-rich particles of magnetite and ilmenite.

Organic fertilizer is constantly extracted from the ocean in the forms of dead sharks, crabs, sea ducks, conchs, and other marine life hurled up by the surf. A host of microorganisms on the beach sets immediately to disaggregate these gifts of flesh into nutrients usable by the island. From the high beach the wind takes over, sifting the sand grains across the full breadth of the barrier, dropping out heaviest first, also transporting nutrients. This lays the substrate across the island for different vegetational communities that, influenced by soil type, nearness to salt spray, elevation, and other factors, will be zoned more precisely than any human planning could manage.

None of this, however, could ever gain respite enough from the salt and wind and waves to get established were it not for *Amophila breviligulata*, or American beach grass. *Amophila*'s virtues caused ancient English and Scottish kings to pass laws that it not be disturbed wherever it grew on the oceanfront. Its seeds, sown along the beach in the drift line of organic detritus you can see washed up along the high-tide mark, have evolved to take root even where summer temperatures reach a blistering 120° F. Once it begins to grow, the more the sand threatens to drift over it, the faster *Amophila* is stimulated to push upward, and the faster it sends out roots to stabilize the sand. Wind-blown sand, the most sterile-seeming of soils, in effect acts as fertilizer for the beach grass; and the more *Amophila* takes hold, the more sand it traps. In this way are born the dunes, and they provide in their lee a place protected enough from the harsh Atlantic elements for the rest of the island to gather its resources, to pursue higher, more stable, diverse vegetational forms.

Grass and sand and wind—all conspire so elegantly to create a rudimentary form of order, the beach dune. Seldom as on the ocean beach is it revealed how the whole of nature's interrelated qualities so exceeds the mere sum of the parts. I wish more of our environmental decision makers would walk on the beaches, listen to the rustling of sand through the *Amophila*, and watch the kinetic little shore birds race back and forth in a dance with the advancing and retreating waves, as intimately synchronized as Ginger Rogers and Fred Astaire. Sandpipers and surf—can you really treat them as anything but parts of the same process? Much too easily our Western, reductionist science looks only at the parts of things. We still assign the study of sand to the geologist, and we assume the wind is the domain of meteorologists and that plants are for botanists, when what we need desperately is more people who understand dunes.

A walk anywhere on Assateague, watching order and life continually being wrested from inanimate randomness, cannot fail to make one think; is it possible that we can be apart from, rather than a part of, a process that seems to connect the subatomic to the intergalactic and blur the lines between life and nonlife? Maybe answering yes would make some feel powerful. It would make me feel lonely.

No one feels lonely in Ocean City, just across the inlet that terminates Assateague at its north end. It is Maryland's premiere coastal resort metropolis, a barrier island whose twelve miles of beach are packed with upward of a quarter-million sun-seekers each weekend. It seems another world from the undeveloped Assateague coastline; but they are linked, perhaps fatally so. Toward Assateague's north end its dunes vanish, as does the vegetation and the wildlife. All the processes of order have broken down here. The north end is retreating before erosion that is proceeding at a cancerous pace. Before another decade has passed the island here will cease to exist, joining the Worcester County mainland, which is now separated from it by a quarter-mile of water.

Even as Assateague's normally stable economy of sand seems to be courting bankruptcy, Ocean City has never done so well, and it considers itself as a model of stability and order. Its economy is booming, with an assessable tax base that is third in the state only to Baltimore City and Rockville in affluent Montgomery County. Its beaches just across from the eroding north end of Assateague are fat and sleek, and its high-rise, oceanfront condos stretch solidly north almost to the Delaware line. Until recently, only a few coastal geologists and people like Judy Johnson, an environmentalist who heads the Committee to Preserve Assateague, would say there was much of a connection between Ocean City and the huge erosion losses of Assateague. In response, the late Harry Kelley, the long-time mayor of Ocean City, once said hotly: "That Johnson woman has her island . . . tell her let me alone with mine."

But just as barrier islands stretch our concepts of what are living systems, they also force a reappraisal of what is stable. Often the forces

of the ocean and its storms become too great for even the normal ordering systems of the beach to accommodate. To survive, the barrier islands roll with the punches, "sacrificing" their front dunes to the
waves, and at the same time extending and building their backside
marshes with sand carried across the storm-tossed island by the same
waves. They do not erode, they just migrate, routinely moving landward before the onslaught of storms, then just as capriciously back to
seaward when seasonal or long-term shifts in nearshore currents cause
sand to accrete on their beaches. Their net movement during the last
fifteen thousand or so years has been landward in response to rising
sea level, as the glaciers of the last ice age melt. Even experienced ob-
servers may not notice the magnitude of such retreats and advances,
because a barrier island beach tends to assume the same shape and
slope as it moves back and forth. This process, a manifestation of ordering, is powerful enough that we have a formal name for it, Brunn's
Rule.

In Ocean City there is no migration at all, because it has used artificial groins and jetties and bulldozers to trap extra sand and "stabilize" its beach. The extra sand, however, was sand that normally would
have flowed downcoast to nourish the beach- and dune-building processes at Assateague. That island's north end is now, quite graphically,
starving to death.

A text on coastal geologic processes says: "It might be tempting to
conclude, given the dynamic nature of barrier islands, that these forces
lead to great island instability; while this may be correct in terms of
man's needs for development, ecologically the contrary is true." In
other words, on a barrier island, long-term stability demands instability. Not to sound like a Zen philosopher, but often it seems that what
we call unstable, or chaotic, may only be order we are not yet able to
perceive. How many times have jungles been described as a "riot" of
vegetation, when now scientists know that regions like the Amazon
rain forest have evolved probably the most specialized, diverse, and
marvelously interrelated ecosystems on the planet? Increasingly,
young physicists such as Mitchell Feigenbaum at Cornell are probing
with computers phenomena like the curl of smoke from a cigarette dissolving into nothingness, the unwinding whorls of a cumulus cloud,
the ventricular fibrillation during a heart attack—and finding that all
may turn out to follow predictable patterns. Nature appears to favor
pathways, even on the way to chaos, that are, for lack of a better word
to describe them, *orderly*.

Ocean City's groined and jettied beach, by contrast, is attempting
to follow a path ordained by no higher power than the Army Corps of
Engineers. So out of synch is the "stability" of the resort town's beach

with the ordering tendencies of the natural barrier island that some think it arrogant and stupid to keep building condos as if the place were built on bedrock, instead of on sand that is badly wanting to shift; and they say the next coastal hurricane will exact terrible tribute, while Assateague will merely roll a bit to landward and come back for more.

Others maintain that engineering, and enough money for beach-building, can protect and prevail; that a new corps project in the works can even help restore the north end of Assateague. It is at least arguable; but the proponents should understand they are building in more than the path of the storm. They are trying to anchor their castles in the face of one of the universe's great compulsions, the tendency of all nature toward order.

Spirits of Place

I passed my first four years of life in a log cabin in the piney woods southeast of Salisbury, holdings improved by two chicken houses. Our circumstances were modest enough, but I expect never to live on a finer street. Ours was dirt; pleasant to the bare feet and a capital lounging spot for the dogs, who could pick up vibrations from approaching vehicles in plenty of time to amble out of the way. After a rain, the packed sandy surface showed the extent of nonvehicular traffic—deer, coon, possum, and rabbit. I loved the whispering sound it made beneath the tires of cars, and the wheels of my toy wagon. Its soft edges melded agreeably with the fields and forest and tadpole-filled ditches on either side. It was organic to the landscape, not a division of it like the smooth, weatherproof blacktop that has since "improved" the old neighborhood.

Since my childhood a third of a century ago, we have almost improved the dirt road out of existence in Maryland: so I was heartened to spend an afternoon north of Baltimore recently, scuffing along one of the survivors with a woman who had decided to make her stand there against the forces of progress and pavement. She had grown up near a big Midwestern city in the 1950s, just long enough ago to get a taste of country before the land began to sprout suburbs. She thought she had recaptured it in the 1970s, moving into a newly built solar home in rural Michigan; but the creek nearby turned out to be contaminated with PCBs, and a giant, high-tension line came stalking over the horizon to complete her second disenfranchisement.

In the 1980s, having moved east to a farmhouse with unimproved road frontage, she was advised of the local highway department's plans to tar her road and her dreams of bucolia. She made a traffic survey. The peak daily flow of fifteen cars seemed hardly to justify the proposed widening and paving. Why pave it? she asked. Why in the world not? replied the road builders. By the time she enlisted the support of enough neighbors to win at least a temporary stay, she had come to realize that the little dirt road was more than a road—it was the thread that bound together the whole, companionable mix of field and woods and creek bottom and cow pasture that typified the area's scenery. It was symbolic of a rural way of life that, curiously, could not be defended on the basis of any environmental law, though it seemed at least as precious as any federally protected endangered species of wildflower or salamander, as worthy of preservation as any clean air or water standards. It seemed you should be able to say—hey, this is a neat place and we don't want it to change—my friend said.

What she had collided with was one of this country's major institutional blind spots in its relations with private land. We are beginning, in the final years of the twentieth century, to get pretty creative at using green-space zoning, agricultural districting, and the like to preserve *quantities* of land; but attention only to the acreage of open space—or even to those lands possessing some unique flora or fauna—does not assure preservation of the landscape's integrity, of its personality. The most personable land need not be confined to true wilderness, of which virtually none remains in Maryland anyhow; and it should not be confused with beauty that is merely spectacular. Some of the greatest charm is to be found in the way some landscapes still exhibit a pleasing balance, a coexistence between our works and those of nature, from a time when neither dominated or overwhelmed the other.

Such jewels lie scattered about the state—little stretches of single-lane road where old trees overhang, utility lines be damned, and the road plays tag with rushing streams along a route shaped by water rather than surveyor's transits, and modest little bridges invite a pause and a look down at every bend (try that with the concrete culverts that encase so many streams now). Also spots like the road in lower Dorchester County which runs from Bucktown to Vienna by way of Bestpitch Ferry, where you emerge from woods and suddenly mount a clattery, humpy, wooden bridge and behold an illimitable panorama of sky and salt marsh that would inspire "The Marshes of Glynn" if Sidney Lanier had not written it already. Farther west, there is the Amish country of Garrett County, where the syncopated clip-clop of church-bound buggies flavors Sunday mornings; and the size and shape of farm fields still are dictated by coexistence with hedgerow and wood lot and stream channels, instead of by the horsepower of four-wheel-drive tractors and the scope of center pivot irrigation. In Southern Maryland, a delightful variety of tobacco barn construction still survives to evoke the heritage of three hundred years.

None of these has much guarantee of lasting out the century without much wider public appreciation and legal recognition of the quality of landscape. No doubt our society can survive the aesthetic loss that occurs when barbed wire supplants split rails, concrete replaces wooden bridges, and power-plant stacks intrude on our vistas; but neither should we underestimate how much the quality of land affects us. The novelist Lawrence Durrell, when he was still a travel writer, coined the apt term *spirit of place* to describe the phenomenon. Place, he maintained, was a critical determinant of culture: just as a particular vineyard would reliably give you a wine with special characteristics, so the landscape of a Spain, an Italy, a Greece, would always give you the same unique civilization even if wiped clean of people and begun again. The countryside would express itself through the human being just as surely as it does through its wild flowers. That relationship between us and our surroundings is worth more consideration than it has gotten, especially considering our present ability to so rapidly redefine our surroundings, even to the alteration of the global temperature and the acidity of the very rain.

How very deeply we and the land's character may be entwined was hinted at in a study a few years ago by John Falk, a psychologist at the Smithsonian Institution's bay laboratory near Annapolis. He devised a test wherein people from vastly different cultures were asked to rate the visual appeal of a series of slides that showed landscapes ranging from desert to rain forest, and arctic tundra to an English park. Invariably, no matter the native habitat of the audience doing the selecting, the parklike setting, with its combination of elegantly spaced trees and acres of open, grassy understory, was most preferred. It seemed to be so universal a preference as to be innate. Falk felt it was more than coincidence that the picture of the park very closely resembled the forested edges of the great African savanna where we are thought to have first evolved.

Such theories would seem at least as fruitful for further exploration as the moon and Mars, but as far as I know we have virtually ignored formal study of the human-land relationship. It is an oversight that perhaps comes from the former living too long at right angles to the latter, increasingly disconnected—from our food by corporate farming, from our energy supplies by nation-girdling power grids, and by concrete and asphalt from the very earth we walk and drive across. Falk could not prove it, he told me once, but out of his work with human landscape preference he had become virtually certain in his own mind that we each become imprinted to a "home" landscape, although not necessarily at birth. He felt it probably began around ten to thirteen years of age. That would certainly explain my own happy fixation with Eastern Shore marshes, because that is about the age at which my father began my induction to the bay's hunting and fishing fraternity.

Since then I have progressed to where I find, like the landscape painter John Constable, pleasure in "every stile, and stump, and lane." Land's personality seems to manifest itself from the commonest settings—the mild-mannered, threadbare elegance of limestone pasture, the grouchy isolation of a thicket, the sleek pile of a spartina marsh, arching its back with feline pleasure as the wind brushes it. I suspect we are all, on some subtle level, engaged in an almost constant dialogue with the landscape around us. Perhaps it explains the regret we instinctively feel at seeing a stream straightened for drainage, a farm encircled by subdivisions, a woods being skinned alive for parking space, or a coal dragline feeding hungrily on the guts of a mountain.

Sometimes I think the spirits of place seize on certain sympathetic people among us to fight the battles against change that the land by itself cannot manage. Their agent usually is beauty. Many of the fiercest and most sophisticated allies the environment has, people whose commitment may now be couched in complex and impeccable philosophies of conservation, initially were recruited by the simple, unadulterated loveliness of a place, a view, or an outdoor experience. Certainly that is how Judy Johnson, the most effective lobbyist for seacoast protection that Maryland has ever had, was pressed into service after an outing at Assateague Island, when she and her nine-year-old son, Reid, now grown, agreed she could do nothing more important with her life than save such a place from development. And if the rockfish in the Chesapeake Bay has a vigilant protector in Dick Russell, a Kansan who never saw salt water until adulthood, it is because of the almost mystical feeling that came over him during his first encounter with a great striper in the crashing Atlantic surf. Hooked by what he calls a transcendent beauty that must not be allowed to vanish. Dick has lobbied tirelessly ever since from Boston to the Carolinas to preserve the rock.

The spirits of place can manifest themselves in a fish, or a storm-wracked beach, an ancient and irreplaceable oak, a quiet dirt lane—or in a whole, subtle, and complex web of associations, such as a farm family might have for the land into which it has poured so much more than seed and fertilizer for generations. We usually think in terms of people saving the environment; but I must wonder if it isn't the opposite—nature presents its charms, like an artful fly is cast to a trout, and we, leaping to the bait, are brought to its defense.

Thoreau Times Forty

Old House Cove, San Domingo Creek, February

S*cuds of cold rain* rile the creek and rattle against the tiny cabin as the well-known writer of Chesapeake Bay poetry crafts one of his most substantial compositions. "Best oyster stew you'll ever get," says Gilbert Byron. "Only cook 'em til their edges curl, and light on the pepper, that's the secret," he says, spooning a dozen fat Choptank River oysters into a pot of steaming milk and butter. "Ahhh, boy that's good. This and bologna sandwiches—I live on 'em. Something medicinal about an oyster stew." Gilbert has made something medicinal, something deeply nourishing, I think, of this whole cove where he's lived more than half his eighty-three years, so close to the water's edge he can doze off at night to the splash of minnows in the shallows at high tide.

He repaired to the woods here on this tributary of the Choptank River in the prime of life, to live and write in Thoreauvian simplicity. I sometimes kid Gilbert that Thoreau was a rank drifter, a transient, by comparison, with his paltry year in residence at Walden Pond. Gilbert has been anchored here forty times as long. He built the cabin in sections in Dover, Delaware, where he was teaching school before the move in 1946. "I wanted to live close to nature and economically, while earning a livelihood as a free lance writer . . . I was also seeking a broader margin for my life," he wrote recently. He bought the land for a few hundred dollars. The cabin, built at a total cost of $133.17, still is his main living quarters, measuring nine-by-twelve feet. It shares the dimensions and snug, tongue and groove construction of the cabin on his old catboat, the *Avalon*, in which he sailed the bay in younger days, gathering material on a culture that even half a century ago was in decline, as shown in "Chesapeake Change":

> I saw white schooners torn apart.
> Degraded into scummy freighters now;
> Old sailors clean fish, scrape and bow
> Or wash beer parlor floors, my heart
> Is sad that men who loved a breeze
> must spend declining years on bended knees.

Between slurps of delicate, buttery stew, we've been talking boats this particular morning. Acquiring ever-faster ones is what rules most discussions I and my contemporaries hold on the subject nowadays, I have been telling Gilbert. We truly would prefer sail, most of us, both for its quiet and its conservation of limited fossil fuels; but speed seems the only way to reconcile our hectic modern lives with the desire to gulp down as much experience as possible of this vast bay on which we live. There are limitations to this solution, it seems—not necessarily horsepower. I talked recently with a man who had acquired one of the very expensive, very high-powered, offshore racing hulls capable of sustained, mile-a-minute speeds. He had actually circumnavigated the Delmarva peninsula in six hours, he said. And how was it, I asked? Exciting, he replied, but no, he had not paid much attention to birds or shoreline or any marine life. Hopping wave tops at 60 MPH requires intense concentration on driving the boat, he explained.

Gilbert, who has had the rare good sense to pick one small corner of the earth to explore fully, has enriched our peripatetic lives beyond measure. In time, all of what is special about the Chesapeake Bay has come to him here in one form or another. This cove has become our Walden, chronicled lovingly and elegantly as few places ever are, in all its moods and seasons, and the comings and goings of its herons, loons, crabs, rockfish, swans, and other natural traffic. Some of his best writing, he agrees, has been about the old watermen who came to the cove, as in "Chesapeake Calendar":

> The gaunt man treads the quiet cove
> Where the peeler sheds.
> His heron eyes and clever mesh
> Net them by surprise.
> He's studied the creeks for sixty years.
> Knows old Chesapeake's
> Natural laws and the color
> Of the soft crab's claws.

And later, in winter:

> Hip-booted men with long tongs,
> Come to the cove again;
> Rake the bar of oysters bare
> Yet seldom the surface mar.

> Men who never wrote a line
> Are the greatest poets ever
> Verses of love inscribed upon
> The bottom of the cove.

He writes, every day the weather permits, at an old, weathered picnic table set up outside the cabin, under an oak of two century's growth less than twenty feet from the lap of the creek's waters. I some-times have fancied this picnic-table arrangement to be Gilbert's secret. I and many others have had the same thoughts he sets down so elo-quently here in his shore-front office. Just the other day back in Bal-timore, inspired by a break in the weather, I marshaled enough won-derfully poetic themes on my three-mile walk workward to lock up the Pulitzer Prize through 1990. Gilbert would be so envious. It was not the first time this had happened. And as always, after trotting faithfully by my side across half the city, my themes, like half-wild animals, balked at entering the newspaper office building with me. I suppose they knew that clapped into journalese, digested by newsroom computers, and sieved through the brains of editors, they would risk emerging tame as lap dogs. Gilbert, who has always remained on the outside himself, knows the secret to harnessing such themes. He seduces the little devils, makes them think he has invited them to a picnic by the shore.

Not that it has been any picnic here, authoring *The Lord's Oysters*—a novel based loosely on his boyhood as the son of a Chester River wa-terman—and several volumes of poetry. The bulk of the last forty years has been "hard scratching," Gilbert says; writing free-lance for small area papers, teaching school, watching all his books go out of print. Self-doubt has visited the idyllic cove plenty of times. Sur-rounded by a culture taught to "go for it," Gilbert—who chose to stay at his picnic table, just watching, listening, waiting—has been lonely at times. But he never truly wanted to move, not even when New York publishers, enthusiastic over drafts of *The Lord's Oysters*, in the 1950s urged him to move there to meet the literary crowd and push the book. "That's the way the Eastern Shore is," he says, chuckling. "It traps you, saps your strength."

A few years ago another writer, not from this area, took up resi-dence in a cabin on another creek of the Choptank River only a half-mile from here. He only stayed for a year, but in that time he did some-thing Gilbert has not been able to do in a lifetime. He published a book on the bay that made a vast sum of money. "We never visited," Gilbert recalls of James Michener, the author of the bestseller *Chesapeake*. "We're not in the same league." After a pause, Gilbert adds, a bit test-ily, as I scribble notes, "Don't take that to mean I think he's a better writer."

As an Eastern Shoreman myself, and a Michener fan of longstand-ing, I read *Chesapeake* avidly, and it is my firm opinion that it doesn't ring nearly so true as a representation of the bay's essential qualities as Gilbert's best stuff. The reason probably says more about the peculiar and elusive spirit of place that resides in the bay than it does about the relative talents of the two authors. Michener's forte is the epic—the settlement of the west, landing men on the moon, caravans across Afghanistan; and as epic, the bay served him poorly. Physically, the Chesapeake estuary is among the gentlest bodies of water of its size, lacking furious currents, rocky shoals, mammoth waves, or even much of a daily tidal drop. As for human settlement, food was always bountiful; and marshes and mosquitoes doubtless posed more threats than Indians or climate.

But now listen to part of Gilbert Byron's "These Chesapeake Men":

. . . These men a sun-tanned, quiet breed,
With eyes of English blue and faces
Lined with many a watch of sunlit waters . . . ;

. . . They seek the imperial shad and the lowly crab,
The oyster, the weakfish, the turtle, the rockfish,
. . . And food for their souls
Which they sometimes find.

In the calling of the wild duck,
In the mating of the kingfisher,
In the sloughing of the soft crab,
In the softness of the water's touch,
In the flight of great blue heron.
In the sculling of the oar,
In the passing schools of fish,
In the belly of the sail,
In the hauling of the seine,
In the taste of oysters raw,
In the soaring fish-hawk's wings,
In the touch of southwest wind,
In the little waves that break,
In the surge against the prow,
In the cliffs of yellow clay
In the setting of the sun
In the quest of quiet harbor—
In the Chesapeake.

There you have it, the real essence of our bay. No Ahabs in dramatic pursuit of white whales, no wrecks of the *Edmund Fitzgerald*; just watermen, the most lapidary juxtaposition of humanity and nature left on the civilized globe; just the subtle and enduring beauty of natural cycles, and the synergism that occurs at the edge where land and water mingle intimately, to effect something greater than the sum of their parts. I wonder, is it Gilbert working his magic on the cove, or the other way around? Who is subject, and who is author?

Even Gilbert has to admit that his poem is not timeless. Fifty years later, he says, there is a generation who will wonder what he was talking about with "the imperial shad," a species nearly vanished, and illegal to even fish for. As for the "lowly crab," it is now the mainstay of watermen's incomes. The rockfish, the state fish and a coveted food and sport species, was not even deemed worth mentioning when he wrote "These Chesapeake Men," he says.

The day, one of the year's shortest, is fast fleeing as Gilbert gropes along a wall packed floor to ceiling with books. Glaucoma has taken the sight of one eye, and the other is going. Expertly, he locates the volume he wants, and reads aloud what is still his favorite poem after nearly a half-century, "Evening Marshes":

> Marsh grass is golden
> Under a late sun,
> And wild ducks' wings
> Whistle with the wind.
> We are one,
> Wild duck and setting sun,
> Marsh grass around the pond,
> Earth smells and shadows,
> Coming cold and early night,
> Evening star and this
> Great emptiness
> Within me.

"I wrote that in 1938 after hunting around Lewes, Delaware. They had a great marsh there, great marsh. I've lost the urge to hunt long since, but the poem's held up. I've still got a good ear and that poem makes the most of it." With his sight fading, he is more keenly aware than ever of poetry's aural qualities, he says. "I still enjoy this cove so . . . the sounds of birds massing for spring migrations . . . the water lapping." In this and other ways, Gilbert says, he has never had it so good. It is as if the world, having galloped past him for so long, has begun to rediscover the virtues of quiet coves.

The Lord's Oysters, reprinted a few years ago, has sold out and is in its second reprinting. His first new collection of poems in thirty years has just been published, along with *Cove Dweller,* a prose account of his first year here, building the cabin. Washington College, where he played football at 125 pounds many years ago, honored him at commencement recently, and public television has made a documentary including him. "I only worry that the PBS thing makes it sound like I'm finishing up," Gilbert grouses. In fact, he has finished a sequel to *The Lord's Oysters*, and is at work on another novel, writing now on yellow legal paper with dark felt pens so he can see what he is doing.

As he puts it, approaching eighty-four, "I've got no mortgage, no kids . . . got Social Security, a few royalties, and every now and then somebody pays me to speak. I'm set for life."

And recently he wrote "All of His Days Are Foggy Now":

He does not fume or rage
against this dying of the light.
When young he loved the foggy days
that shut out most of his world,
a world he could never cope with; a world he would never bargain
   with.
Now he sails his white skiff across the blue reaches,
and bikes along lanes green with spring, listens to birds he no
   longer sees.
The eyedrops provide misty landscapes,
the Impressionists he could never afford.
Meeting a lone biker, he muses,
"All of the girls are beautiful now."

Ensorcelled in Garrett County

It is slightly embarrassing for an Eastern Shoreman to admit, but two of my most affecting exposures to unadulterated natural beauty have come as far from the bay as you can get and still be in Maryland. On the high plateau of Garrett County, within just a few miles of each other, are the place where the state's autumn begins and a place where you wish summer would never end.

Brenneman's Grove, October

You can hear fall's glorious marching band tuning up here on Western Maryland's high plateau, fixing to parade east across the state, playing licks so hot only winter can quench them. Among the lordly, old sugar maples that rule the grove, the air is sweetly clangorous with the ring of hard, bright sunlight and crisp air, cold fires forging an orchestra of autumnal tones.

Logically, everyone knows you can't really *hear* fall's coming. Logically, what we have here is lowering temperatures and shortening daylight degrading the leaves' chlorophyll, revealing the carotene, xanthophyll, anthocyanin, and tannin to render autumn's colors. But logic never has penetrated the eerie and arresting atmosphere within virgin forest groves like this one, spared the timberman's axe for its maple sugar production. Early on, the gods of mythology chose to live in such groves. Groves were the sacred precincts of the Greeks, and the first temples of the Romans, who, Pliny wrote, "adored them no less devoutly than images that gleam in gold and ivory." It seems that half the victims in mythic tragedies were guys who messed with the natural order of groves; so perhaps I had best pass on to you exactly what the ancient maples at Brenneman's told me about how the Maryland autumn is born.

Only a few weeks ago, you would have sworn these bland, green hills could not carry a simple melody. They droned on like August's cicadas, and the blue haze of deep summer pooled stagnantly in their boughs. Then, a few of the younger, more excitable maples began tootling brassily, going giddy in just a few branches at first, then starting to really jam, back and forth, building oranges on golds on reds, soaring toward an otherworldly luminosity; and down in the creek bottoms, the willows, flushing green-golden, bent to lullaby to the rushing water, "Fall's a-comin'."

The tune was so infectious. Color leapt to color. Before long, in just one night—whang!—like cymbals clashing, an old spreading beech went shimmery all over. Its reverberations were answered by a rich and resonant chord from deep in the forest, as a whole stand of oaks turned majestic scarlet; and with a flourish as mellow and full as French horns, every tulip poplar within hearing distance began committing alchemy, green into purest gold. The volume increased. The whole mountainside blasted the clotted chlorophyll of monotone summer to the nether ends of the chromatic scale. The forested hills emerged, suited in splendid tweeds, their full instrumentation revealed. There were gums—sweet, sour, and black; a great clump of aspens all a-tremolo. There were dogwoods and sumacs and three kinds of elm; birches and beeches and five kinds of oak; and the maples—oh my, the maples, virtuosos spanning whole octaves of color, setting all the Appalachians to music.

A surge of piercing, crystalline air is all it takes to snap the whole show into formation and march it down off the plateau, severing with a snap the last, torpid traces of August, charging the whole state with a crackling kinesis, ushering in a time of color and clarity, harvest and migration. Across Carroll and Baltimore counties, lumbering harvesters regurgitate brassy mounds of shelled grain into waiting trucks in the field, as chevrons of Canada geese scud overhead. In the bay, tongers are grappling the bottom for fat oysters, even as the clearing water reveals the last run of blue crabs scuttling for the bottom and hibernation.

The wind plays its own tunes of the season, from the scuffle of sere leaves on city concrete to soughing overtures through the boughs of pines. And all across Maryland, people will feel a restlessness, an exuberance, a deep stirring that they can't quite explain. Is it the great symphony, dimly sensed, that creates their nameless anticipation? Many of us, living outside of groves, would scoff at such a notion. But consider some things that science already has documented—the subsonic singing of great whales which spans whole ocean basins; and the echoes from Atlantic and Pacific surf used by some high-flying birds to navigate down the Mississippi flyway. There may be much music in this world that is nonetheless sweet for eluding our own poor audition.

Back on the Garrett plateau, I often think of one man who must have heard the autumn symphony at least occasionally. Leo Beachy, an early photographer who loved these hills and lived his life not far from Brenneman's Grove, wrote in a letter to his cousin Isabelle on a fall day almost seventy-five years ago: "For the past few weeks I have been burdened with an emotion to go out on the hills with my camera and record a wonderful picture—I know not what—but something to carry a story of God's wonderful creation." At the time, Beachy could no longer walk because of a virus known later to medicine as muscular dystrophy; but for all that, I suspect his greatest frustration was facing the brilliant firestorm of a Garrett County autumn armed only with black and white film.

Frazee Ridge, June

MEMO TO THE EDITOR:

Your reporter in Garrett County has been ensorcelled by a June day. A force greater than the call of duty has made him to lie down in green pastures, feet propped on a rock, head cradled by a sheaf of fresh-cut hay. He realizes he was dispatched here to address a host of vital issues, from strip mining and deforestation to the merits of centralized sewage treatment versus septic tanks.

They can wait.

There are more important questions here today that can be grappled with only from a supine position in consultation with daisies and buttercups so bright I swear you could sight them from space orbit. To wit:

—Can physicists explain how an eruption of bobwhite from the hedgerow I just passed could impart a tingling motivation to half the mountainside, despite representing an infinitessimal part of the whole scene's mass and energy?

—Is the fecund dishabille of a sun-spangled hardwood forest aesthetically superior to the needle-carpeted order in an adjacent copse of hemlocks, which greedily sponge up all available light for their own darkly brooding purposes?

—How many shades of green can nature mint? Are the alpine pastures lapping upward, like gentle surf, into forested coves, or is it the reverse—is the woods' arsenical green bleeding, madraslike, down the slopes?

—Why do we perceive a cornfield as so pleasantly natural when it is really the quintessence of a laboratory-bred monoculture, sown in the most regimented fashion imaginable? The earth up here in June can respond to sun and rain in so many tongues—elm, oak, goldenrod, and trailing arbutus to name only a few—isn't it a terrible imposition, being lashed by the plow into shouting summer after summer, in a monotone, "Corn"?

It is a superb vantage point your reporter has chosen to ponder these critical matters. It is near the crest of a high ridge where the light somehow amplifies color, and the very hush welling up from the valley sounds its own pure, exultant note in the adyts of the spirit.

Admittedly, there are distractions in getting down to business here. Last night, when your correspondent pitched camp he was interrupted repeatedly by the singular transformation of a rising moon— from a horizon-filling round of orangey cheddar, to lemony gold gouda, to palest whey as it passed its apogee (talk about food for thought). And around dawn, it seemed a shame to get moving before all the pale watermelon and cantaloupe striations of the eastern sky had thawed to a warm, brilliant blush.

And just as that show was ending, here came the sun, sloshing over the ridgeline and flowing down onto the cool, moist pasture bottoms like acid striking lime, setting the whole landscape aboil with fantastic vapors. Transfixed, your reporter let the warming, kneading rays of the sun supple his consciousness, sending it straying to other seasons he had experienced here, when a hard virginal crust of snow rendered the meadow an eye-averting lake of light, and the surface of the ridge was coruscant under a hard blue sky that crashed down to meet it with the keenness of a guillotine blade . . .

But by now, dear editor, I know you will be asking yourself that standard question of our trade: Is this news?

Well, no one held a press conference on it, and no important government officials said it yesterday. But when we get to the point where a fine day in June is not worth writing about, will there be anything left worth calling a press conference for?

All Minny's Fault

Sugar Loaf Mountain, Spring

Perhaps our values will catch up with Minny Pohlmann's someday. Maybe in a less materialistic age she would long since have had honor and recognition. As a modern American success story, however, she has been mostly a bust, an oddball, a mild embarrassment to some of her well-to-do-neighbors, whose estates and farms around Sugar Loaf Mountain encompass some of Maryland's richest rural heritage. At age sixty-two, Minny is in debt, has deliberately squandered a small fortune, traded retirement savings in the bank for nothing more tangible than the integrity of a landscape, and has invested totally in maintaining "the mountain's beautiful serenity—it looks like a pregnant woman reclining," she says.

Sugar Loaf Mountain proper, which at 1,280 feet in elevation dominates the Frederick–Montgomery County border for miles around, already is irrevocably preserved from development by the trust of its wealthy former owner, Gordon Strong. Strong, a Chicago banker who was heir to a fortune from the Atchison, Topeka, & Santa Fe Railway, was captured by the mountain one perfect day around the century's turn as he bicycled through the nearby Potomac River foothills.

It was then, and still is, a curious property of the Sugar Loaf that despite its prominence above anything else in the landscape for miles around, one can approach quite close before sighting it. The explanation surely lies in the dips and rises of the surrounding land, and the winding, forested roads, which still carry traffic through the countryside. Nonetheless, the effect is quite magical when one turns a corner and the mountain springs out from behind a copse of maples, or rears its shaggy bulk from behind a groomed field of grain. If you choose your routes well through the region ruled by the Sugar Loaf, you can play hide-and-seek delightfully with the great mountain for most of an afternoon. I suspect it was just such an exercise that impelled the young cyclist Gordon Strong to devote most of the rest of his long life to buying the entire mountain, piece by piece, as his private park, which he later opened to anyone who wished to share the beauty of its views.

Strong was not the only powerful person entranced by the mountain. In President Franklin D. Roosevelt's first term, Secretary of the Interior Harold Ickes seized on the idea of acquiring the mountain, only thirty-two miles from Washington, as a presidential retreat. "A handful of people will benefit from it if you do that," Strong told Ickes, "thousands can enjoy it if I keep it." Not one to turn down a request without offering alternatives, Strong suggested alternate sites for the retreat, including a spot in the nearby Catoctins that became Roosevelt's Shangri-la, the present-day Camp David. I find it pleasant to think, drinking in the panoramas from atop Sugar Loaf, that with all the power of the American presidency, and all that is written about the restorative powers every occupant of the office seems to find in the natural beauty at Camp David, that we, the people, got the first choice of retreats in the region.

But if the mountain was protected under Strong's trust, no such terms applied to the farmland at its foot that was sold to the private trustees who manage Sugar Loaf by elderly neighbors of Minny. The old couple had neglected to put any restrictions on the land's use because they assumed it would be treated as the mountain it adjoined. The trustees, however, anticipating that it could be a ready source of money if it were needed in the future, got approval to subdivide for development the seventeen acres of the farm that fronted on Sugar Loaf Mountain Road, a winding dirt track along the preserve's eastern flank. If anything, the development, by establishing a precedent for more zoning change in the rural landscape, would have enhanced substantially the dollar potential of Minny's fifty-four acres, located not far away on the other side of the road. There are few surer tickets to wealth than owning developable farmland within commuting distance of Washington. But Minny and her late husband, Ken, were never much good at extracting profits from the land—or perhaps they just defined profit differently than most.

They came to the valley at the foot of Sugar Loaf in 1952, Minny says, following a period of enormous impact and questioning of their values after their first-born son, aged three and a half, had died of cancer in 1948. "The land gave Ken stability. I still think he never would have lived as long as he did—he had heart problems—if not for the farm. He was never happier, never freer, than in the spring when he was bouncing along on his tractor, mowing, pipe clenched between his teeth, sailor's cap on his head. Actually, he never got much mowed in the spring, because he was always stopping so he wouldn't harm birds' nests. " The Pohlmanns kept their land in grass, raising cattle instead of joining the movement in agriculture to continuous cropping of corn, which maximized income but, all too often, soil erosion as well. To support them, Ken commuted to a regular job in Washington as a pension analyst for the United Mine Workers.

If they never made much of a living from the soil, the Pohlmanns still were nourished more than most of us, one suspects, by the landscape. Minny tells of winter mornings after ice storms when the forest on top of the mountain glistened like diamonds; of spring's new green on the slopes and fall's blaze of colors; and rising with the sun in the fleeting, precious cool of summer mornings, watching the light play on the mountaintop over a mug of coffee on the farmhouse porch—and of something else that a nation of urban and suburban dwellers has almost forgotten—the beauty of the night sky when the surrounding land is completely dark, unbroken by street lamps and security lights.

She could not let a development come between her and the mountain, so Minny bought the land back from the trustees at full development price, $5,000 an acre. Payments on the loan she took out take all the interest on her savings and soon may leave her only Social Security to live on. Those tempted to help Minny out should be warned before reaching for their checkbook. This is a bad investment by all conventional methods of accounting loss and gain. Your prospective business partner's value system is dangerously antithetical to the concept of land-as-commodity that has helped make America grow. Minny's plans for the land, once she owns it free and clear, are to turn around and slap a perpetual conservation easement on it, in effect devaluing the price back to open space, thousands less than she is paying for it. "I believe, like the Indian prayer, that the earth does not belong to man. Man belongs to the earth," she says. "We are part of the community, not the dictators." Also, be warned, if you would throw in with Minny Pohlmann, that she has more irons in the fire by far than this one seventeen-acre parcel. She is working to ensure the rural nature, through easements and zoning and public ownership, of a chunk of countryside, fifteen thousand acres and twenty square miles, around the majestic mountain here. Nor is it just acreage she aims at perserving; it is nothing less than *country*—in the sense that the conservationist Aldo Leopold defined country as "the personality of land."

"Personable" is not a bad way to describe the region anchored by Sugar Loaf Mountain. Physically, it is rolling Potomac Piedmont that in an age of huge and featureless grain farms has retained a nice balance between wood lot and smallish cornfield and pasture. Hedgerows and thickets and occasional windbreak plantings of dark cedar trees lend pleasing definition to the interstices of ridge and stream valley.

Culturally, a lot remains of the old stone bank barns and huge, white clapboard farmhouses, stone fences, and silos typical of the area's early farming community.

Once Minny took me down to where the Monocacy River flows by the mountain and into the Potomac. We stood near the archeological site of an old Indian village at the confluence. Looking back upriver we could see the old C&O Canal Aqueduct still standing from the days of barge traffic. In line of sight, behind that, was the trestle for the nation's first railroad, the Baltimore and Ohio; and high in the sky, over timeless Sugar Loaf, cruised the French, supersonic Concorde, descending to Dulles International Airport. It was a rare window through time and cultures, all inextricably part of the countryside's unique personality.

"Worth keeping, huh," Minny says. She and other citizens of the region have made a good start. Minny—often at her own expense for lawyers—has been instrumental in down-zoning a corridor of land critical to wildlife habitat from industrial use to open space only; also in down-zoning more than three thousand acres that she subsequently interested the state in preserving as the Monocacy Natural Resources Area. Other fights loom. The state is considering the region for a new power-plant site. The tall stacks of the plant would rise to within a couple hundred feet of the mountain's peak elevation. But Minny feels that the citizens opposing the plant will prevail. The mountain, she says, makes a strong rallying point.

The mountain—and Minny Pohlmann, she might have added. Ed Weseley, a long-time environmental activist in these parts, says he doesn't know a person anywhere, who is not a millionaire, who has done as much as Minny to preserve land. That, however, is not the nicest thing anyone has said about her, Minny says. The nicest thing was when the zoning lawyer for a prominent developer pointed his finger at her in a public hearing on preserving another big chunk of the Sugar Loaf region and said, "Minny Pohlmann, all this is your fault."

Watermen's World

Late Winter, aboard the Hayruss IV

It was nearing midnight when Garland Phillips gave in to Nature for the first time in eighteen hours. The bay was locked in ice from the coldest winter in fifty years. That night, from the Potomac River to the

Chesapeake and Delaware ship canal, not even the big ships bound for Baltimore harbor were moving. For hours the twin diesels of the *Hayruss* had howled unceasingly, a lone speck bellowing protest across the frozen, moon-washed emptiness of the Chesapeake Bay. The lights of Tilghman, home port, twinkled and beckoned only a few miles away. Again and again, Garland slammed the throttles forward, lashing the fifty-foot fiberglass fishing craft into five-inch ice, and the *Hayruss* would shudder and crash forward a few more yards.

Two miles from Tilghman her fuel ran out. In the silence, her captain slumped at the wheel. It was the first time man and boat had stopped moving since 5:30 A.M. Garland's weariness lasted about thirty seconds. Snapping upright, he radioed ashore on the CB to his wife, Adrienne—Pete, he always called her: Pete should phone Bobby, an oyster tonger with a boat sturdy enough to come out and tow us; also, get the local fuel distributor out of bed and tell him to have two drums of diesel on the dock in an hour; get to the store before it closed. Pick up net twine and extra groceries, enough for three nights. We had to be forty miles back up the bay by daylight, nets ready to fish. It was the first time in a week that the ice had yielded enough for the *Hayruss* to clear port. Garland's sonar had located an enormous school of rockfish off Worton Point in the upper bay, and who could tell when more cold weather and heavier ice would again "slam the door to the meat locker," as the watermen say.

Within minutes, the unflappable Pete radioed back that everything was under control. Garland, who is forty-five, looked delighted as a small boy who has been told he can go back out and play again. Not that we were out for the sport of it; not at a time when the Coast Guard, and sanity, had virtually shut down waterborne commerce in Maryland. In the stern of the *Hayruss,* an etiolated moon pooled coldly on more than a ton of sleek, silver- and black-striped rockfish, which were bringing close to a dollar a pound, dockside. Pete had also arranged for a local fish dealer to send a truck to meet us at 2:00 A.M. to unload the rock. They would be in New York's Fulton Fish Market by midmorning. It was an impressive though hardly record-setting catch for the *Hayruss.* In the next few days Garland would more than triple it. "Got to go hard when you can go, got to get 'em when you can in winter fishing," Russell Phillips, Garland's father and a crew member, told me. Come with him again next winter and he would show me some real fishing, Garland had joked when I left the boat, numb and exhausted, one cold, starlit morning. We never did it. Eleven months later on 9 February 1979, with heavy ice on the bay, the *Hayruss* went down in sixty feet of water, drowning Garland and four crewmen. It happened so fast, they found two of them still in the pilot house.

I had gone fishing with Garland because I heard he was the best and the biggest the bay had ever seen—the ultimate blending of technology and know-how, the high point of an evolutionary process among the watermen who had been netting in the bay for three centuries. *Hayruss IV,* named after his mom, Hazel, and his dad, Russell, had been built to Garland's specifications. Her thick fiberglass could buck ice that would stop the most foolhardy captain on a traditional wooden workboat. The boat's $80,000 price included nearly $10,000 of fish-finding sonar and all-weather navigational gear. With twin Caterpillar diesels, she could cruise the length of the bay and back in a day without straining. Four comfortable bunks, shower and head, microwave oven, electric baseboard heat in the cabin, and color television made staying on the water overnight a minor consideration. It might seem extravagant by traditional bay standards, Garland told me; but he considered it his office—an office where he would be spending a major portion of his life. It might as well be comfortable.

For all that the boat impressed, the most extraordinary thing about the *Hayruss* was Garland. As a group, the captains of the bay's forty-boat fleet of winter rockfishermen have always been the high rollers, the hardest goers, the nomads among Chesapeake watermen. Pursuing a mobile and elusive quarry in a season ruled by storms and ice, they live with the prospect of failing to make gas money for weeks at a time, but also with the lure of making two years' pay in a week. They look on the bulk of bay watermen, who harvest the sedentary clams and oysters each winter, as prehistoric hunters must have looked on the rest of the tribe who plodded daily from the village to hoe in the fields.

Some oystermen said after the drowning that Garland had been too greedy, wanting always to be "big boy of the day," as the top-catching captain is sometimes called. For a fact, he was competitive. I remember his joy one morning before dawn, as the *Hayruss* roared north, past Rock Hall, the center of the winter fishing fleet since white men first began pursuing the rockfish. All the captains there were iced in, or considered themselves to be, Garland said, and it was clear that it made his day to be the only one out after the fish. He was not given to reading poetry, but I told him he should look up "Winter Fisherman," written decades ago by Albert W. Dowling, a Rock Hall native and poet:

It is not need for bread alone that drives
A man from fireside to the ice's flow,
But goading inner appetite that thrives
On hazards which the meek will never know,

An eagerness that spurns and scorns the weak
And welcomes winters on the Chesapeake.

Garland and *Hayruss*, many thought, were the wave of the future
for watermen, pointing the way to bigger, mobile, more efficient harvesting of the bay's resources. In retrospect, they seem more like the
beginning of the end.

It is New Year's Eve, nearly six years since the *Hayruss* went down. I am
back on Garland's old upper bay stomping grounds, fishing aboard the
Seawitch, a forty-footer belonging to Ronnie Fithian, one of Rock Hall's
ablest young fishing captains. Ronnie, thirty-three, remembers icy
winter nights he spent tied to Garland's stern off Devil's Head, north of
Worton Point, waiting for the dawn light by which to set their deadly
efficient drift nets dancing with the tide. Even fiercest competitors
would buddy up for added insurance under those conditions. "We'd
stay out fishing 'til the food and fuel ran out," Ronnie said. "That ice'd
be coming down out of the Susquehanna on ebb tide, hit the bow, it'd
knock you out of your bunk. One year the Coast Guard cutter came up
to tell us they had restricted the bay to large vessels only. But we
wouldn't budge. We were catching rock. It seems like the times you can
make money are the times you shouldn't be out there."

On this day, however, the proud winter fishing fleet is just going
through the motions. The *Seawitch*'s nets are ragged and unmended.
The power winder that pulls the heavily anchored mesh from the bottom is broken. There is no need to fix anything anymore. A morning's
work has netted four small rockfish. Some of the nets are full of menhaden, "trash fish," but the crew doesn't bother to untangle them, just
heaping the whole affair up on the deck. A cold rain begins to fall. To
our north, the blast furnaces at Sparrows Point huff and flare. On the
Bay Bridges a couple miles south, morning rush-hour commuters from
the Eastern Shore stream through the toll gates. The last net is hauled,
and then it is done—done for the year, done for the season, done,
maybe, forever. For the first time in history a moratorium, effective
midnight this night, has been imposed by the state on all catching of
the state fish, the rock.

We docked back in Rock Hall, where television stations from Baltimore and Washington were setting up to record the end of an era. I
noticed another condo project going up, on waterfront land that used
to be owned by one of the best winter rockfish captains on the bay.
More pleasure craft slips were going in at another location on the small
harbor. "Can't compete with weekend sailboaters for space on the waterfront," Ronnie had said in disgust on the way in. Room to tie up

workboats like the *Seawitch* was going to get pretty scarce, he reckoned. No one, I knew, would lament the precarious future of the watermen any more than the weekend sailors and vacation home owners and party-boat fishermen. It is in large part the charm, both real and fancied, of working fishing villages like Rock Hall that draws them, in ever-swelling numbers, to the half-dozen or so major watermens' communities that remain on Maryland's Eastern Shore.

At no point in the bay's history have watermen been more valued—or more endangered. They fascinate us moderns in ways perhaps similar to any big, predatory animal that embodies wildness and, by roaming free, signifies that at least a corner of the planet remains in working, natural order. Imagine the sense of accomplishment and the thrill that would come were we able to repopulate our forests and parks in Maryland with the bear and mountain lion that once held the franchise there. Of course, they would have to observe some limits. They could not eat the cows from adjacent dairy farms, or frighten and maul campers, or otherwise let their making a living interfere with the millions of our citizens who now use those same outdoors for pleasure and sport. Of course we know that is impossible. Top predators in nature simply need more space and resources to be themselves than we can afford them outside of the remaining wilderness back country and jungles. It is why we have zoos.

But what we long ago found unthinkable on land, we continue to celebrate on the water. *Waterman*—the unique, all-purpose term we use to describe the object of our affection is tribute to the scope of his appetite for natural resources. Preying on oysters, crabs, rockfish, eels, clams, terrapins, even bloodworms—virtually every variety of marketable flesh that grows in the bay—the Chesapeake waterman is a true top-of-the-food-chain predator, the closest thing to a great white shark this estuary supports, the nearest subculture in America to the hunter-gatherer society that we left behind for herding and agriculture nine thousand years ago.

And how we love the images of the men and the boats and the independent life style, still attuned to natural forces, that having watermen around perpetuates. It is a luxury that few developed regions on earth enjoy—not just oysters on the half shell, but oysters on the half shell caught by salty captains under full sail in century-old wooden skipjacks; not just rockfish stuffed with crab meat, but rockfish and crab meat that come from little towns and islands where Elizabethan English still tinges the speech, and the quaint harbors are the stuff of picture postcards.

The existence of watermen is perhaps the most powerful symbol we have that our bay still flourishes. To lose them would be to lose a powerful impetus for maintaining our environmental standards. It is so often said that we all benefit from clean water, without defining how clean, that few people stop to think that most uses of the bay do not require the highest levels of purity and productivity. Shipping, power-plant cooling, recreational boating, even swimming—all these can flourish in aquatic systems ranging from filthy to mildly degraded. Even sport fishermen seem well on the way to accepting bluefish, which have scant commercial value, as the declining rock's replacement for the premiere game fish of the estuary. An ocean spawner, the blue, unlike the rock, need not spend its most pollution-sensitive, larval and juvenile phases here. Neither do those who fish for recreation need to catch tons a day like a Garland Phillips or a Ronnie Fithian; the mere anticipation of a fish is often enough to sate their cravings and insure their returning, to spend hundreds of dollars on yet another expedition.

Of all the human users of the bay, only the waterman absolutely requires resources of a quantity and variety that presuppose a natural system in top, year-round condition. Put another way, the waterman is to the rest of us bay dwellers what the canary was to coal miners, who carried them down the shafts, depending on the bird's exquisite sensitivity to leaking gas to give them an early warning of disaster. If watermen are flourishing, it is a sign that the bay's integrity still holds.

Top predator and reliable canary, the waterman would certainly seem worth keeping around, a fitting symbol of the kind of bay we want to preserve. But as the bay's resources have declined to historic lows among several species, watermen have also become symbols of plunder and greed. These are among the most dispiriting and confusing of times for the waterman. At once, we have made his preservation a prime objective of an unprecedented drive to restore health to the bay's waters, and also have portrayed him as an unconscionable over-harvester of increasingly scarce fish and oysters. We want him to remain a perfectly ferocious, free-ranging natural animal—but also, please to go easier on eating the deer. It is enough to confuse any symbol.

Because watermen could only benefit from cleaner water, there is a tendency to think they are natural allies of everyone who would stem the bay's environmental decline. The truth is more complicated. The reason is contained in the essay "The Tragedy of the Commons." It remains, twenty years after it was written by the genetic biologist, Garrett Hardin, one of the most compelling and troubling statements to emerge from the modern environmental movement. Hardin tells the parable of a pasture (translate bay for our purposes) that is open to all. Each herdsman (waterman) will reasonably try to keep as many cattle (catch as much seafood) as he can on this commons. It is an arrangement that may work until society banishes disease, famine, war, and poverty to the extent that population, as well as people's demands for a higher living standard, begin steadily to rise.

As the pressure on the commons consequently begins to increase, each herdsman rationally asks what he gains by putting one more head of cattle there. The answer is that it is in his interest to do so, because he gets virtually all the gain from selling an extra cow, whereas the loss resulting from overgrazing is shared among all the users: "The rational herdsman concludes that the only sensible course for him to pursue is to add another animal to his herd. And another . . . But this is the conclusion reached by each and every rational herdsman sharing a commons. Therein is the tragedy. Each man is locked into a system that compels him to increase his herd without limit—in a world that is limited . . . each pursuing his own best interest in a society that believes in the freedom of the commons. Freedom in a commons brings ruin to all."

Watermen, in addition to operating in a commons, know well that their bay is a fickle bank for anyone who would stockpile current abundance of a natural resource in the interests of conservation. Fish and crabs may migrate to other states, with looser harvest laws. Shellfish cannot do that, but almost every waterman will tell you from painful experience how he planned to come back next month, or next season, to exploit a rich bed of clams or oysters, only to have it discovered by other watermen, killed by a hard winter, or by a spring freshet that fatally lowered the salinity, or—increasingly—saw it wiped out by pollution. The only resource that is any good to you is one in the boat, the watermen will say.

Bound to the unpredictable comings and goings of nature, he survives not by trying to conserve, but by making hay while the sun shines. Also, he is extremely adept at "switching off," at turning quickly to catching other species when the one he has been preying on declines—as he knows in his bones it will, sooner or later. Garland Phillips, who thought farther ahead than the average waterman, had planned for the ultimate switch off—moving *Hayruss* out of the bay— as long ago as 1978. Garland had invested in fish-finding sonar that could operate at depths found in the ocean. He had a sense, I think, of how hard people like himself were pushing the system in the Chesapeake.

To the environmentalist, the waterman's normal reaction to scarcity—fish harder while they last—is appalling; but the waterman is following his evolutionary dictates. Also, some of the best money to be made comes as a species declines, because its scarcity drives the market price up. In 1986 oystermen took fewer bushels from the bay than they had since the 1840s, but at prices that made it one of their more profitable winters. Rockfish netters in 1984 caught only a tenth of what they did a decade before, but sold them at prices many, many times as high.

For all this, the commercial watermen will never fish a species into extinction, the rockfish netters like to say. They would switch off to catching something more abundant long before that low a level of population was approached. Only the sport fisherman could afford to catch the last rockfish. For a long time, the state's lawmakers seemed to buy this proposition as the watermen and conservationists wrangled over the bay's diminishing supplies of seafood.

By 1984, however, the string was beginning to run out on the watermen. For the first time in history, the state banned them from taking any more rockfish. The species no longer was reproducing well, for reasons only poorly understood. Many watermen lamented that if pollution from the cities had been controlled years before, there would be no need for ending their centuries-old fishery. The state reassured them that restoration of water quality to aid the rockfish was a major reason the legislature had just passed a massive program of laws and expenditures aimed at combatting the pollution of the Chesapeake Bay. Neither side, however, fully appreciated that the traditional kinds of pollution targeted by these programs were not necessarily the ultimate poison that destroys large, fierce predators. In 1983 the public got a look for the first time at confidential statistics that the state kept on who was catching how much of the bay's rockfish. It had been generally known that it was split about 50–50, between sportsmen and commercial netters. Even so, it was shocking to see that 10 percent of the commercial share had gone to two netters, and that perhaps forty or fifty watermen were accounting for the great bulk of all commercial landings.

Never mind that even small catches were said to represent an important option for hundreds more of the bay's 4,500 watermen. The sport fishermen were aroused—and there were 900,000 of them. They had finally seen the predators up close and found that, for symbols and canaries, they had awfully sharp claws and long fangs, and needed tons of the resource to fill their bellies. By contrast, more than a third of the sportsmen, a state creel survey showed, did not even catch a rockfish, and most of them did not catch more than four fish.

Galvanized by this sort of information, the state's sport-fishing interests achieved their first semblance of unity in calling for a moratorium to give the rockfish breathing room to rebound. From the sportsmen, some of whom came from as far away as Boston, the commercial men heard accounts at public hearings of the rockfish's "transcendent beauty . . . infinite mystery," and of connections formed between angler and fish "vital to the soul." The watermen left some of those meetings shaking their heads in disbelief.

Ultimately, it was not the poetry of the sportsmen that would beat the commercial men, but the growing numbers of the former, all of them now demanding their share of the pie. This would prove as deadly to the netters as any toxic spill. And unlike toxics, no one even thought that the idea of more and more recreational users of the resource was a bad thing, or to be regulated. Such freedom to use a commons, as Hardin said, ultimately brings ruin to all; and his essay has not retained its power and currency all these years because he wrote just about some medieval system of cowherding.

He extended his reasoning to the very planet, the ultimate commons, in which our human herd busily multiplies, pursuing what individuals, families, and corporations, as well as local, state, and national governments, see as their various rational self-interests. And he asked, how long, in a world of finite natural resources, could growth of such a herd continue without inevitable ruin to the earth. At our peril, we assume the plight of watermen signifies nothing more than the fading of a vestigial life style, the inability of big predators and civilization to mix; for watermen are also our canaries. Their problems may be symptomatic of greater perils that could befall the greater commons, the 64,000-square-mile watershed of the Chesapeake, of which the bay, lying at its bottom, is a reflection.

Perhaps we will, in years to come, clean the more recognized pollutants from our waters, and perhaps that will bring the rockfish and the oysters back. The numbers of sport fishermen and others who want to share our waters for fun will have continued to increase, given current population trends in the "Bos-Wash corridor" development that stretches between New England and the District of Columbia. Meantime, there is a fishing moratorium in effect on the bay, and any waterman who wants to make a living through the winter will have little option but to catch oysters. He will not feel lonely, because by 1984 only one river system in the bay, the Choptank, still contained substantial quantities. From Rock Hall to Crisfield the tongers and dredgers homed in on the remaining beds like starving black ducks on shelled corn, working literally shoulder to shoulder. It was the rational thing for each to do in a commons like the Maryland bay, whose resources belong to no one and to everyone; but few thought the oysters could stand it for long.

Despite all their problems, the top predators we call watermen are not likely to fade away quietly like the bear and the mountain lion, who could not speak up for themselves; and the rest of us are not prepared at this point to give up such evocative symbols without a struggle. Perhaps some sort of limited-entry system could be worked out to curtail the watermen's use of the commons. Then one will quite literally have to be a "born waterman" to harvest seafood. Or perhaps jaded urbanites will vie to purchase from native watermen their inherited right to work the water, as one buys a seat on the New York Stock Exchange.

Or maybe, in our affluence, we will decide it is worthwhile to memorialize the waterman in a sort of Colonial Williamsburg on the bay—Watermen's World, we could call it. It could be built where the old, forgotten fishing town of Rock Hall once stood, and be replete with glassed-in, underwater lounges from which to view in action the techniques of authentic oyster tongers, who would go out and put their catch back on the beds after dark, to grapple them up again the next day for throngs of tourists, which seem to grow larger every year.

The Clatteringest Old Bridge

Hooper Island, October 1977

Soon they are going to replace the longest, narrowest, clatteringest old wooden bridge in Maryland. It connects upper Hooper Island to middle Hooper Island, and, no matter how far you've come, crossing it is the most memorable part of your trip. It is 1,178 feet long; 10-feet, 8-inches wide; decked with 3-by-10-inch creosote planks of old growth, heartwood loblolly pine, clinched to 4-by-14 stringers with 8-penny spikes. It has lovely white wooden railings . . . but all that scarcely does it justice. For that, you would have to be a newly licensed driver, trepidly negotiating the steatopygic gantlet of summer crabbers who bend unconcernedly over both railings, giving no quarter as they lean to dip crustaceans flippering on the tide. Somehow, no hind ends ever were fractured there, although a couple of windshields were sharded by the long, wooden handles of crab nets.

To do the bridge justice, you would need to have hearkened, miles out on the lower Dorchester County marshes, to the rolling thunder from vehicles rippling across the planks, indistinguishable from a brewing storm to the untutored ear. Years ago, late on a blowy winter night, when no one but a game warden was likely to be driving about, the bridge muttered a warning to some youthful duck hunters who had stayed in the marsh a few hours later than they should have.

Some of the bridge's character is personified by Robert Meekins, its tender for years. Sunup to sundown, seven days a week, crab season, oyster season, he was there, straining at the long, iron crank rod, whose hollow end slipped over a steel nut set in a plank of the fifty-foot center span. Walked round and round for several minutes, the crank smoothly pivoted the center span to let the larger workboats through. If, as sometimes happened, Meekins could not be raised by horn, shout, or, more recently, radio, the captain desiring passage between the bay and the Honga River had the option of tying to the bridge, hopping up, and cranking it open himself. Sometimes in a high wind, and later on when the gears in the pivot mechanism began to go bad, Meekins would have to get his wife to crank with him, he recalled. Between them, they kept it open all the time. A few years ago the county electrified the center span so that all the Meekinses had left to do was to push a button.

The new bridge will be longer, wider, higher, sturdier, and faster; two broad lanes of prestressed concrete, the only 60-MPH stretch on a whole island otherwise regulated to about 30 MPH by its twisty, shoulderless road that follows the contour of the bay and river shore. The bridge will eliminate the need for a draw, rising to thirty-five feet at the channel, a massive upswelling from the horizontality that stamps most of lower Dorchester County. It will be too high for crabbing or fishing. Pedestrian and recreational uses are not to be encouraged, says the feasibility study by a city planning firm. Meekins once caught 560 pounds of rockfish on a handline off the old bridge. Being two-lane, the new bridge will not need the pullover for a single car built into the center of the old structure, one of the pleasantest spots in the state to turn off the motor and the lights at night and listen to geese in concert and the sound of the Chesapeake Bay sliding by.

The primary consideration for replacing the old bridge was cost, according to Leonard Dayton, the Dorchester County Commission president. It just took too much maintenance with the higher speeds and heavier vehicles of the modern age. The availability of federal bridge-safety funds for virtually all of the project did not hurt either. No doubt a wealthier county, or one so developed that little of its traditional life styles remained, would have gone to great lengths to preserve a bridge like this. Dorchester County is neither of those. It is a working county, just as the old bridge has been no frivolous, picture-postcard bridge. Its 250 vehicles a day consist mostly of school buses, seafood delivery trucks, and local watermen going from Hoopersville to Fishing Creek and back. Nostalgia is gone from the scheme of things today, Dayton said.

Robert Meekins said that the bridge really isn't that old, though it

has seemed so in an era of modern materials, when even local watermen have been opting for fiberglass workboats over wooden ones. It
was built in 1941, on the remains of the bridge that was ripped away in
the hurricane of 1933. The bridge tender perished during that storm.
Jim Riggins was his name, Meekins said, adding that the tide "riz so
fast" that Riggins was carried away right with the draw house, which at
the time was on the bridge's center. They found him in the house up
the bay later on.

Thomas A. Flowers, a poet, storyteller, and county commissioner
whose family came from Hooper Island, said that his father, born in
1893, could remember when a man was able to step across the marsh
where now a quarter-mile of water flows beneath the wooden bridge.
He seemed somewhat less enthusiastic than Commissioner Dayton
and other county officials about the big, new span. But how do you
stop a federal plan? he asked. He said the bridge, because of its federal
funding, had to meet design standards determined by Congress, not
by the subtle natural forces that still shape most of life on the island.

I said goodbye to the bridge and the bridge tender. Meekins said
though the bridge was getting some age on it, it was strong yet. He
would retire when the wooden bridge was yanked from the water. The
Coast Guard navigation folks would not permit it to remain, even with
its center span fixed open, as a place for crabbers and rockfishermen
and goers to goose concerts. "Everythin' has an endin'," the bridge
tender called after me.

Hooper Island, 6 September 1980

A group of bureaucrats, the top officials of the federal and the state
Department of Transportation, are gathered here today to dedicate the
mountainous curve of concrete that is visible from virtually any point
on the island, and from as far off as the Patuxent River on the other side
of the bay. Its cost has risen, during construction, sevenfold from an
initial estimate of $500,000, and the county's share has soared from
$125,000 to $900,000. The money, one cannot help thinking, would
have paid for a lot of pine planking and creosote, and a lot of paint jobs
for those old white railings. Heads bowed, the officials' coats whip in
the breeze off the Honga River as Commissioner Tom Flowers begins
the opening ceremonies with this invocation: "Father, today we are
gathered here to dedicate a bridge that is a monument to man's stu-
pidity, a monument to man's waste, a monument to governmental in-
terference and inefficiency . . . " Faces flush red among the officials,
but heads remain bowed. As a *Baltimore Sun* editorial would ask later:
"How do you interrupt a prayer, after all, especially when the man delivering it is right?"

And Flowers continued: "For there is no need for such an elaborate structure as this is . . . which is so out of keeping in the peaceful and lovely environment of south Dorchester . . . our great Creator and Father bless this bridge, and those who will use this structure to meet their needs, knowing that wind and wave and tide are daily at work destroying that which has been built."

Fishing Creek, September 1982

I had driven over the bold new bridge on my way down to Hoopersville, almost to where the road peters out in the whispering marsh, where my friend Chandus Rippons runs his crab house. In two years it has come to seem more ridiculous, rather than more familiar, to me. Watch out for the traffic bottleneck if you take the bridge at Hooper's, I tell people. The bridge is bad? they ask. No, the bridge is fantastic, it's just the rest of Dorchester County, I say. The bridge and its approaches are so well bulkheaded against erosion (federal standards and all that), they are bound to outlast the rapidly eroding island above and below them. Someday tour boats, passing, will point it out as the famous bridge to nowhere.

Chan and I stroll from his crab-packing plant over to his house at Hoopersville. I say how much I missed the old bridge, and how it was a shame they had to get rid of it. "Get rid of it? Get rid of it!" Chan said, eyes twinkling. "C'mon around with me to the p'int [point] yonder," he says, motioning toward some land on the other side of an abandoned oyster house. There in stacks are great sections of bridge. Chan says he thinks tourists are beginning to discover the island and, when they come, will want to eat at the little marina he is planning. He thinks they would flock to a restaurant built out over the water, built on the old sections of the longest, narrowest, clatteringest old wooden bridge there ever was.

Saving the Bay

GARRETT COUNTY, MD.—My friend Meg, the product of a comfortable upbringing in Washington, D.C., had just moved with her husband, Chuck, onto Frazee Ridge, a spectacular place of alpine meadows, big woods, and mountain farms in the remotest corner of far Western Maryland. It was around the time for harvesting and bagging the corn, and, seated inside the farmhouse of her in-laws, she heard someone hail the arrival of a flatbed semi: "Here comes the truck with sacks on it!" How nice, Meg remembers thinking, rising to walk outside; if Saks delivers way up here, maybe there's hope.

That was a decade ago. Meg has long since moved her family to Hagerstown—fled some of the most unspoiled natural surroundings that Maryland has to offer. The thing Frazee Ridge could not provide was company on all those long nights alone, going slightly batty raising two little kids while Chuck commuted home only on weekends from his job ninety miles away. The toughest thing about it, I suspect, came to be listening to occasional weekend visitors say for the thousandth time, as they prepared to return to the city, how they wished they could live forever in the pristine solitude of Frazee Ridge.

ETHIOPIA—All you read about it nowadays is the hunger and the poverty and the hopelessness; but those great, soaring, twisted ridges of the Abysinnian highlands form some of the most breath-taking scenery on earth, with a climate year-round to match the finest of Maryland's spring and autumn. Its thousand-mile Red Sea coast is fringed with coral reefs the equal of anything in the Caribbean. By Land Rover, by foot, and by camel (and never again by camel), I was privileged to spend years exploring that fantastic mountain kingdom during a tour of duty in the U.S. Army. From waters clear as air we caught rainbows of fish and sweet lobster. We came upon mountain valleys perhaps never before visited by Westerners.

It was high adventure and untrammeled beauty, I recalled at a recent reunion with some army buddies; but the more we talked, the more we realized what else had made our time in that far-off mountain kingdom so special. It was the sure knowledge of returning, anytime we wished, superheated and dust-covered, to collapse in air-conditioned comfort and to lather up in hot showers, and swill icy beers with steak and French fries at the Little America—right down to the miniature golf course and bowling lanes—maintained at gargantuan expense and effort in the Ethiopian vastness by the U.S. government.

PARRAMORE ISLAND, VA.—You could land jumbo jets on the expanse of white, packed sand beach here, stretching unpeopled for more than a dozen miles. Back of the dunes, the broad marshes are full of ducks and tangy salt oysters, and deer roam ancient forests of cedar and pine. This crown jewel of all the mid-Atlantic coast's bright string of sea islands, owned by a private nature trust and inaccessible to most people, seemed like paradise on a recent camping trip. We luxuriated in the thought about half a day before we began to rearrange paradise.

First, we scooped sand from the backside of a dune and propped old cedar logs around it to make a comfortable lean-to for shelter from the wind. Were we to be there much longer, we decided, we would chop one of the tall pines to bridge several of the island's deep marsh creeks for more convenient travel. A couple creeks had barren, sandy bottoms, swept clean by the tides. There we would transplant a few beds of oysters from muddy locations, so they would grow better and be convenient to our campsite. A nearby high marsh, if diked, would make fine pasture for a few head of cattle, and for crops . . . and on and on the planning went, customizing the Garden of Eden.

The best of both worlds is what we seem really to crave. A little farm on Frazee Ridge with excellent schools and a large shopping center not too far away; trackless wilderness with a return each evening to a first-class hotel; and a sweeping view of unspoiled ocean coast in all directions—from the deck of our condominium. The best of both worlds, the natural and the manufactured—who could argue with pursuit of that; and, by extension, with the extraordinary technological and economic progress that has enabled it. Even such a proponent of wilderness as Aldo Leopold had to concede that "wild things had little value until mechanization assured us of a good breakfast, and science disclosed the drama of where they come from and how they live."

The best of both worlds. It seems to imply an unalloyed good, but it also means there is a balance to be struck, and limits to our encroachment on the natural world of the Chesapeake region. To avoid facing this squarely is to risk bankrupting the Save the Bay movement that bids to become our environmental drumbeat through the remainder of this century. "Will we save the bay?" It is the question I am most asked since the landmark conference in 1983 when citizens, scientists, and their elected leaders met from across the watershed in Fairfax, Virginia, to discuss a six-year study documenting widespread and accelerating environmental declines in North America's greatest estuary. I try to be optimistic. I tell people that since then we have committed more money and human resources to reversing the bay's downtrends than at any point in our history on its shores. It is nothing short of inspirational, I say, that on one of the bitterest weekends of winter nearly one thousand people in Pennsylvania, a state that owns not a square inch of the Chesapeake, braved icy roads and paid $10 each to attend a conference on how they could contribute to the bay's cleanup. Their concern is critical because, through its mighty Susquehanna River, Pennsylvania contributes not only half the fresh water of the Chesapeake Bay, but also enough pollution, mainly from its bountiful agriculture, that any meaningful cleanup of the bay will be literally impossible without a huge effort from the third of its watershed that lies in Pennsylvania.

I also tell people about more subtle, though no less important, moves afoot, such as the meeting one night to discuss pollution control between a concerned farmer from the Amish country in Lancaster County, and his counterpart from Virginia's tidewater, down on the Rappahannock—the two connected across 250 miles by a skein of water, flowing river at one's end, almost ocean at the other's; connected by their mutual caring about the whole of it.

I tell my questioners how we are upgrading our treatment of sewage to levels well beyond any legal requirements in some cases; also controlling the sediment from land development, regulating even the polluted storm water that runs from the asphalt and concrete covering our communities; and recruiting small armies of technicians to help farmers keep their soil and chemicals on their land, instead of in our water. I recount how conservationists finally prevailed in 1984 in the bitterest natural-resources controversy in Maryland history since the Oyster Wars of the 1880s. They won a moratorium to stop all fishing for the troubled state fish, the rockfish, until we can once again make its spawning waters clean.

I note that where a problem—and its solution—can be defined, we are not grudging of money to pursue it. Baltimore's Back River was chosen a century ago as the dumping spot for the region's sewage, precisely because it had such poor flushing action that it would not let the wastes escape to the rest of the bay. The river became, in effect, the final stage of sewage treatment for the city; and many still feel that is a cost-effective strategy, especially because Back River never was the finest of waterways even in more pristine times. But citizens and government have overwhelmingly rejected that option, and we are preparing to spend a third of a billion dollars, maybe more, to upgrade the sewage-treatment plant in hopes of reclaiming Back River. Our sleaziest tributary, perhaps, but if money can buy it back, we'll take it, thank you.

Who could ever doubt that we want to save the bay? It is, after all, what makes this region, for so many of us, the best of both worlds. But having told people who would save the bay all of the above, I also caution them that the 1983 conference to save the bay was preceded by similar conferences in 1968 and in 1977. Like the third conference, the first two ended on hopeful and enthusiastic notes; indeed, the years following the first of those gatherings witnessed the greatest surge of both federal and state antipollution legislation and spending in history, part of the dramatic rise of the modern environmental movement. I tell them what Bill Hargis, a long-time bay scientist, said of those years. We were making famous progress in fighting pollution, he said—moving upstream, with tremendous effort, at about three knots—only the current continued to run downstream at five knots. His point was that we do not perform our bay-saving in some laboratory where all parameters are under our precise control; we are not in a game where the forces of pollution take time out while we huddle on countermeasures. It is why, finally, I warn those who hope to save the bay that its epitaph has already been written, if not yet chiseled in stone.

There are a number of ways in which that proleptic epitaph can be stated, but I think it was particularly fitting the way it came from the mouth of a real-estate agent from the boom-growth bay-shore county of Anne Arundel. She was testifying against controversial new state legislation designed to limit the amount and the type of development of the most environmentally sensitive waterfront areas of the bay and its rivers. She feared this would affect her livelihood but also wanted the lawmakers to understand that it was as much in her interest as anyone's to want a healthy Chesapeake Bay: "We need the bay to stay clean and beautiful, so that people will continue to move here to enjoy it," she explained. Very nicely, and in all sincerity, she had defined the best of both worlds as we conceive it today in the Chesapeake region—that is, without limit on the number of those who would seek it, or on the share of the natural pie each would expect.

Irrevocably, and more than most bodies of water, our Chesapeake is "a people's bay," as William Ruckelshaus, director of the U.S. Environmental Protection Agency, called it at the 1983 conference; and therein lies both its infinite charm and the seeds of its destruction.

Compare the Chesapeake Bay to Puget Sound, San Francisco Bay, Delaware Bay—to almost any of the world's other great bays, gulfs, estuaries, and inland seas. You will be hard-pressed to find another where the water twines more extensively with the land in dozens of rivers and thousands of creeks; where the depths are as moderate, the tides as minimal, the seas as kindly, the bottoms as hazard-free, the seafood as abundant; where these and a dozen other factors, such as proximity to the nation's capital, conspire half so well to create water so eminently usable for so many purposes by such a large and growing population.

Our bay is a convivial bay, an accessible bay, a *tasty* bay. I know a single cove on a Talbot County tributary where the property owners harvest silver-kerneled sugar corn, tart and robust tomatoes, succulent canvasback duck and Canada goose, plump oysters the color of cream, sweet soft crabs and firm-fleshed rockfish, as well as deer, coon, muskrat, quail, and rabbit; and a nearby poultry house grows Perdue Oven Stuffer Roasters! Such a cornucopia. I often decry Captain John Smith's overquoted "heaven and earth never agreeing better to frame habitation for man" as a shameless bit of anthropocentricism—as if God and Ole Ma Nature had just been setting the table for fifteen thousand years or so in hopes that a crowd of unwashed Europeans would settle down for an extended free meal. But honestly, this bay and the ample regions it waters and drains do almost beg to be used.

And use it we have. Waterfront, water view, water access, water privilege—nothing sells lots better than proximity to the shoreline. To the waterman, the bay is twenty-seven million pounds of oyster meats annually, and fifty-five million pounds of crab meat atop that. It is a vast and economical heat sink for power plants, the largest of which, Calvert Cliffs, sucks three billion gallons of bay water a day across its nuclear core to cool it. Our bay is highway and harbor to two of the world's great shipping complexes, at Norfolk and Baltimore; and the setting for millions of individual fishing and hunting trips each year. To the biologist it is a world-class laboratory; to the industrialist and the sanitary engineer, an economical source of the dilution that once was considered the ultimate solution to pollution. It is a federal and a military bay, a proving ground for big guns at Aberdeen, a bombing and strafing and shelling range for naval jets and destroyers at Bloodsworth Island; its depths are convenient to the Pentagon for underwater demolition experiments, which occasionally have blown up weakfish by the ton, and oysters by the bar; and it is home port, near its mouth, to the U.S. Navy's Atlantic Fleet.

So many things the bay means to so many users, yet one thing it becomes for all of us—the ultimate sink, the settling basin, the end of the road, for the sediment and chemicals and wastes that flow from our activities on the land; flowing from across a drainage basin that extends north as far as the New York Finger Lakes, south nearly into North Carolina, and west almost to Tennessee. The intimate connection between how we live on this land and the quality of the waters that drain it is a profound lesson we have learned belatedly; and with the knowledge has come almost agonizing recognition of a fundamental irony of public environmental policy toward the Chesapeake Bay: we hold its waters and their denizens to be a public trust, to be held in stewardship for future generations; while the surrounding land, most of the massive, 64,000-square-mile watershed, remains a free-market commodity, its highest and best use largely determined by the short-term economics of individual gain. To the greater public interest, vested in state and federal government, has gone most of the rule over the water of the watershed; but land-use decisions remain the province of a thousand town and county governments, none of which wants its water to end up like Baltimore harbor, but most of which will fight to the death to retain the option to use its land just as intensively as the state's largest city, should the opportunity arise.

Grow or die is the watchword by which every political jurisdiction proceeds. Attract development. Increase the tax base. Stoke the economy. And of course, "Save the Bay"—no political platform would be complete without it. It is, after all, nothing less than the best of both worlds that we want, isn't it? The catch, of course, is that, even assuming the most technologically advanced and zealously enforced pollution controls (quite a big assumption), we are nowhere near the point where each additional resident does not constitute a net draft against the finite natural resources of the Chesapeake and its surrounds. We can only influence the degree of withdrawal from our natural bank accounts, not the direction of the cash flow.

And so, the people keep on coming. The many uses and seductions of the edge, where land meets water, draw people so powerfully that nearly half the planet's population has settled on 5 percent of its land mass—the 5 percent that is mostly adjacent to coastlines. In the United States, fully three-quarters of us soon will live within fifty miles of an ocean or Great Lakes coast. And the heart of the heart of all this, the bay with perhaps the greatest amount of shoreline edge for its size of anyplace on earth, is none other than the Chesapeake. Compare the ratio of our bay's shoreline to its length with almost any similar coastal water body in the world. Usually these others show an edge that is two, three, or four times their greatest length or width; but on the Chesapeake, the ratio is nearly 35:1.

If humankind, concerned about a global population well on its way to doubling, were to order up a test case of how intensely we can exploit natural systems without irretrievably ruining them, we could have done worse than construct a scenario such as the one we will be living out for the next several decades around the Chesapeake Bay. The population in the bay's sprawling watershed now is about twelve million people, with the bulk of them, predictably, clustered as close to the water's edge as they can afford. The modern history of our failure to stem the bay's environmental decline has been not so much a case of ignoring the adverse impacts of this population as it has been underestimating the *rate* at which changes were occurring. The population in the five-state watershed, which took 350 years of European settlement to reach eight million people, required only thirty years more, the last 8 percent of our time here, to grow by 50 percent to twelve million; and we could double that within the lifetimes of many readers.

A similarly striking trend has marked our use of the watershed for agriculture, now recognized as a source of the rain-washed silt and chemicals that pollute the bay, on the whole, more than our sewage. At first glance, farming's impact appears to have decreased in modern times. Acreage in farms dropped a whopping 40 percent in Maryland alone in the last fifty years. But the soil that remained in tillage has been pushed harder to extract ever greater yields. Use of nitrogen and phosphorus fertilizers, both major pollutants in the decline of the Chesapeake's aquatic life, soared by 250 percent per acre. The same thing happened in Pennsylvania, and, in an average year now, more than eighty million pounds of nitrogen and phosphorus are washed down the Susquehanna River alone. During the same period, equally rapid shifts were occurring from a farm economy based on livestock and pastures to one based on sowing grain crops. That meant more exposed soil washing into the bay. In 1982 the federal government confirmed that after fifty years of voluntary soil conservation, erosion from farmland stood at its highest rate ever. In Maryland in the latter half of this same period, the destruction of forests, which filtered soil and fertilizer pollutants from runoff headed for the bay, proceeded at the highest rate in northeastern America.

The problem is not just more of us, but more of us each expecting more. Consider the impact on the Chesapeake Bay from an item at the center of the American dream, the home. In the decade 1970–1980, while Maryland's population grew by about 8 percent, the amount of undeveloped farm and forest required to house each person grew at triple that rate—clear reflection of the increasing demand for a rural or suburban home setting with a large lot. The more affluent new bay-dwellers were, the more they consumed the countryside of the watershed. Nearly two-thirds of all the land that changed from open to developed space went to house a mere fifth of the population growth.

Most of this development took place on land outside areas where water and sewers were planned, mocking the "comprehensive land-use plans" county governments like to trot out as evidence they have achieved "controlled growth."

Other areas in which the desire for a higher standard of living exacerbates the impacts of growth are not covered by any plans at all— we do not usually even connect them as cause and effect. Yet just as surely as we all want more air-conditioning, more power plants on the water's edge are needed; and as each of us aspires to a boat (I have one, and *need* two more), we must have more and bigger shorefront marinas. And we all, quite naturally, hope someday to have a vacation home at the shore, or at least a vacation, which means more bridges and roads and cars to get us there. Eventually, it all means fewer untrammeled natural coves in the shoreline and bends in the rivers.

It all comes back to wanting Frazee Ridge and Parramore Island, but, if you please, with a shopping center, good schools, and lots of modern job opportunities in close commuting distance—and while they're at it, can't they do something about the traffic, which seems to get worse every year! More people, seeking the best of both worlds— and scarcely one among them does not earnestly subscribe to balancing the developed with the natural. It is a curious kind of balance though, that must be refigured, however minutely, every time another soul is added to the watershed. Each time it is struck anew, we seem to be left with a little more concrete and a little less nature.

Now, I am optimistic that, with even a little luck, we will soon see some payoff in more fish and cleaner waters from the massive and technologically sophisticated Save the Bay campaign, on which the states of the watershed have launched themselves. But it is short-term optimism. Talk to the scientists whose research has laid the foundations for the next wave of pollution controls, and they will tell you that it will not be many years before the population trends and life-style demands again outstrip any gains. Many may say to that, "So what if they do? We will be ready at that time to respond with whatever degree of bay-saving is required."

That is not such a bad approach to a number of ongoing problems, such as regulating the nation's money supply, or maintaining its road system. We operate that way often enough that a Yale economist, Charles Lindblom, even gave it a formal name, "muddling through," in a famous article published in the 1950s. At its best, Muddling Through recognizes that we are not really all that good at divining long-term, comprehensive solutions to problems—there are too many variables and imponderables involved. Instead we make admittedly incomplete, imperfect decisions, followed up by almost constant, incremental midcourse corrections. It is essentially how we run this country, for all our talk about long-range planning.

But consider the flaws in Muddling Through if we really desire no further degradation (indeed, we want restoration) of the environment in the bay region. First, it is the character of an estuary, where rivers war constantly with the ocean for dominance, that the plants and animals living there routinely and quite naturally undergo dramatic declines and rebounds from year to year, as the dynamic environment there favors now this one, now that. Thus a true environmental problem usually is confirmed only after a downtrend is firmly established. The virtual disappearance, between 1969 and 1972, of the bay's submerged aquatic grasses, one of the estuary's major life-support systems, did not begin to be sorted out from natural ups and downs until the late 1970s. It was around the end of that time that I shared a beer with Walt Boynton, a bay scientist with a remarkable gift for explaining complicated environmental problems to laypeople.

What did he think had happened to the grasses? I asked, knowing that research into the mysterious disappearance had just begun, but also knowing that no scientist heads into a project without some pretty good hunches, which they call hypotheses when they are seeking grant money. Walt sucked on his beer and said, after a long pause, "Too much shit and too much dirt is what I think it will turn out to be, but it'll be four or five more years before we can prove that to where anyone will be able to do something about it."

Walt was right on both counts. The killer turned out to be a combination of chemicals in treated sewage, combined with the same chemicals and the dirt washing off millions of acres of farms in the watershed. By the time Maryland, Virginia, and Pennsylvania had been convinced to make major commitments to control the problem, it was 1983; and, depending on which state one is talking about, it will be anywhere from 1988 to the end of this century before major reductions begin to occur in the pollutants that have been killing the bay's grasses. Thus, changing course in the way we use the land and water across an immense watershed can take a generation or more. And during that time the causes of the problem continue. It is one reason we end up "progressing" at William Hargis's three knots against that unrelenting, five-knot current.

Similarly, as we turn the watershed increasingly to human use, we permanently foreclose valuable options for reversing pollution. On the Patuxent River, at 110 miles the longest waterway wholly contained in Maryland, it was determined a few years ago that in dry summers treated sewage from booming upstream growth centers would soon make up around 75 percent of all the fresh water flowing down the river, with implications for the rich seafood-harvesting areas of the lower Patuxent that made even the sanitary engineers wince. A bold commitment was made by upstream sewage authorities to quit using the river as a waste sink. They would begin to spray the sewage, after treatment, on the land, allowing the soil to filter out the final traces of harmful pollution. Environmentalists cheered. But it never came to pass. The region in question already had developed to the point that the considerable acreage required for spraying the sewage simply could not be assembled.

Finally, we have always put a good deal of faith in the bay's *resilience*, its ability, given half a chance, to recover from an environmental insult. Our faith is not without a basis. When the Chesapeake Bay Foundation was making a movie about the bay recently, there was an office joke that it could not decide whether to call it *Fragile Paradise*, or *Sturdy Sewer*. So many times in recorded history, this or that species has been knocked back by natural events or pollution, only to resurge to record levels. You wonder at all that we have wrecked in the bay's environment; but even more, you wonder at how much survives.

Yet, if we look at the bay's natural defenses of a century or two ago, we must recognize that, like any veteran of many tough rounds in the ring, our modern Chesapeake has lost forever the ability to take a punch like it once could. Consider the haymaker delivered by Tropical Storm Agnes in late June of 1972. The worst flooding in perhaps two centuries across most of its huge watershed blasted the estuary for days on end with unheard-of volumes of choking silt, farm chemicals, sewage from ruptured lines, and fresh water—the latter as deadly a pollutant as any of the others to salt-loving aquatic species. Agnes would have been a rude shock to the Chesapeake's system in any age, but, coming in modern times, it almost surely was far more devastating.

The forest—which once covered virtually 100 percent of the watershed, unsurpassed among all types of land use in filtering pollutants and absorbing the runoff from storms before it reached the bay—had been reduced by nearly a third when Agnes hit. Similarly the bay's stocks of oysters, once so vast it is estimated they could filter and cleanse the bay's entire volume through their gills every week or so, were now reduced to perhaps 5 percent of their former glory. The great reaches of underwater grasses, which had existed continuously in the bay for at least one thousand years, were already highly stressed by pollution when Agnes hit. They never bounced back, and with them went their ability to absorb several sewage plants–worth of nitrogen and phosphorus, two chemicals that have increasingly plagued the bay ever since. Fifteen years later, people will still say of this bay problem or that, "Things haven't been the same since Agnes." The truth may be that Agnes wasn't the problem so much as the incapacity of the modern bay—shorn of its biological filters and buffers, destabilized and stressed already to the limit—to handle the insult.

Sometimes the loss of resilience has been more concrete. In the last century or so the bay has lost hundreds of miles of prime spawning rivers to big dams, notably on the Susquehanna, where rockfish once mounted as far as the Juniata, and shad and herring ran all the way past Binghamton, New York. As a result, the fish simply have a lot fewer windows at which to place their bets for a successful hatch. And in addition to the major dams we know about, it is estimated there are more than nine hundred blockages, small dams, culverts, and so forth, closing innumerable miles of small spawning streams all over the bay region.

Breathing space for the bay to rebound has even been lost in court, as recently as the Bruce Decision in 1971, which released the watermen of every Maryland county to oyster and crab outside their county waters. It quickly created a more mobile work force, with bigger, bay-ranging boats that can now exert tremendous pressure within a matter of hours on any new "hotspot" where the beleaguered oysters and other species try to stage a comeback.

Beyond the loss of resiliance that our demands on the bay have created is another type of pollution that should give special pause to the very people who rail the loudest against controls on growth and private land use. It is the loss of freedom, and it is the inevitable price that a civilized society exacts as it tries to infinitely expand the use of finite resources. Simply put, the more family that moves into your house, the more rules you all have to live by to keep from each other's throats. As Nick Carter, a minor philosopher and environmental permit writer for the state of Maryland, has pointed out, there are so many uses impacting the bay, the rivers, and the land that, to compensate, we regulate. Thus we now need a license to fish in the bay, a half-dozen stamps and permits to hunt; and we have rules that tell us what kind of detergent (nonphosphate) we can wash our clothes in, a soaring fee for boat registration, and serious talk of requiring licensing for boaters and creel limits on certain species of bay fish. If we double and someday triple the population in the watershed, I would expect lotteries to determine who got to camp on Assateague Island, shoot many species of duck, or take home a rockfish; and only cars with license plates ending in odd numbers will use U.S. Route 50 to the beaches on the first and third weekends of each summer month.

Will we save the bay? It seems unimaginable that we can restore it to any level of quality that existed much before the late 1950s. Even if the restoration could be done, the sacrifices would be too great, and I imagine the expectations of today's public would be mostly satisfied before that point. Most scientists I talk to think it unlikely we can do more than hang on to most of what we've still got left, and many feel all we can do is slow the present rate of decline. I sometimes remind people that if we even save half of what the Chesapeake is about during the next several generations, we'll still have more than most regions of the world.

I know from experience that this kind of speculation strikes the politicians and the bureaucrats as pessimistic, and smacks of criticism of their ability to carry out the public mandate, which clearly is to save the bay. But they miss the point, which is that so much of what is changing the Chesapeake Bay simply remains beyond the current or envisioned scope of our political-legal system to deal with it. Doubters might wish to read the final report of the first modern bay conference held in 1968. It posed five basic policy questions which, had they been clearly answered, might have made it unnecessary to gather fifteen years later to plan one of history's largest environmental salvage operations. They asked, regarding the bay:

How many people do we wish to house on the shores?

How many tons of food do we wish to harvest, and what kinds?

How big a ship do we wish to accommodate (implications for dredging and dredge spoil disposal)?

How many pleasure boats will be operating?

How many acres of wetlands should we preserve?

We have not yet faced up to any of those questions, with the exception of wetlands, soon after protected by law, and are only beginning to recognize them as legitimate issues. How big? How many? How much? Those questions seem almost to paralyze us, so directly do they suggest limits to our pursuit of the best of both worlds. They confront a faith in perpetual progress, reinforced by nearly two millennia of a Judeo-Christian tradition that sees the earth as planned for the benefit of humanity.

As a boy I listened as old market gunners on my native Eastern Shore cited Genesis, about the Lord assigning man dominion over the fish and fowl of the earth, to justify their inalienable right to continue slaughtering wild ducks without limit. Today, most of us chuckle at such attitudes, even as we shake our heads ruefully over the latest bulldozing for another road, or shopping mall, or sprawling housing development, and remind ourselves that growth, after all, is going to come whether we like it or not; and that people do have the right to realize as much profit as they can get from their land. Sometimes people question whether it has to be this way; but they are easily dismissed by proponents of growth as having gotten their piece of the countryside, and now wanting to keep others out. I wonder sometimes whether the boomers of such continued progress wouldn't have sunk Noah's Ark, trying to add more cabins on the deck.

Will we save the bay? I know that we will always be trying; but "saving the bay" can become almost a state of grace, like tithing, allowing us to proceed comfortably with business as usual in the rest of our lives. My feeling is that we must broaden our definitions of environmental quality to include far more than the standards set forth in clean-water and clean-air laws. We must fundamentally reexamine our striving for the best of both worlds, for numbers without limit. There are signs that we are beginning to do so, but make no mistake: in our incipient efforts to grapple with limits in the watershed of the Chesapeake Bay, we are embarked on waters fully as uncharted as anything Captain John Smith encountered nearly four centuries ago.

Epilogue

About the time I conceived this book I made my first trip to Martha's Vineyard, to help deliver a boat back to the Chesapeake Bay. It was late autumn, nasty weather, and I ducked into a local bookstore to escape a rain squall. Signs in the window were touting "the Christmas season" on the Vineyard. The place, evidently, was on the verge of attaining enough popularity to shed the typical Memorial Day to Labor Day cycle of resort towns. The heady prospect of a year-round tourist economy beckoned.

Inside, I was astounded by the quantity and quality of publications on Martha's Vineyard and its environs—coffee-table books, poetry, history, diaries, essays, fiction, whaling, architecture, calendars. A number of the talented authors were people who "summered" on the Vineyard, I was told. Seldom has a small island been more thoroughly or lavishly celebrated, I thought.

Later, I began to realize what that really implied. To produce and support such a body of local literature and photography absolutely required a community grown large and affluent enough to have supplanted much of the original Martha's Vineyard. If a lot of what used to be there hadn't vanished, would there be the nostalgia necessary to sell half the attractive volumes on display—or the stimulus to undertake them?

Anyone who is more than a casual browser in Maryland book-stores will note that literature and photography of the Chesapeake have begun to flourish in recent years, even as the bay and its old life styles have continued to erode. I told all this to my good friend Tom Wisner, the bay folksinger, poet, and storyteller. He sent me this graph, which he said charts a prosperous, if remorseful, future for writers like me.

The Bay's Changing Bounty

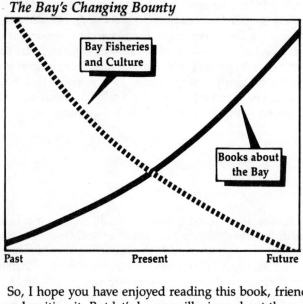

Bay Fisheries and Culture

Books about the Bay

Past   Present   Future

So, I hope you have enjoyed reading this book, friend, as I have enjoyed writing it. But let's have no illusions about the process we're both part of.